Silent Victims

Recognizing and Stopping Abuse of the Family Pet

Pamela Carlisle-Frank
Tom Flanagan

UNIVERSITY PRESS OF AMERICA,® INC.

Lanham • Boulder • New York • Toronto • Oxford

**Copyright © 2006 by
University Press of America,® Inc.**
4501 Forbes Boulevard
Suite 200
Lanham, Maryland 20706
UPA Acquisitions Department (301) 459-3366

PO Box 317
Oxford
OX2 9RU, UK

Library of Congress Control Number: 2005937540
ISBN 0-7618-3397-8 (paperback : alk. ppr.)

To Mai-Tai
and all the innocent companion animals
who have suffered from the
type of cruelty unique to the human animal species.

Contents

List of Tables

Foreword

When I was asked to write this *Foreword* I was both honored and humbled. Dr. Carlisle- Frank and Tom Flanagan are people I respect very much. Both are, in an unfortunate way, recognized veterans in the battle to break the connection between animal abuse and violent crimes. This book is a very much-needed weapon in that battle.

I graduated from Veterinary school in 1973, coming away with a solid base of scientific and medical knowledge, as we knew it to be then. More importantly, what I did not know I knew where to look it up. But in one important area I was totally clueless. And that is the so-called connection, or link, between animal abuse and violence to people. In fact, while Veterinary schools now provide students with extensive material on the topic, rarely was animal abuse mentioned then and certainly we had little if any formal training on how to recognize it ourselves.

All that changed for me in 1997. I had, of course, witnessed and suspected animal abuse in practice settings and had a vague awareness of the link between it and violent crimes, that there were people out there who started their life of crime by abusing animals and graduated to serious mayhem and murder. But the dots began to be connected at a daylong seminar that I attended. Presenters ranged from Social Workers to Animal Law Enforcement Officers. Topics and examples varied from kids who shot at pigeons to satanic, ritualistic killings and Jeffrey Dahmer-type cases.

There was a sudden feeling of total inadequacy, that I was an experienced practitioner of 25 years who was pretty uninformed about a serious societal problem with its roots in my profession. What had I missed over the years? What had my ignorance allowed to occur? What could have I prevented?

After attending another seminar on the link a few months later I became convinced my profession needed much more enlightening on this very grave problem. Not only did we need to protect our patients but our clients, friends, families and communities as well. I organized a shortened version of the two seminars I had attended and it was presented at our State Veterinary Medical Association Annual Meeting. In attendance were people of many professions whose jobs involved service to animals and/or people. From this came the development of Link-UP Education Network, a non-profit coalition of people who again provide service to animals and/or people. It began as a loose-knit discussion group but quickly became more. We have presented 4 day-long seminars ourselves with many nationally known speakers, have organized an emergency foster care network for animals of violence victims who need to immediately leave the danger they are in, and have presented numerous other training sessions with our members as speakers. LUEN has been included in the National Crime Prevention Council's "50 Strategies To Prevent Violent Domestic Crime."

I am very pleased that a book of this nature and magnitude has been written. It has a target readership as stated in the introduction. I would urge everyone to read this book, not just Veterinarians, Physicians, Social Workers, etc. Everyone needs to be aware of the Link. The Postman who notices mail building up, the meter reader who overhears or sees that something is not right, the Fireman who is inspecting a building for safety or the teacher who hears something from a student that could mean animal or human abuse at home all may be able to intervene or contact someone who can. Those who care about animals or people must be aware that abuse is not confined to someone else's community or neighborhood. It may be next door, it may be occurring in the home of a close friend or even a family member. It could even be in your own home. So read carefully and heed what is written. If this book aids you in preventing the suffering of even one animal or person, imagine what it will do for society as a whole.

James Knight, DVM
Ware, Massachusetts
May 20, 2005

Preface

MAKING THE LINK

As I write this preface, news has just crossed my desk that the Canadian Veterinary Medical Association (CVMA) has declared that veterinarians have a moral responsibility to report suspected animal abuse to appropriate authorities. This seemingly simple statement sounds obvious to some, outrageous to others. But it represents some remarkable progress for those of us who have been working for many years to get what we call "the Link" between animal abuse and interpersonal violence recognized as serious, legitimate, an early warning sign, an aspect of family violence, and a rationale for implementing more effective prevention and intervention strategies for people—and animals—at risk.

The CVMA position statement, while historic, pioneering and welcomed, also indicates that we have a long way to go. But progress is being made, and the book in your hands is another important step in that right direction.

How did we get here? Where are we going? And what can you—the reader—do to help prevent family violence by looking at it through the lens of animal abuse, cruelty and neglect? Some of the answers to these questions will be found in this book. Others are sitting in your imagination, waiting to be born and implemented, triggered by an idea or a comment or a model in this book that gives you an Aha!-moment as you realize you can incorporate these concepts into your work.

As I speak to people all over the world who work in the human care giving professions, most of them had never really thought about the implications of animals in the lives of their clients or patients. Yet when presented with case studies and the overwhelming evidence that a person's acts of animal abuse frequently are precursors to acts of violence against people, they experience an

'Aha!-moment.' They can then all recall a case or two that, at the time, did not seem particularly significant, but now, through this new lens, they see what they had missed.

More importantly, they can see implications of how they can use this new information to better inform current and future cases.

When confronted with the statistics about the ubiquitous presence and emotional significance of pets in the lives of contemporary families, they begin to realize that omitting questions about animals from risk assessments, intake forms, patient histories and other documentation leaves out a significant part of many persons' lives—and ignores a large number of family members whose lives might be at risk.

The past two decades have seen a surge in interest in the links between how animals are treated and the parallel, often intersecting, abuse of women, children and elders. This interest is multidisciplinary, creating an exciting cross-fertilization of ideas—and a maddeningly frustrating inability for professionals to communicate across disciplinary barriers and turfs. This interest is also nothing new: what you're about to read was espoused 40 years ago by Margaret Mead, 250 years ago by John Locke and Immanuel Kant, 700 years ago by St. Thomas Aquinas. It's not rocket science. It's common sense.

Your goals in reading this book should be to identify ways you can incorporate its concepts into your work, whether you're in humane or human services. You may also wish to consider ways to expand these ideas by developing in your community a multi-agency working group that can have an impact upon policy and professional practice.

COMMON THEMES

Borrowing from ideas articulated by Becker and French (2004), let me share with you four dominant and interrelated themes that have emerged from research over the past two decades:

1. Redefining animal "cruelty" as part of the continuum of abuse within the family. This has implications for animal care and control officials, veterinarians, child protective services caseworkers, adult protective services officials, domestic violence personnel, women's shelters, law enforcement, and the criminal justice system.
2. Animal abuse perpetrated by children who show later aggressive and deviant behavior.
3. Animal abuse as an indicator of the coexistence of child abuse, domestic violence and elder abuse.

4. The therapeutic potential of animal-assisted interventions with children in post-abuse cases and in prevention efforts with at-risk youth.

As you read this book, you will see these themes repeated over and over.

COMING FULL CIRCLE

Let me return for a moment to the new CVMA position statement. As of this writing, veterinary associations in the U.S., Canada, the United Kingdom and New Zealand have boldly gone where professional groups in human medicine have been somewhat uncomfortable for 40 years: describing the responsibilities in recognizing and reporting family violence. The CVMA position statement is a significant step forward from earlier policies: while saying veterinarians have a *moral* responsibility to report suspected animal abuse, it notes they do not have a *legal* responsibility. But the CVMA believes veterinarians should have this legal responsibility so as to put them on an even par with human health professionals, and it urges local veterinary associations to lobby their provincial governments for this responsibility. It further encourages colleges of veterinary medicine to teach "the Link" to better inform and prepare tomorrow's vets. "Veterinarians may be able to play an important role in breaking the cycle of family violence," says the position statement. (CVMA, 2005)

This is significant progress. And these issues recall similar challenges that were overcome by physicians, dentists, and other human healthcare professionals in the 1960s and 1970s when research began to indicate that child abuse and domestic violence were medical issues amenable to public health solutions (Arkow, 2003).

The good news, and the irony, is that the animal protection field is coming full circle. As many readers know, the child protection field emerged from the animal protection movement. Emboldened by the success of the ASPCA's "Little Mary Ellen" case in the 1870s, societies for the prevention of cruelty to animals began assuming a dual responsibility for the protection of children as well—an interest that remained intact until federal legislation in the 1970s created our current child protection system which is largely under government control (Arkow, 1999; Costin, 1991).

Today, many animal protection organizations are back in the child (and woman and elder) protection business. They're recognizing animal abuse not just as a violation of an animal's integrity, but as a public health and safety issue. More importantly, the legislative, law enforcement, criminal justice, education, social service and other communities with which they work are making this connection as well. By putting animal abuse into a contemporary context and language that these other fields can more readily understand, we're advancing the welfare of animals, women, children, and elders—all the silent victims.

Today's Link efforts are informed not so much by emotionalism nor by morality, but rather by solid research. This research is growing, compelling, and global in scope. For example, an Australian study (Clarke, 2002) of offenders found that animal abuse was a better predictor of sexual assault than previous convictions for homicide, arson or firearms offenses, leading the researchers to propose that risk assessment frameworks could be established based upon known information about incidents of animal cruelty—assuming, that is, that these incidents were made known to law enforcement officials (which, unfortunately, they are not.)

Another Australian study (Dadds, et al., 2004), after finding that 30% of school-age children surveyed reported partaking in cruelty to animals, simply declared, "cruelty to animals may be a particularly pernicious aspect of problematic child development."

Other new research is emerging in South Africa, Italy, Scotland, Canada and, of course, the U.S. Space does not permit a full literature review here, but an extensive bibliography of writings about the "Link" can be accessed at www.animaltherapy.net.

DIRECTIONS FOR THE FUTURE

As the "Link" field matures and as efforts in this area begin to gain some traction, some apparent patterns for future growth and development are beginning to emerge. General public awareness of the "Link," and more detailed involvement by the various professions involved, are continuing and accelerating. We are seeing growing participation among veterinary associations, schools of social work, the field of animal law, mental health interventions, probation and parole officers, people working with juvenile offenders, and prosecutors.

For example, the vast majority of participants in one study (Risley-Curtiss, Holley & Wolf, 2004) said that their animal companions provide them with emotional support, unconditional love and companionship, and that they consider their animals to be family members; this finding has tremendous implications for social workers who traditionally have not considered a holistic, multi-species look at the families they work with. Similarly, child psychologists, school counselors, probation officers, and a myriad of other professions who fail to include the animal component are missing a potentially significant factor in their clients' lives. Assessments that do not include attention to individuals' relationships with their pets are missing essential elements of their interactions with their environments, and are failing to identify and draw upon critical resources for their clients' health and well-being.

I believe the next generation of issues that the field will have to address include:

1. Veterinarians: practitioners will need specific training on identifying the clinical signs of Non-Accidental Injury (NAI) (Arkow & Munro, 2006). They will need practice management skills in learning how to approach clients to gather information about suspicious cases, training on what to do with this information once they obtain it, and professional support to help resolve their justifiable concerns about economic issues, confidentiality constraints, and security fears. The CVMA position statement is a significant step forward in this regard. Veterinarians can learn much from the similar experiences of the human medicine field.

2. Animal shelters: animal care and control facilities charged with the responsibility and authority to investigate and prosecute animal abuse will need reliable, institutionalized systems of reporting animal abuse data to state and possibly federal law enforcement agencies. This will create a database, similar to uniform crime statistics already in place for many crimes against humans. Systems are already in place in many areas for the reporting of other public health concerns, such as rabies, and perhaps these can serve as models for animal abuse reporting. Two U.S. Surgeons General have observed that sociological, law enforcement and criminal justice approaches to violence have resulted in "unmitigated failure," and suggested that a public health strategy might be more effective (Koop & Lundberg, 1992; Novello, Shosky & Froehlke, 1992).

3. Animal-assisted interventions: Much of the field of animal-assisted therapy and animal-assisted activities has shifted in recent years toward targeted interventions directed at at-risk youth, providing these teens with opportunities to resolve conflicts non-violently through positive reinforcement behavior modification to make shelter dogs more adoptable (Duel, 2004). What is unknown is the effectiveness of these programs. Much research is needed to evaluate the long-term successes and failures of these strategic interventions.

4. Community coalitions: Many local groups have organized to provide inter-agency cross-training and cross-reporting protocols, linking child protection, domestic violence, animal protection and elder abuse agencies. But few of these coalitions have achieved the critical mass, infrastructure

or institutionalization necessary for widespread sustainability. Few coalitions seem to take advantage of the availability of federal funding—either in the U.S., through the Community Oriented Policing Services (COPS) and Violence Against Women Act (VAWA) funding vehicles, or in Canada, through the National Crime Prevention Strategy. Child protective services continually seems to be "the missing link" in participating in these coalitions, for reasons that have yet to be fully articulated.

5. Advocacy: The increase in the number of states that have made some forms of serious animal abuse felonies is impressive, but there are no indications yet that these states are experiencing either a decrease in animal abuse or an increase in reporting or prosecutions. Various initiatives are underway to increase the number of professions mandated to report suspected family violence, with immunity from civil and criminal liability for making such reports in good faith; as yet these initiatives have not been undertaken systematically. Canadian efforts to redefine animal abuse as a crime of violence rather than a crime against property have been repeatedly stymied. Application of the child protection model, in which the former term "cruelty" has been widely replaced with the more contemporary "abuse" and further subdivided into "physical abuse," "emotional abuse," "sexual abuse," and "neglect," and in which a nationwide system of mandatory reporting procedures has been institutionalized, has not been widely replicated in the animal protection system.

6. Training: Colleges of veterinary medicine, law schools, schools of social work, and law enforcement training academies should be the next logical areas where "Link" training must be introduced into curricula. Instructors, ideally, should present this training from those fields with the appropriate language and credentials necessary to gain widespread acceptance in those professions.

UNANSWERED QUESTIONS

It would be naïve to think that paying greater attention to the welfare of animals will solve the many societal problems facing our communities: Debbie Duel, former humane educator for the Washington, D.C. Humane Society, once described to me her challenge in trying to reach inner-city youths. "How can I go into a classroom and teach children to be kind to animals," she asked, "when these kids are afraid to walk to school because of drive-by shootings?" (Arkow, 2004) I haven't found an answer to that question yet.

But the fact, or at least the hope, remains, that if people do not care about each other, perhaps we can get them to be a little more considerate by caring about animals. There's a kernel of goodness in most people, and judging by the number of people who call a social services agency to intervene because they're concerned about the welfare of animals, we can use this spirit of compassion to intervene and prevent many forms of family dysfunction.

Given the themes and the evidence emerging from research, professionals in a wide array of disciplines can no longer afford to ignore the links between animal abuse, child abuse, domestic violence, and elder abuse. These forms of violence can no longer be seen or treated as mutually exclusive; they can, and often do, coexist and these linkages have serious implications for public policy and professional practice. A collaborative effort by the community holds great potential for making progress where individual efforts have been lagging. Acknowledging "the Link," addressing it in policy, and institutionalizing it in practice offers new opportunities to safeguard both the two-legged and four-legged members of the family.

Phil Arkow
Stratford, New Jersey
May 15, 2005

Acknowledgements

We would like to thank several people whose assistance and support helped make this book a reality. Among them are James Knight, DVM, Phil Arkow and Joshua M. Frank, Ph.D. We are also grateful to Patricia Keelen and Joanna Sinclair for fact-checking the resources, Jennifer Petruzzini for her creative touch and for making sure all the 'i's' were dotted and the 't's' were crossed, and Jodi Banfelder for her fieldwork insights. We would also like to acknowledge all the people who gave so generously of their time for interviews and to answer our many questions. Thanks also to our colleagues at HAVEN and BBC Worldwide Americas, especially Catherine Mirra.

Introduction

Every week somewhere in the country a story of animal abuse is so horrific it catches the attention of the media. A dog is found wandering through a suburban neighborhood, broken and bloodied, his eyes cut out by a 10-year old who "wanted to see what would happen." A group of college students duct tape firecrackers to a defenseless rabbit and then hurl the animal in the air after lighting the fuse—the victim is the pet of the key perpetrator. A kitten is found strangled and nailed to the front door, a message to the spouse of a domestic violence batterer that she is next. A dog is found dead, frozen to the ground in the middle of winter. His emaciated body is tethered to a pole, the chain around his neck there for so long it has grown into his skin. While many adults have seen at least one sensationalistic news piece in recent times detailing some horrific case of animal abuse or neglect, most people would be surprised to learn that such stories are far from isolated incidents. In fact, abuse and severe neglect of companion animals is actually a common occurrence in the United States. Unfortunately, far too much of the abuse and neglect that happens to these creatures never makes the local news. And, sadly, far too often animal abuse and neglect goes unnoticed by those who can intervene and stop the suffering.

You may have heard about the link between animal abuse and violence directed toward people. But how much do we really know about animal abuse, the perpetrators, or what to do to put an end to it? Over the course of the past decade researchers have documented a myriad of factors associated with animal abuse—factors that law enforcement and animal welfare professionals have known anecdotally for even longer. Unfortunately, while some of this information has made its way to those people who can do something about it, many professionals have yet to learn about the antecedents and consequences, as well as the red flags and the solutions for helping to stop animal abuse and neglect. The need to get the word out about animal abuse is precisely the reason we felt there was a need to write this book.

WHO SHOULD READ THIS BOOK?

This book is written for those professionals who are the most likely to come into contact with the victims and/or perpetrators of animal abuse: law enforcement, humane officers, counselors, family therapists and other mental health professionals, domestic violence caseworkers and shelter managers, animal control officers, district attorneys, judges, veterinarians, school teachers, child and family service case workers, fire department officials, animal welfare advocates, and many other professions can all gain from the information offered here. Students enrolled in victims of violence courses and those training to focus in law enforcement, counseling, social service work, family services and veterinary sciences will also find this book of value. This book is also intended for anyone committed to stop abuse and neglect of the victims who have no voice to speak for themselves.

I SIGNED ON TO HELP PEOPLE, NOT ANIMALS

Some people have asked, "With all of the violence directed toward humans, should we really be worrying about pets?" As we will see throughout this book, luckily there is no need for the goal of helping humans and the goal of helping companion animals to be competing or conflicting efforts. With a cooperative spirit and a coordinated plan, professionals can address the issues surrounding the welfare and well being of both human and non-human victims of violence. In fact, as we shall see later, helping animal victims of abuse can actually aid in helping human victims, making it easier and more effective to assist them in their recovery.

WHAT TO EXPECT

This book is designed to give professionals, students, and laypersons an overview of the most critical scientific and anecdotal findings about the factors surrounding animal abuse. The goal is to provide readers with the findings and strategies that are the most useful and effective in everyday, real-world settings. The research findings presented in this book include notable studies on animal abuse, perpetrators, and abusive environments, as well as the possible causes and outcomes thought to be linked to animal abuse. Included are discussions of recent research on the attitudes, perceptions and beliefs of animal abusers conducted by author Dr. Carlisle-Frank, in her work with the Foundation of Interdisciplinary Research and Education Promoting Animal Welfare [FIREPAW]. Officer Tom Flanagan outlines some real-life tales from the street, as well as strategies and techniques for recognizing and addressing animal abuse. Flanagan draws from his seminal work with the acclaimed Link-UP program, which brings law enforcement together with multiple municipal agencies to cooperatively and effectively resolve problems involving animal abuse.

What are the factors associated with animal abuse? Chapter One offers an overview of the magnitude of the problem of animal abuse and highlights some of the key antecedents and consequences of this serious social problem. Chapter One also examines why specific professions must learn to recognize the red flags of animal abuse and to become actively involved in stopping it.

Chapter Two explores where animal victims tend to come from as it explores some of the key trends and tendencies of the violent home environment in which pets are victimized. Domestic violence may be a key place you will find animal abuse, but not all family violence perpetrators batter the family pet. Chapter Three explores the trends and tendencies that may help identify those batterers who are most likely perpetrators of animal abuse.

What happens to cause kids to torture, abuse, and kill companion animals, even their own pets? Chapter Four explores the key factors associated with child and adolescent perpetrators of animal abuse. But overt abuse is not the only way companion animals suffer. Chapter Five explores the problem of severely neglected animals and offers problem-solving strategies for recognizing and helping companion animals suffering from severe neglect.

Some forms of animal abuse catch the attention of neighbors long before social service or law enforcement officials ever become aware it is going on. This form of animal abuse often involves filthy, odorous conditions created by large numbers of neglected and sickly animals living inside a person's single-family home. The cause? A condition that has come to be known as "animal hoarding." What compels people to collect animals to the point of causing them harm? Chapter Six explores the curious topic of hoarders and hoarding animals and Chapter Seven offers techniques and solutions for intervening and resolving hoarding cases. This chapter will teach you how to recognize the red flags of potential hoarding cases and how to solve the problem of hoarding in your community.

Now that the problems and causes of animal abuse have been explored, what can professionals do about it? Chapter Eight discusses how professionals can learn to recognize red flags and find those animals, individuals and families who need help. Chapter Nine offers tools and strategies for developing multi-disciplinary partnerships and seeking solutions for abused pets, and Chapter Ten offers valuable, practical resources to help professionals to network, come together and problem-solve when encountering suspected animal abuse and neglect cases in their communities.

Chapter One

Sticks and Stones Will Break Their Bones: Why We All Need to Get Involved in Stopping Animal Abuse

Many Americans have seen at least one sensationalistic news piece in recent times detailing some horrific case of animal abuse or neglect in their community. Unfortunately, far too much of the abuse and neglect that happens to these innocent creatures never makes the local news. As a consequence, those people who do not work with animal abuse-related issues on an ongoing basis often find it surprising to learn how prevalent animal abuse and neglect is in our country. Abuse and severe neglect of companion animals is actually a common occurrence in the United States (Flynn, 2000a). A frequently cited estimate attributed to the Humane Society of the United States (HSUS) places the number of animals abused in the U.S. each year in the hundreds of thousands (Robin, 1999). As of the summer of 2004 there were 2,440 animal abuse cases and 2,778 animal abusers listed on a national online animal abuse database (Gerbasi, 2004). Unfortunately, since animal cruelty reports are neither uniformly collected nor maintained, there is no way to determine precisely the number of animal cruelty cases reported nationwide each year (Davidson, 1998). Just as important, far too often animal abuse and neglect goes unnoticed by those who are in the best positions to intervene and stop the suffering. Even when professionals on the frontline suspect animal cruelty may be occurring, many are unaware how urgently their involvement is needed to stop the abuse. The need to provide those professionals most likely to come into contact with victims and/or perpetrators of animal abuse with the latest findings about animal abuse and abusers, how to recognize it, and practical techniques and solutions to stop it is precisely the reason we felt there was a need to write this book.

Over the past two decades researchers have amassed a good deal of information about the factors surrounding animal abuse. In fact, the current body of research and articles about animal abuse and its link to violence directed at people is quite sizeable these days and continues to grow. The findings from empirical studies and theoretical papers can now be found in scientific journals in a variety of fields. They are so plentiful, in fact, in the time it takes for this book to go to print there will already be several more new resources beyond those cited in this and subsequent chapters. Given the vast amount of studies and findings available today it is hard to believe how relatively new the body of knowledge about animal cruelty actually is.

Animal cruelty became a part of my vocabulary long before FIREPAW ever existed. It was back in 1985 when I first became aware of the horrors of animal abuse. It was at the residential treatment home for severely emotionally disturbed children and adolescents where I worked. The kids there, it turned out, had no shortage of stories about cruelty to animals—both those they witnessed and those they inflicted themselves. A few years later, while reading the assignments of upper-middle class students enrolled in a Victims of Violence course at a major university, I was struck with how eerily similar their stories of animal abuse were to those of their troubled counterparts. Back then there was a smattering of professionals who were writing about the significance of animal abuse as a marker for potential violence overall, but the issue was certainly not grabbing any headlines.

Now, two decades since I first learned about the youngsters' disturbing tales of animal abuse, the landscape has changed dramatically. The college students in a family violence course I taught recently were still surprised to learn about the significance of pet abuse and its link with violence directed toward humans, but by then there was no shortage of research findings and anecdotal reports from professionals in the field to convince them.

Students are not the only beneficiaries of the comprehensive body of literature now available on the topic of animal cruelty. Thanks to the scientific findings and practical insights from practitioners in the field a myriad of professionals can now become active players in stopping this abuse. With ample information now available the next step is to reach those professionals who are most likely to encounter animal abuse to (1) make them aware of how much their involvement is needed to speak up and take action on behalf of these victims, and (2) give them the tools and strategies to make it happen. Researcher Clifton Flynn (2000a) has pointed out that animals and human infants are the only victims of systematic discrimination and exploitation who truly cannot speak on their own behalf. The silence, Flynn argues, makes it easier for all of us to ignore their plight and its relation to our lives. Can we go on remaining silent? Absolutely. But then we must acknowledge that we too have become victims.

WHAT IS ANIMAL CRUELTY?

What do we mean when we talk about animal "abuse" and "neglect"? Scientists researching the topic of animal cruelty have used variations of definitions for what constitutes animal abuse, most commonly including acts that are deemed socially unacceptable, deliberate and as causing unnecessary suffering and harm inflicted on animals. This and similar definitions fall short when one includes animal hoarding under the rubric of "animal abuse" as it can be argued that those persons who suffer from mental illnesses such as obsessive compulsive disorder do not harm animals deliberately. For the purpose of this book we define animal abuse broadly as any act that contributes to the pain, suffering, or death of a companion animal or that threatens the welfare of that animal (Vermeulen and Odendaal, 1993). With this broad definition we account for abuse that is physical (including sexual in nature), mental (as in the case of causing extreme and/or prolonged stress to an animal), active abuse or passive neglect, direct or indirect, and intentional or unintentional (Agnew, 1998).

As further clarification we have included for consideration seven definitions of animal cruelty proposed by Merz-Perez and Heide (2004). The authors state that the definitions are not mutually exclusive and that they are intended to establish distinct conceptual parameters for a more clear understanding of the various manifestations of animal cruelty. The definitions are intended to broaden our understanding of the warning signals for both intervention and future research.

1. Passive cruelty: individual observes acts of animal cruelty but neither participates nor intervenes
2. Participatory cruelty: Individual actively participates in an act of animal cruelty
3. Perfunctory cruelty: a child commits an animal cruelty act either alone or with same-aged peers in which the targeted animal is perceived to be an object or "target", devoid of sentience
4. Parochial cruelty: regionally or culturally inspired acts of animal cruelty (such as dogfights or cockfights)
5. Partitive cruelty: conceptual compartmentalization of animals to justify animal cruelty
6. Psychological cruelty: animal cruelty that results from the particularities of the individual's subconscious, unconscious, intellectual, emotional or pathological manifestations
7. Predatory cruelty: purposeful, planned and often sequential acts of animal cruelty. The authors offer as an example killing animals purely for the sake of killing.

As a footnote to this section it is important to mention that researchers have called for the establishment of standardized definitions and measures of animal abuse (Ascione, 1998b). Such standardization will be useful for scientists and practitioners alike, as it will help with consistency of both communication and understanding in what is frequently a complex phenomenon.

WHAT IS ANIMAL ABUSE COMPRISED OF?

Animal abuse cases resulting in convictions have reported such cruelties as beating, stabbing, burning, drowning, hanging, fighting, hoarding, poisoning, shooting, throwing against a wall or out a window, neglect (including intentional starvation of an animal and neglecting to provide adequate water, shelter, stimulation, emotional attention, and veterinary care), torture, choking, mutilation, bestiality and kicking (www.Pet-Abuse.com, 2005).

WHY DOES ANIMAL ABUSE HAPPEN?

There have been numerous empirical studies and theoretical papers over the past two decades focused on uncovering the possible antecedents of animal abuse. The studies have tested theories about the factors that may precipitate animal abuse using a variety of subjects from diverse backgrounds and under a wide range of settings. Other researchers have replicated many of these studies with completely different subjects and the results were still found to be statistically significant. So if there are so many possible factors associated with animal abuse, which are right? Some may be better at explaining certain scenarios, while other factors may be better at explaining different types of settings surrounding animal abuse. The most likely possibility however is that a combination of several of these factors may be at play depending on the type of animal abuse and abuser encountered.

Ignorance and Inability to Empathize

Many people are unaware that animals experience suffering and pain. The depersonalizing or objectifying of animals perpetuates such ignorance. Animal abuse may be more prevalent among those individuals who have difficulty with empathy—especially with the ability to empathize with the pain experienced by animals (Ascione, 1992). Agnew (1998) has argued that many people are ignorant about the fact that animals experience adverse consequences to being abused and therefore have difficulty empathizing with the pain felt by animals. Herzog and Borghardt (1988) found that many people believe animals do not experience pain, therefore leading animal abusers to often deny or minimize the pain experienced by the animals they abuse. Believing that animals are not sentient beings may contribute to the belief that abusing companion animals is not a serious matter (Herzog and Borghardt, 1988).

A Lack of Adequate Coping Skills

It has been suggested that those who engage in animal abuse tend to be more sensitive to stress and strain (Agnew, 1998). Batterers may abuse the family pets to reduce stress or to get revenge against the perceived "cause" of the stress. One of the primary stressors for abusers may be the pet's own behavior. Research findings have indicated that animal abusers frequently report the animals' "bad" behaviors as a reason for abusing them (DeViney, Dickert and Lockwood, 1983; Kellert and Felthous 1985; Felthous and Kellert 1987).

Animal abuse may occur as a release of frustration and anger by individuals with poor coping skills. The family pet is often a scapegoat for such individuals, especially in homes with ongoing domestic violence (DeViney, et al., 1983; Kellert and Felthous, 1985; Vermeulen and Odendaal, 1993; Adams, 1994; Carlisle-Frank, Frank and Nielsen, 2004a).

Perpetrators are Socialized to Abuse

One theory to explain the causes of animal abuse states that it may occur more often by those individuals who have been socialized to do so—either through reinforcements, rewards, praise from family or friends or punishment such as being belittled as a "sissy" for not abusing animals (Zahn-Waxler, Hollenbeck and Radke-Yarrow, 1984). This argument is based on the social learning theory which basically says that we learn our beliefs and behaviors through the role models we are exposed to and the reinforcements and punishments we receive from others in our social world such as family, teachers, religious institutions, peers, neighbors, the media, and so on. Children will often mimic their parents' treatment of animals. If abusive behaviors toward the family pet are condoned or rewarded children may learn that animal abuse is the optimal behavior.

Also drawing from the social learning theory Agnew (1998) has argued that the causes of animal abuse result from (1) ignorance about the abusive consequences to animals, (2) the belief that abuse is often justified, (3) the perception that animal abuse is personally beneficial. Agnew also argues that other factors may be at play including individual traits such as the person's ability to experience empathy, the abuser's socialization, personal level of stress, the individual's level of social control including his or her attachment to animals, his/her commitment to conventional institutions (family, school, etc.), the species and breed of the animal victim and the abuser's social position.

Abuse is Beneficial and Justified

What sort of benefits could come from abusing animals? Perceived benefits might include forcing the animal to comply with demands such as not barking or clawing the furniture. Benefits could also include achieving an elevated position among peers or gaining compliance and control over a spouse or girlfriend (Adams, 1994). The coexistence of violence, power and control issues found in other violent scenarios are likely operating in animal abuse cases as well (Solot, 1997). Another perceived benefit of animal abuse for abusers may be that it demonstrates masculinity for some individuals such as aggression, domination and control. Animal abusers interviewed by researchers have revealed they have abused animals to impress others with their capacity for violence, improve aggressive skills, and to exercise total power and control (Kellert and Felthous, 1985).

People may believe that animal abuse is deserved or justified in certain cases. Usually this is because the animal has done something they do not want or because the animal possesses characteristics they do not like. Retaliation against an animal people believe has "wronged" them in some way or to stop unwanted behaviors or to act against a certain species or breed the perpetrator dislikes (like cats) have also been reported (DeViney, et al., 1985; Kellert and Felthous, 1985).

In short, it has been argued that animal abuse is most likely to occur when perpetrators are unaware of the consequences their abusive behavior has for animals, perpetrators do not think their behavior is wrong, and they believe there is some benefit from their abusive behavior (Agnew, 1998).

Sense of Entitlement

Some people believe animals are not worthy of moral consideration because humans are superior and should have dominating rights to do what they want with animals (Serpell, 1986). The belief that animals are private property and should therefore be off-limits to outside interference may be another contributing factor as to why people justify doing whatever they want to their companion animals (Agnew, 1998).

Personality Dysfunction

Animal cruelty is one of numerous behaviors that indicate extreme personality dysfunction with poor impulse control (Lembke, 1994). Animal abuse may occur as a result of personality characteristics such as impulsivity, sensation-seeking tendencies, a tendency for irritability, and tendencies of low self-control (Gottfredson and Hirshi, 1990; Agnew, 1998).

Religious and Regional Subcultures

Religious practices and regional subcultures such as those rural subcultures where hunting is encouraged (Pope-Lance and Engelsman, 1987; Herzog and Borghardt, 1988; Bowd and Bowd, 1989; Statman, 1990; Adams, 1994; Agnew, 1998; Flynn, 2002; Carlisle-Frank, et al., 2004a) and urban subcultures where dog-fighting and cockfighting are viewed as acceptable forms of behavior may foster a generalized belief about animals that devalues their ability to experience pain.

Key Motivations to Abuse Animals

The key motivations for committing cruelty to animals according to researchers Kellert and Felthous (1985) are:

- to control an animal
- to retaliate against an animal
- to satisfy a prejudice against a species or breed of animal
- to express aggression through an animal (such as training dogs to fight)
- to enhance one's aggressiveness/to impress others with one's capacity for violence
- to shock people for amusement/to entertain friends
- to get revenge against another person
- displaced hostility (from a person to an animal)
- nonspecific sadism

Attitudes, Perceptions and Beliefs about Animals

And finally, as we will see in more detail in Chapter Three, animal abuse may occur from the perpetrators' attitudes, perceptions and beliefs about animals (Carlisle-Frank, et al., 2004a). This may include viewing companion animals as objects or property rather than as sentient beings with feelings and preferences, believing that the family pet is the primary source of one's family and personal problems, and the belief that the family pet intentionally disobeys the perpetrator because the animal lacks respects for the perpetrator's authority.

WHERE IS ANIMAL ABUSE OCCURRING?

Animal abuse has been reported in urban, rural and suburban communities across the country. It crosses all educational, ethnic and socioeconomic barriers. Research studies have found that animal abuse within the context of domestic violence has been reported to occur to victims residing in urban, rural and suburban settings as well (Quinlisk, 1995; Ascione, 1998a; Flynn, 2000b; Carlisle-Frank, et al., 2004a).

WHO IS DOING ALL THE ABUSING OF ANIMALS?

Reports from researchers and law enforcement tell us animal abuse is primarily being done by the following groups:

- Domestic violence batterers: A number of studies and articles have documented the pervasiveness of violence directed towards pets in abusive homes (DeViney, et al., 1983; Kellert and Felthous, 1985; Zahn-Waxler, et al., 1984; Lockwood and Hodge, 1986; Ascione, 1993; Adams, 1994; Arkow, 1994a; Beirne, 1995; Boat, 1995; Arkow, 1996; Lockwood and Church, 1996; Ascione, Weber, and Wood, 1997a,b; LaCroix, 1998; Robin, 1999; Ascione and Arkow, 1999; Flynn, 2000a,b; Ponder and Lockwood, 2000; Turner, 2000). This group of animal abusers is predominately males (Kellert, 1980; Galvin and Herzog, 1992) but females are also perpetrators of violence against pets. Threatening to kill or harm or actually killing or harming companion animals is not uncommon in violent families as the batterer uses the animal to control or manipulate his or her partner (DeViney, et al., 1983; Kellert and Felthous, 1985; Zahn-Waxler, et al., 1984; Ascione, 1993; Adams, 1994; Carlisle-Frank, et al., 2004a). Animal abuse has been found to occur within both heterosexual and same-sex partnerships (Renzetti, 1992);
- Individuals with personality disorders such as conduct disorder or antisocial personality disorder (Ascione and Lockwood, 2001);
- Children and teens: Primarily males (Flynn, 1999a; 2001; Miller, 2001); Animal abuse has been found to be most prevalent among preschoolers, de-

creasing during childhood until age 16 (Achenbach, Howell, Quay, and Conners, 1991);

- Adult women and men engaged in compulsive hoarding behaviors: Approximately 75% of animal hoarders have been found to be females (Kuehn, 2002);
- Adult women and men with unrealistic expectations about how animals should behave and/or have a need to control the animals' behavior: (DeViney, et al., 1983; Zahn-Waxler, et al., 1984; Ascione, 1993; Adams, 1994; Carlisle-Frank, et al., 2004a);
- Adult women and men who engage in both passive and active neglect of their companion animals;
- Adolescents and adults (most often males) who are prone to engage in a range of criminal activities including delinquency, property offenses, drug offenses and public disorder offenses (Arluke, Levin, Luke and Ascione, 1999; Henry, 2004; Merz-Perez and Heide, 2004) as well as violent offenses (Kellert and Felthous, 1985; Felthous and Kellert, 1987a; Merz-Perez, Heide and Silverman, 2001; Merz-Perez and Heide, 2004).

High rates of animal cruelty have been reported by violent offenders including rapists and perpetrators of sexual homicide (Tingle, Barnard, Robbins, Newman and Hutchinson, 1986; Douglas, Burgess and Ressler, 1995). The FBI perspective on animal cruelty: since the 1970's investigation and prosecution of crimes against animals has been an important tool for identifying people who are or may become perpetrators of violent crimes against people. The FBI views cruelty to animals and cruelty to humans as a continuum. Additionally, the FBI has interviewed multiple murderers. Self-reports indicated that 36% of multiple murderers tortured and killed animals as children; 46% did so as teens (Lockwood and Church, 1996).

So who is abusing animals? In short, perpetrators of animal cruelty can be young children, teenagers, young and middle-aged adults or senior citizens. And, while animal abusers can be female, the overwhelming majority of perpetrators are male (Flynn, 2001).

Animal abuse statistics:

A 1997 study by the National Humane Society found that . . .

~30% of animal abusers also harmed a child, wife or girlfriend
~90% of animal abusers were male

The majority of animal abuse victims were dogs.

Of the 1,677 animal abuse cases and 1,863 perpetrators analyzed in a Humane Society of the United States study, male perpetrators were involved in the majority of animal abuse cases including intentional animal cruelty and animal fighting cases. Additionally . . .

56% of the cases were intentional
44% involved extreme neglect
76% of all cases had perpetrators who were male
92% of intentional abuse cases involved males
91% of animal fighting cases involved males
62% of hoarders were female
48% of neglect cases involved females

And finally, there is a limited amount of research that seems to indicate that ethnicity and education may affect the tendency to tolerate animal abuse. The results seem to suggest that Caucasians and well-educated individuals have less tolerance for animal abuse than other ethnic groups and those individuals with less education (Kellert, 1980; 1983; 1985; Galvin and Herzog, 1992; Nibert, 1994).

WHO CAN RECOGNIZE AND IDENTIFY POTENTIAL RED FLAGS OF ANIMAL ABUSE?

Certain professions are in a unique position to recognize and identify potential red flags for animal abuse and to probe further and/or seek input from other investigative agencies. In particular those professions who are most likely to come into contact with victims and/or perpetrators of animal abuse including veterinarians, social service workers (including child, elderly and family services), law enforcement (including humane investigators and animal control officers), professionals from the penal/legal system, animal welfare advocates, domestic violence caseworkers, fire department officials, and counselors/therapists. It has only been relatively recently—over the course of the past two decades—that the link between animal abuse and violence directed toward humans has started to become an issue of importance for professionals working in law enforcement, district attorneys and judges, municipalities and legislation and social service agencies (Lockwood and Hodge, 1986). Unfortunately, while the word has certainly gotten out about animal cruelty there are still many professionals from these groups who are unaware of the prevalence of animal abuse, its link with violence directed toward humans, or the impact animal abuse has on those people directly affected or the effect it has at the macro level—our society as a whole. Equally problematic is the fact that many professionals are (1) still unaware of how critically their participation is needed in stopping animal abuse and (2) unable to locate an organized system within their community with which to report their suspicions of animal abuse. Chapter Nine will offer strategies for professionals to establish a solution-focused network within their community to address animal abuse. For now, however, let's take a look at the professions who are most likely to encounter the red flags of animal abuse.

DOMESTIC VIOLENCE CASEWORKERS, THERAPISTS AND COUNSELORS

Domestic violence caseworkers, counselors and therapists are in the frontline for identifying animal abuse. Chapter Two will present more details about the findings but for now let it suffice to say that numerous research studies and surveys of both domestic violence victims and domestic violence shelters over the past two decades have found that of those victims with pets anywhere between 23% and 91% of victims reported having witnessed their partners either threaten to harm or actually harm or kill their companion animals. Additionally, one study surveying domestic violence shelters across the country found that while reports of pet abuse were common among domestic violence victims, few shelters routinely ask victims about the abuse of their pets during the intake interview (Ascione, Weber, and Wood, 1997b). If you are working as a domestic violence caseworker or counselor or you are a therapist treating previous victims of domestic violence, chances are high that a good percentage of these individuals have experienced threats of harm or actual harm to their companion animals.

Veterinarians

Veterinarians are one of the frontline professions for identifying animal abuse. A number of key features have been found that can act as red flags, alerting veterinarians to probe further and/or notify authorities of the potential for animal abuse. A study of veterinarians' perceptions conducted in the United Kingdom sought to determine the extent of Non-Accidental Injury (NAI) in companion animals seen in veterinary practices and to ascertain the characteristics veterinarians had recognized (Munro, 1996). Another objective of the study was to identify the features of NAI syndrome. Anonymous questionnaires were sent to a random sample of small animal practitioners.

Non-accidental Injury (NAI) was acknowledged by 91.3% of the 404 participants. Another 48.3% reported having either suspected or actually seen NAI
cases. Sexual abuse and suspected cases of Munchausen syndrome by proxy
(a disorder whereby individuals cause others—usually their children or pets
—to become sick or injured in order to garner attention and sympathy) were
also reported (Munro, 1996; Munro and Thrusfield, 2001).

Factors revealed in the study as raising suspicions or facilitating recognition of NAI:

* implication of another person
* features of the animal's history
* referral agency involvement
* behavior of owner
* behavior of animal
* nature of injuries
* socioeconomic status of owners

In the majority of reports the reason for suspecting animal abuse was a
combination of these most commonly reported features:

Implication of a particular person. The person bringing the animal in for examination often implicated a family member. In some cases owners of the
   animal actually admitted to harming the animal.
Violence in the home. This was a feature that aroused suspicion in veterinarians of NAI.
History inconsistent with the injury. The presentation of injuries that were
   markedly inconsistent with the animal's history that was given was seen as
   a major feature of NAI in animals. The author noted that the same clinical
   and pathological features of animal abuse emphasize similarities to diagnostic features for child abuse (Munro, 1998).
Behavior of the animal's owner/guardian. This was another key feature in
   raising suspicion of veterinarians for NAI. The study respondents' descriptions included witnessing behaviors such as "implausible and aggressive,"
   "obvious discomfort and embarrassment," "uneasy," "reluctant to give animal's history," "lack of concern," "angry on questioning," and "not reacting as expected to the news."
Repetitive injuries. This feature aroused particular suspicion and was seen as
   an important factor. Either the animal was presented for surgery more than
   once with injuries or different ages of injuries were noted during examination. Some animals were presented numerous times, each time with a different injury.

Multiple occurrences within the same household. Respondents reported concern about other animals who had also suffered injury or death under unexplained circumstances in households suspected of animal abuse.

Socioeconomic Status. While cases of NAI were more common in low-SES cases NAI were also reported among highly educated professionals.

Munro (1996) has called for the establishment of diagnostic criteria within the veterinarian field to separate accidental and deliberate injury to animals.

FIRE DEPARTMENT OFFICIALS

Fire department professionals are often on the frontline for recognizing two specific types of animal abuse: (1) animal hoarding and (2) animal abuse as a symptom of conduct disorder. The latter often comes to the attention of fire officials because another common symptom of this disorder is fire setting. The upcoming chapters on hoarding and child/adolescent perpetrators of animal abuse offer the key antecedents, consequences, and red flags for recognizing these types of animal abuse. It is recommended that fire officials offer information about how to recognize signs of potential animal abuse to their firefighters as well as establishing a network of professionals within your community so that the appropriate agencies can be notified when potential animal abuse is identified.

LAW ENFORCEMENT/JUDGES/PROSECUTORS

Law enforcement officers come in to contact with perpetrators of animal abuse on an ongoing basis. While many municipalities have educated their law enforcement officials about the red flags of animal abuse and the link between animal cruelty and violence directed toward people, unfortunately there are still some law enforcement agencies that are uninformed. Still others do not place animal abuse as a high priority. But there are also a couple of key issues at play that can run interference with law enforcement officers taking direct and speedy action against suspected animal abusers. Anecdotal reports from members of the community contacting FIREPAW and interviews with animal protectionists tell us many times law enforcement is not even aware of recent animal welfare laws at the state and county-wide level and therefore do not always respond to animal cruelty complaints that might be covered under those laws. Is this an accurate account? Or could it be that law enforcement officials are aware of the laws but believe they lack support to take any real action? The answer oftentimes is a little of both.

While the criminal justice system is starting to acknowledge animal cruelty as a serious offense (Sauder, 2000), there is still a problem protecting animals due to reluctance by the legal/penal system to enforce animal anti-cruelty laws. When legislators, prosecutors and judges are reluctant to legislate and enforce the current animal anti-cruelty laws, law enforcement may follow suit. After all, what is the point of conducting arrests and investigations when past history tells law enforcement the cases are going nowhere?

Many states have enacted felony-level statutes for animal cruelty for "certain" forms of animal abuse (Ascione, 2001). According to experts on animal anti-cruelty laws, however, most of these laws lack the strength to be much of a deterrent. Each of the 50 states has legislated animal laws primarily designed to punish people who commit animal cruelty according to the Animal Legal Rights Survey of the Animal Welfare Institute. These laws were enacted on moral grounds as opposed to being created for the protection of animals. Therefore, many of these laws as they are currently written and enforced afford animals only the minimum of protection (LaCroix, 1998). According to LaCroix, scholars of animal law agree that the current anti-cruelty laws fail to provide animals adequate protection and have little to no effect on deterring perpetrators from abusing animals. The two primary reasons for this lack of protection for animals are (1) the primary goals of animal cruelty laws have traditionally not been to protect animals, and (2) legal professionals have historically been reluctant to legislate and/or enforce these laws.

Why would legal professionals be reluctant to enforce the current animal anti-cruelty laws through the legal/penal system? The primary reason is that the pervasive attitude (among policy makers, legislators and society at large) has been that animals are not a top priority. Another reason is that legislators have difficulty agreeing on the definitions of what constitutes abusive and cruel treatment of animals. This in turn has lead to difficulty in the interpretations of current animal anti-cruelty laws and subsequent enforcement of these laws. Another reason there is a generalized reluctance to enforce animal anti-cruelty laws is that the penalties are frequently misdemeanors. Felony offenses, not misdemeanors, are what grabs and holds the time and attention of prosecutors. While some states have adopted felony laws and harsher penalties for animal cruelty in recent years (Frasch, Otto, Olsen and Ernest, 1999) overall, misdemeanor-level charges and weak sentencing still prevail. Additionally, a lack of funding and manpower as well as confusion over just who has the authority to enforce the animal anti-cruelty laws causes sluggish reactions to animal abuse cases: Within a single community law enforcement, municipal animal control and humane investigators from animal shelters and animal welfare organizations may all be involved at some level with intervention and prevention of animal abuse and enforcing local animal anti-cruelty laws. Delegating just which agency has authority to do what has lead to a breakdown at the systemic level and the subsequent lack of enforcement of animal anti-cruelty laws. Finally, a lack of available resources to properly train law enforcement how to recognize and intervene in animal abuse cases has left many communities with inconsistent and unpredictable enforcement of animal anti-cruelty laws (LaCroix, 1998). In short, there is not a lot of support or incentive in many communities for law enforcement to vigorously pursue and enforce laws to protect animals from cruel and abusive treatment. Chapter Nine will offer an overview of some successful programs already in place that have overcome the obstacles involving law enforcement and legal/ penal professionals.

WHY ANIMALS FREQUENTLY SUFFER IN SILENCE

We have already seen that weak anti-cruelty laws and the subsequent reaction to them helps to prolong the suffering of companion animals. Some programs such as the one headed up by my co-author, have had tremendous success in conviction rates for animal cruelty cases but many more have not. Arluke and Luke (1997) conducted research over a fifteen-year period from 1975 to 1990 in the state of Massachusetts on the extent and outcomes of animal cruelty cases. Less than half of the cases of animal cruelty actually resulted in a conviction, only one-third of those perpetrators found guilty were fined, and only 10% of perpetrators received jail time. Psychological counseling or community service occurred in only a small percentage in the sentencing of perpetrators found guilty of animal abuse.

But anti-cruelty laws that lack robust penalties and support are not the only reasons animal abuse is so prevalent. Some of the other primary reasons animals continue to suffer in silence stem from the fact that lawmakers and law enforcers do not live in a vacuum. These people must be accountable to the people in their communities. According to Flynn (2000a) society tends to value animals less than people so abuse of animals is not taken as seriously as it should be. If the public makes it clear they wish their tax dollars to be spent on human-related rather than animal-related problems, it is challenging at best for those creating and enforcing the laws to do otherwise.

Unfortunately, part of the reason members of the general public do not always support attention and energy being directed to stopping animal abuse is they simply have no idea about the extent of this societal problem. This is in large part because the media only reports a small percentage of animal abuse cases so the general public has no concept of how prevalent cruelty to animals actually is (Flynn, 2000a).

Additionally, those professionals who are most likely to encounter symptoms of abuse and help animal victims are often poorly informed about the need for their involvement, the red flags or warning signs to look for, or even what steps to take when they do become aware of suspected animal abuse. This is understandable. The interviews we have conducted with domestic violence caseworkers, law enforcement and veterinarians reveal that most professionals are too busy with their daily responsibilities and keeping up with the professional conferences and literature of their own field to research and dig their way through mounds of literature in the social, behavioral and animal welfare sciences to keep up with the findings on animal abuse.

Still other professionals may be well aware of the red flags surrounding animal abuse but are concerned with the reporting risks . . . some are working without the support of their own agencies, ancillary agencies or the community in general. Still others may feel they lack the training to report a case definitively as animal abuse to authorities. These are all reasonable explanations. They are also key reasons to develop community partnerships made up of multiple professions with the primary goal to work to end the unnecessary abuse of animals. As we will see in Chapter Nine, such multi-disciplinary partnerships allow for the proper training and cross-training to recognize animal abuse as well as facilitating open communications with and support of other agencies. Community partnerships comprised of multiple professionals assure that more than one agency will become involved, thus facilitating prompt investigation and appropriate action.

WHY HELPING ABUSED ANIMALS IS CRITICAL— EVEN WHEN THERE ARE HUMAN VICTIMS IN NEED

As a society we are finally moving toward recognition that cruelty to animals can result in great harm not only to the animal victims but also to their human caretakers, the perpetrator, and society as a whole. It has not only been the scientific community whose interest has moved in this direction. The general public has also given increased attention to animal cruelty in the last decade (Vollum, Buffington-Vollum and Longmire, 2004). In fact, the public has begun to express concern over both the effects on animals and the potential for human harm (Ascione and Lockwood, 2001). This is evident in a 1996 survey of American households conducted by the Humane Society of the United States (HSUS) that found:

- 42% respondents believe animal cruelty is a moderately to extremely serious problem

- 71% Americans surveyed supported the idea to make animal abuse a felony
- 81% of respondents felt enforcement of animal anti-cruelty laws need to be strengthened

Some of the specific reasons compelling us to come together and take action to stop animal abuse include:

1. Children who witness abuse of their pets by their parents may have an increased likelihood to go on to abuse animals themselves and/or they may have an increased likelihood to go on to become violent toward people.

Severe, intentional animal abuse increasingly is recognized by society as being symptomatic of a mental disorder and psychological assessment and treatment are now required or recommended in an increasing amount of such cases. This is increasingly true in animal hoarding cases and cases of extreme neglect to animals but it is especially true for animal cruelty cases. The reason is that according to researchers and psychologists at organizations such as Society and Animals Forum (a.k.a. Animals and Society Institute; previously Psychologists for the Ethical Treatment of Animals, PsyETA), Doris Day Animal League (DDAL), and the Humane Society of the United States (HSUS), animal cruelty is often one of the first warning signs of future aggressive behavior and violence directed at both animals and humans. The results of numerous scientific studies have demonstrated that a link exists between animal cruelty and violence directed toward humans and an increased likelihood for children who witness or commit animal cruelty to become violent toward animals and/or people in the future (Flynn, 1999a; Arkow, 2003).

2. Children who witness animal abuse in their own homes may go on to lack trust in the system and those in authority when professionals in a position to intercede do nothing.

Children and adolescents are not empowered in our society. They are dependent on those in authority to step in and take action to protect them and the ones they love—including their companion animals. When professionals who can help choose to look the other way and hope someone else steps in this can cause young people to develop learned helplessness. Why should they risk telling adult authority figures about abuse—or any other criminal activity, for that matter—when nothing is done to help them or their pets? Developing learned helplessness about the effectiveness of authority figures could affect a young person's entire future. A lack of trust for those who are meant to help and protect them can affect their future relationships with employers, loved ones, friendships, and even their level of involvement when others need their help. In short, when young people lose trust for authority and traditional helping sources such as law enforcement, medical/veterinary professionals, and family service professionals it has the potential to adversely affect their entire community and society as a whole.

3. Spillover effect to rest of community/Larger social problems arise from the violence in general directed toward animals.

There is now societal pressure on legislators to create and enforce animal cruelty laws. This is because our society is finally beginning to realize that violence in general is pervasive and dangerous for everyone. Those who perpetrate violence behind closed doors whether it is directed at people or animals, eventually come outside with the rest of us. Their poor impulse control can be seen in the form of road rage, violence in the workplace, angry acts directed at neighbors, and a host of other deleterious behaviors. Perpetrators of animal abuse are among us every day and if left unchecked we are all vulnerable to be on the receiving end of their outbursts.

Just as perpetrators do not live in a vacuum, neither do their victims. Family members of animals who are abused are also among us. Witnessing a beloved family member being threatened or abused can cause significant stress to the pets' guardians. This stress can translate in to a myriad of behavioral and physical maladies and can spill over in to the school classroom, the workplace, and everywhere else the witnesses go. If the witnesses to animal abuse are children it may cause serious developmental and behavioral problems—problems that if left unchecked may affect those in the child's neighborhood and entire community for years to come.

There are also added financial burdens resulting from animal abuse. Violence directed toward animals, like violence directed toward people, costs communities a significant amount of money.

There are costs associated with veterinary care and costs to house animals who have been abused, as well as costs to euthanize those animals whose injuries are too severe to save. If the caretakers cannot afford to pay these costs the community frequently picks up the tab. There are also costs associated with counseling for family members who have witnessed the abuse of a beloved companion animal. Such therapy is critical and can be long-term—especially if those witnesses are children.

Animal abuse that occurs as a result of conduct disorder can be dangerous and even deadly for the entire community. As we will see in Chapter Four, one of the antecedents of animal abuse is children and teenagers with conduct disorder—a disorder where one of the primary markers is animal abuse. When those in a position to do something about it ignore animal abuse, there is an increased likelihood that the deviant behaviors will escalate. Left unchecked, conduct disorder is likely to result in more violence, possibly in the form of fires intentionally set to private homes.

In the final analysis, animal abuse is embedded in a complex content. Whether it is obvious or covert we cannot escape the spillover effect of this violence at the community and societal levels.

4. Suffering of innocent victims who cannot speak for themselves about what is happening to them is occurring. Moral and ethical considerations dictate that intervening is the right thing to do.

As researchers Ascione and Lockwood (2001) have stated, "Cruelty to animals must be taken seriously as a problem in its own right, independent of what it may tell us about the potential for human harm." One does not have to be an animal advocate to appreciate this. When innocent creatures are suffering from being tortured and abused, we must take action. We have a moral and ethical obligation to stop the cruelty directed toward all creatures whenever possible. If not us, then who?

5. Human victims' well-being frequently hinges on their animals' well-being and safety.

Helping abused animals does not have to run interference with efforts to help human victims. In fact, helping animal victims can actually make helping their human counterparts more effective. The reason is because so many people are bonded with their companion animals. Human victims of domestic violence may be especially attached to their pets because of the comfort and solace their companion animals offer them (Ascione, 1998a; Flynn, 1999a; Carlisle-Frank, et al., 2004a). Human victims will experience far less stress and worry about their decision to leave the batterer if they know there is compassion and concern for their animal family members. In short, helping animal victims does not negate nor lessen the assistance to human victims, and in fact, may make such efforts more effective.

SUMMARY

As researcher Clifton Flynn (2000a) has argued, professionals who study and work with families must attend to animal abuse for seven key reasons:

1. animal abuse is a serious antisocial behavior frequently committed by children and teens
2. animal abuse is a relatively common occurrence in childhood
3. animal abuse has the potential for negative developmental consequences
4. animal abuse is correlated with violence directed toward humans
5. animal abuse is related to (and may be a red flag for) family violence
6. the well-being of innocent companion animals is at stake

7. addressing the problem of animal abuse will help lead to a less violent society overall for both human and non-human animals

In summary, the reason helping animals is critical even when there are human victims in need all comes down to this: stopping the suffering of animals
benefits everyone, and not helping will sooner or later cost all of us a very serious social price.

A FINAL THOUGHT

If you are a student or a relative newcomer to your profession, this may be the
first exposure you have had to the topic of animal abuse and its link to violence
directed toward people and a host of other serious social ills. If you are a seasoned professional, you have likely been exposed to the general findings about
this topic but can benefit greatly from a more comprehensive look at the findings about the antecedents, consequences and potential solutions to the problems
associated with animal cruelty in your community. No matter what point you are
coming in at, the following chapters are designed to offer a user-friendly, at-a-
glance, encapsulated overview of the wealth of findings now available on the
topic of animal abuse, real life tales from the street from a seasoned law enforcement officer working on the frontline with animal abuse cases, red flags for
recognizing potential animal abuse, strategies for tackling the problem, and finally, resources for learning more to begin your own multidisciplinary partnership to stop animal abuse in your community. As researchers have argued, although the connection between animal cruelty and human problems has been
well established by case research, many professionals are still unaware of the
magnitude of the problem. It is most important to share this information with
those professionals in the frontline who are in a position to recognize the red
flags: veterinarians, law enforcement officers, animal control officers, humane
agents, fire officials, domestic violence shelter workers, therapists, counselors,
elderly and family services professionals and child welfare professionals. As
Lockwood and Hodge (1986) have argued, "It is also important to get people
from these professions talking with one another." It is a primary goal of this book
to offer the informational and resource tools needed to do just that.

FROM IN THE TRENCHES

The text that you are now holding in your hands came about through the collaboration of two authors writing from somewhat different backgrounds but focusing on the same objective. My own personal words will come to you from the

perspective of someone who has been there and done that for a period of over thirty years. My stories and statements come from a purely "on the street" point of view. Very little classroom or academic theory will have an influence on my uncensored descriptions that will follow throughout these writings. My aim is to reach as many people as possible from the myriad of disciplines spread across the entire makeup of today's society. As you read along I hope you will note the many different agencies and people that I call upon for assistance during the various investigations. I hope you will also be very much aware that no professional working with animals and people can say, "It will never affect me." No one is immune from involvement; it can come at you from any number of unsuspected sources. The Link-UP Program that you will see mentioned more than once as we go along came about because of the need for multiple agency involvement in many of these situations. If anyone has doubts about that often-heard statement, "It Takes a Village to Raise a Child," let me assure you, many sections of this book will re-affirm that phrase through this one: "It Takes a Village to Solve Social Problems." Police departments, fire departments, animal control officers, humane agencies, shelters, veterinarians, medical staff, judges, lawyers, social service agencies, domestic violence programs—they all play a part right along with everyone else that makes up a local community. No one is "outside the loop" shall we say, when it comes to the problems or the solutions of animal cruelty. We all have a part in putting a stop to it.

Who are the "Silent Victims" that we are talking about? There is more than one, but on the top rung of this book we are speaking of animals. Animals are unable to conduct verbal communications with us other than by crying or barking. Contrary to the claims of some people, I have never met anyone capable of talking with an animal, although I have never spoken with an animal that refuted that statement. Animals and children, our silent victims, cannot speak out for help and their crying is often stopped before others can hear their plight. Our silent victims reach that point from many different sources of origin. Some of them are mistreated from the very beginning of their lives; others become victims slowly over a long period of time. Different problems can develop on the part of the instigator leading to the victimization of perfectly innocent animals. We will discuss some of the more likely triggers that may activate a situation throughout this book, and of course give you the tools you will need to protect these victims and stop animal cruelty in your own neck of the woods.

TALES FROM THE STREET: REAL-LIFE SILENT VICTIMS

It may be a bitter cold night in the middle of January or a hot and humid afternoon in July when the silent victim comes to your attention. They don't pick their time and you don't get to put it off until the timing is better. I have responded in both of these circumstances as well as many more varied settings, but I want to describe these in particular. It was nice and warm and I was enjoying a night off and listening to the wind howl outside my house when my work phone rang. First thoughts were do I just ignore it and wait for a voice mail message to come through? Nope, that won't work, someone is calling that number for a reason and my job is to answer it. I pick up the phone and see the calling number. Good thing I looked, because it's my boss calling. "Hello," I say hoping he is only passing along a minor work-related message. No such luck. His opening statement is, "There's been a shooting at. . ." and he gives the address. It is a house we've watched for quite a long time because of suspected criminal activities but we could never get a good look at it. He continues on by saying, "The police want us to meet them as they think there are dogs in the house." "I'm on the way," I reply and close the phone-cover. Dressing warmly for a possible cold and long night I head for the location, about fifteen minutes away. When I arrive on the scene the street is blocked with police vehicles, ambulances, animal control vans, a fire engine, and the ever-present media. I see my bosses' vehicle and make my way down the street.

"What have we got besides a lot of confusion?" I ask.

"The police are in the house conducting a search for the guns. Three people were shot and are at the hospital, and the perpetrator is in custody at the local district."

We now wait outside the building. It's a building I know very well from years of responding to incidents that happened all through the surrounding streets. I think to myself that I would like to have a dollar for every violent incident I responded to in this area during my time with the police department. The police come out of the house. The gun has been located and is in the process of being properly removed by members of the ballistics unit.

A former partner of mine is one of the detectives and upon seeing me he calls out, "I thought you retired so you could stay home on nights like this."

My response is, "Old habits are hard to break. Plus I knew you couldn't handle this all by yourself."

He laughs and says, "Good luck in there. The place is a dump," and he is off to the warmth of the station. We now get permission from the officer in charge of the scene to enter the building. I have waited many years to go through this door, but I don't think I would have made tonight my first choice. As we enter, the first thing I notice is there is no interior lighting in the hall. Good thing I have a flashlight. On goes the light and I observe what was once a beautiful wooden staircase in front of me leading to the upper floors of the building. Located to the right of the stairway is a hallway leading into pitch darkness, presumably to the back of the house. To the right of the hallway is a high entranceway to what was once possibly a living room. I walk into this room and do a slow scan with my flashlight, not like any living room I've seen in quite some time. I realize I have walked into a motorcycle repair shop with a large old-fashioned barber's chair located in the middle of the room. No animals in here, so we will leave it for later. I leave the room and proceed down the hallway, which is cluttered with piles of clothes and junk along its length. The hallway ends at the back of the building in what used to be a kitchen but now has most of its appliances missing. I hear some talking from a doorway off the kitchen and proceed over to find a flight of stairs leading to a basement.

As I am about to start down the stairs one of the animal control officers comes up and says, "Glad you are here, wait until you see what we found." I follow him down the stairs and around some support columns into an area illuminated by emergency lights running in through an open basement window. I look around and see dogs attached to huge cement blocks by massive chains. Quick count totals about five adult dogs. The most interesting thing is they are not making a sound. Not a growl, bark, or snarl can be heard. I look around behind me and see a screened-in pen containing a number of puppies. The basement looks like an indoor kennel fully stocked with dogs.

The fellow from animal control motions toward the front corner of the basement and I observe a wooden enclosed area of substantial square footage. Upon closer inspection I see that it is an official size pit used for dog fighting and the flooring and walls have blood stain splatters clearly visible. My years of thoughts about this location are suddenly confirmed. A heavy-duty bolt cutter is retrieved from my vehicle and we cut the chains and remove the animals after photographing each one. Animal Control transports the dogs to the city shelter where they will receive an examination the following morning by a veterinarian. The puppies are removed from the pen and placed in carriers to also be transported to the city shelter.

To provide a quick synopsis of the rest of our actions that night, here's what was done before we left the scene: An elderly bed-ridden woman was removed from a second floor bedroom to the hospital for evaluation. A young woman and her three young children were removed to a temporary shelter from a room they were renting in the building. A pound of marijuana was found under an old oil tank during the search for the firearm and removed by police. The building was found to be uninhabitable due to no heat, running water, or electricity. The inspection services division of the building department boarded it up. A police officer was posted outside to guard the building as no owner could be located and an arson threat had been received.

As to the fate of the silent victims, half the adult dogs were unable to be saved due to extensive untreated wounds. The other half of the adult dogs was too aggressive to be adopted and had to be humanely euthanized. The bright spot in the entire picture was that the puppies had been removed from the situation in time to all be adopted out. Half of the silent victims were lost in this situation but the person responsible did not get away with it. In addition to being charged with the shooting of three people he was also on parole from the Federal Prison system at the time and was quickly returned to their custody while awaiting his new court appearance. Another plus was that his dog-fighting operation was shut down and additional individuals were identified as participants leading to more successful investigations. The woman who was bedridden and the young woman with the three children can also be counted as silent victims in this situation and they too were saved before it was too late. The location was under suspicion for a long time and it took a totally unexpected incident to get to the silent victims, but at last it was finally accomplished. Some of the victims were saved—all of them were relieved of their suffering. And as we shall see throughout this book, it took the cooperation of multiple agencies and professionals to make it happen.

Chapter Two

Where Silent Victims Frequently Come From: What We Know About Animal Abuse in the Violent Home

Domestic violence continues to be a serious problem in the United States. Despite the fact that U.S. Department of Justice statistics indicate that law enforcement, criminal justice, social service, and public educational efforts have begun to have a positive impact and that the number of violent crimes by intimate partners against females nationwide declined from 1993 to 2001 (the last year for which statistics are available), professionals working in the field know only too well how prevalent and dangerous violence in the home continues to be—approximately one-third of all police work continues to be related to domestic violence and over one-half of the aggravated assaults are from domestic violence calls.

Sadly, humans are not the only victims of domestic violence. There have been a number of studies and articles documenting the pervasiveness of violence directed towards pets in abusive homes. . .

(For those of you who are feeling ambitious and would like to learn the specifics, here is a sampling of some of that research: Kellert, 1980; DeViney, Dickert, and Lockwood, 1983; Katcher and Beck, 1983; Zahn-Waxler, Hollenbeck, and Radke-Yarrow, 1984; Carmack, 1985; Kellert and Felthous, 1985; Voith, 1985; Lockwood and Hodge, 1986; Kidd and Kidd, 1987; Bryant, 1990; Ascione, 1993; Adams, 1994; Arkow, 1994a; Beirne, 1995; Boat, 1995; Arkow, 1996; Lockwood and Church, 1996; Ascione, Weber, and Wood, 1997a; b; LaCroix, 1998; Ascione and Arkow, 1999; Robin, 1999; Flynn, 2000b; Ponder and Lockwood, 2000; Turner, 2000) . . . and the relationship pet abuse has with abuse of the human victims of family violence (Walker, 1979; Ganley, 1985; Veevers, 1985; Browne, 1987; Finkelhor, Williams, and Burns, 1988; Walker, 1989; Dutton, 1992; Renzetti, 1992; Siegel, 1993; Schenk, Templer, Peters and Schmidt, 1994; Adams, 1995;

Ascione, 1998a; Davidson, 1998; Jacobson and Gottman, 1998; Arluke, Ascione, Levin and Luke, 1999; Flynn, 1999a; Flynn, 2000c; Carlisle-Frank, Frank and Nielsen, 2004a; b).

In fact, according to the research findings, it appears that animal abuse definitely tends to be more common in families where child and partner abuse are present (DeViney, et al., 1983; Ascione, 1993; Adams, 1994; Beirne, 1995)...

COMPANION ANIMALS LIVING IN VIOLENT HOMES:
AN OVERVIEW

The majority (approximately 60%) of American households have at least one companion animal (AVMA, 1997). That's over 375 million dogs, cats, birds, gerbils, rabbits, mice, rats, hamsters, reptiles and fish currently living with us. The majority of people consider their companion animal a member of the family (Cain, 1983; Albert and Bulcroft, 1988; Siegel, 1993; Carlisle-Frank, et al., 2004a).

Research indicates that attitudes about pets are developed within the family context (Schenk, et al., 1994). Unfortunately, this not only applies to non-violent households but to violent families as well (Carlisle-Frank, et al., 2004a; b). That means that pets sharing our homes frequently share the risks as well as the benefits (Boat and Knight, 2000). When companion animals are considered members of the family within violent households it can make them vulnerable to violent threats and attacks from other family members (Flynn, 2000a).

Pets are particularly important when human family members are enduring stressful life events. This may be especially true for women who have been victimized by battering partners and losing their pets may create an additional trauma for these women (Flynn, 2000b). This trauma can be even worse if the women experience guilt over not being able to protect their beloved pets. As with non-violent families, women living in violent homes have reported that their companion animals were more than just pets and were members of the family (Flynn, 2000b; Carlisle-Frank, et al., 2004a). The majority of female victims of domestic violence not only consider their pets to be family members, but sometimes refer to them as their children or babies (Flynn, 2000c). According to researcher Clifton Flynn's (2000b) study surveying women at a domestic violence shelter, the data clearly revealed that companion animals were an important source of emotional support for women coping with violent relationships. This was especially true if the pets had been abused.

In a different study, most women seeking assistance at a domestic violence shelter reported they were "very close" to their pets that had been abused by their partners (Ascione, et al., 1997a). This is really not so surprising. As Boat and Knight (2000) have pointed out, attachment is the key element in the human-animal bond. Adults report pets are instrumental in coping with stress and abuse. Pets can make owners—especially those who are victims of family violence— feel connected and safe. Domestic violence victims have also reported that pets have a calming effect and relieve their stress (Ascione, et al., 1997a). Additionally, the batterer may isolate female victims of domestic violence. Battered women with pets may substitute the lack of relationships with other humans by closely bonding with their companion animals (Flynn, 2000b).

Companion animals are completely dependent on their family in order to have basic necessities just to stay alive. This makes them especially vulnerable to being abused in violent homes. They are, by and large, unable to protect themselves from abuse, making them easy targets. Additionally, abuse of animals is often hidden from view. Animals are unable to solicit aid outside the home, to alert others or identify their abusers (Agnew, 1998). One expert in the field of domestic violence has concluded that companion animals should be included among the hidden victims of family violence (Gelles, 1997).

Our interviews with domestic violence caseworkers and the findings of our study surveying battered women at domestic violence shelters reveal a host of horrific tales of animal abuse. When Ascione and his colleagues (1997b) asked female victims of domestic violence to discuss their pets and other animal-related issues, the victims revealed batterers had tried to run animals over with the car, forced women to have sex with dogs, threatened to throw animals out the window of a multi-story building, and slowly starved animals to death. Battered women have reported their pets have been hit, kicked, shot, drowned, nailed to doors, poisoned, and thrown out of a moving car (Ascione, et al., 1997a). The types of pets that have been reported as being victimized by domestic violence batterers include cats, dogs, birds, rabbits, gerbils, hamsters, and reptiles. Additionally, reports by children with pets living inside violent homes have revealed "frequent pet turnover," an unexplained loss of pets, pets who die mysteriously or simply "disappear" (Boat, 1995).

As horrible as the acts of animal cruelty are they must also be considered within the context of the entire picture of family violence (Arkow, 1996). According to the Humane Society of the United States (HSUS) animal cruelty is one link in the chain of family violence (Turner, 2000).

Domestic violence intervention professionals have begun to recognize animal abuse as a part of dysfunctional family constellations. Abuse to companion animals is a key factor for identifying batterers of female partners and/or children (Browne, 1987; Statman, 1990). Many published articles reporting anecdotal observations describe abuse, torture and killing of companion animals as related to battering of female partners and sexual abuse of partners and children (Browne, 1987; Gelles and Strauss, 1988; Dutton, 1992).

Researchers warn that where there is pet abuse there is an increased likelihood of child, partner, and/or elderly abuse (DeViney, et al., 1983; Boat, 1995; Ascione and Arkow, 1999). Numerous articles and accounts from interviews with professionals in the domestic violence field cite animal abuse and torture and killing of animals in cases of child-abusing families, partner battering, sexual abuse of children and coerced bestiality between abused partners and their favorite pets. Additionally, animal abuse when either perpetrated or observed by children has the ability to create a generalized desensitization to violence. Research indicates there is a connection between violence to children and violence to pets (Boat, 1995). Children who observe such abuse may imitate these violent acts by abusing animals themselves (Arkow, 1996).

Law enforcement and social service professionals may find that children in domestic violence families are more willing to share information about abuse to their pets than to themselves (Turner, 2000). The law does not explicitly recognize parental cruelty toward a child's pet as "emotional maltreatment" and neither legislative nor appellate courts have adequately addressed this issue. Additionally, there exist relatively few cross-reporting mechanisms between animal and child protection agencies (Davidson, 1998). Therefore, a victim-specific approach by professionals is no longer an acceptable method for dealing with family violence. It is dangerous to focus on protecting one type of victim while failing to identify and protect other family members who are also at risk (LaCroix, 1998). In short, all potential victims within violent households—including the family pets—must merit investigation, intervention and protection.

Abuse of the Family Pet: The Extent of the Problem

Violent Homes with Companion Animals: Trends and Tendencies of Animal Abuse

According to the American Humane Association, every year more than a million children are confirmed victims of abuse and/or neglect in the U.S. At the same time, untold numbers of companion animals living within the same violent families also fall victim to abuse. At least one expert has estimated that humane agencies investigate thousands of cases of animal abuse and neglect every year (Arkow, 1996). Let's take a look at some of the research findings:

- In a study that surveyed women at a domestic violence shelter in Utah 71% of women reported their partners threatened to hurt or kill or had actually hurt or killed at least one pet (Ascione, 1998a).
- A separate study of women at a battered women's shelter in Utah found 52% of batterers in violent families threatened to hurt or kill the family pet and 54% actually hurt or killed their companion animals (Ascione, et al., 1997a).
- The Center for the Prevention of Domestic Violence in Colorado Springs, Colorado found 23.8% of battered women at a domestic violence shelter and 10.9% of women seeking restraining orders, counseling or support services observed cruelty to pets by batterers (Arkow, 1994a).
- A study interviewing women at a domestic violence shelter in North Carolina revealed that 46.5% of batterers threatened to harm or actually harmed the family pets (Flynn, 2000b).
- A study of families meeting the New Jersey state criteria for child-abuse/neglect found that 25% of family members admitted someone in the household had injured a pet at some time. In an additional 38% of families with child abuse and/or neglect a caseworker observed evidence of animal abuse or neglect first-hand that was not reported in the interviews. Additionally, 34% of participants indicated some pets they had owned previously had either been abused or neglected. In all, 60% of families were identified as having had at least one family member who met the criteria for abuse of the family pet (DeViney, et al., 1983).
- A study surveying victims of domestic violence shelters in New York found that 53% of victims reported their companion animals had been threatened or were actually abused or killed (Carlisle-Frank, et al., 2004a).
- A report by the Community Coalition Against Violence in Wisconsin revealed that 80% of women surveyed at domestic violence prevention centers reported batterers had been violent toward animals (Quinlisk, 1995).
- A study interviewing victims of partner abuse revealed that 71% of women with pets observed partners threatening to hurt or kill or actually hurting or killing the family pet (Ascione, 1996).
- A national survey conducted by the Humane Society of the United States (HSUS) of domestic violence shelters revealed that 91% of advocates have heard female victims talking about incidents of pet abuse (Beckett, 2005).
- The American Bar Association Commission on Domestic Violence estimates approximately 4 million women experience serious assault by an intimate partner each year. Using conservative estimates of approximately 3 million women abused by their male partners every year in the U.S. (Browne, 1993), Ascione has argued that if just 50% of these violent homes have companion animals (a conservative estimate) then an average of 71%

partner cruelty to animals (Ascione, 1998a) represents hundreds of thousands of families where companion animal victimization (actual or threatened) is a reality for animals, children and women. Using these parameters, this could conceivably mean there are a couple of million companion animals who are victims of domestic violence each year.

- In interviews with mothers seeking safety at a domestic violence shelter in Utah, Ascione and colleagues (1997a) found:
  - 52% of women said their partners threatened to hurt their pets
  - 70% reported the batterer had either threatened or actually hurt or killed their pets
  - 54% of women reported actual hurting or killing of their pets by batterers
  - These women reported multiple incidents of abuse to pets
  - A FIREPAW study surveying women at domestic violence shelters conducted by Carlisle-Frank and colleagues (2004a) found that:
  - 43% of women with pets reported that batterers abused their pets through physical punishment described as punching, hitting, choking, drowning, shooting, stabbing, throwing against the wall/down the stairs.
  - 30% of women reported that abusers verbally threatened to either kill or hurt the pet
  - 26% of women reported the abusers denied food and/or water to the animal
  - 26% of women reported abusers denied their animal veterinary care
  - 48% of women reported pet abuse occurred "often" during the past 12 months
  - 30% of women reported that abuse to the family pet had occurred "almost always" during the   past 12 months
  - Victims whose pets had been abused reported that abuse to the family pets occurred an average   of 51% of the time violent outbursts had taken place over the past year
- According to one scholar (Adams, 1995) the types of abuse occurring to companion animals within domestic violence scenarios include the following:
  - cats are more likely to be stabbed or disemboweled
  - dogs are more likely to be shot
  - cats and dogs may be victims of hangings (dogs with choker chains)
  - pets may disappear or die mysteriously
  - batterers have chopped off heads and legs of cats and stepped on puppies
  - cats have been nailed to the front door
  - batterers may actually beat their partners with the family pet
- In one study 80% of domestic violence victims reported batterers had abused pets by kicking, beating, punching, mutilating, extreme neglect and

killing of pets. Animal abuse was done in front of female victims in 87.7% of the cases and in the presence of their children in 75.5% of the cases (Quinlisk, 1995).

- Interviewing women at a domestic violence shelter in North Carolina, Flynn (2000b) found that 40.2% of women had pets at one time during an abusive relationship.
- In a study of battered women and their pets, Ascione (1998a) found that 71% of women interviewed reported their partners had either threatened or actually hurt or killed one or more of their pets. Women reported that batterers threatened to put the kitten in a blender, bury the cat up to its head and mow it, starve a dog to death, and shoot and kill the cat; 57% of victims' partners had actually harmed or killed pets; 32% of women reported their children had hurt or killed pet animals. Children's behavior toward abusing pets included sitting on kittens, throwing kittens against a wall, cutting a dog's fur and tail, pulling a kitten's head out of the socket and sodomizing a cat, among other things.
- One study interviewing female victims of domestic violence revealed their pets had been threatened and/or harmed or killed and that the animals suffered physical, sexual and psychological abuse and death at the hands of the batterers (Flynn, 2000b).
- Psychological abuse to companion animals included indirect abuse such as pets having to watch women/children terrorized and battered—something that is stressful for animals. Direct abuse included batterers intentionally terrifying and intimidating pets including shooting at them (Flynn, 2000b).
- Physical abuse to companion animals included kicking, beating, punching, throwing animal against wall/down stairs/across room, sexual abuse, choking, and even burying animals alive and feeding them gun powder (Flynn, 2000b).

Dynamics of Violent Home Environments

- Approximately 30% of domestic violence victims reported that violence from the batterer directed toward them increased over time and that this included batterers' willingness to include abusing pets during violent rages (Ascione, et al., 1997a).
- Family violence, which includes abuse to partners and their pets, has also been reported in research of lesbian households (Renzetti, 1992).
- Interviewing women at a domestic violence shelter in North Carolina Flynn (2000b) found that 33% of pet abusing homes also had ongoing child abuse.
- In 88% of families receiving services from the Division of Youth and Family Services in New Jersey due to child physical abuse, the pets were also

abused. In two-thirds of the cases the abuser had killed or injured the animal to discipline the child (DeViney, et al., 1983).

Common Perceptions, Beliefs and Attitudes Regarding Pets

• Interviewing women at a domestic violence shelter Flynn (2000b) found the majority of women (73%) said their pets were very important for emotional support. Women whose pets were abused were more bonded with their animals than women whose pets had not been abused.

• A FIREPAW study surveying women at domestic violence shelters (Carlisle-Frank, et al., 2004a) found that 71% of respondents whose pets had been abused reported they felt either "terrible" or "mildly upset" about the abuse that occurred to their animal.

Common Consequences of Animal Abuse Within Violent Homes

• A study of battered women found that 20% of women with pets and 40% whose pets had been harmed delayed seeking shelter out of concern for their pets (Flynn, 2000b).
• In a study that surveyed women at a domestic violence shelter in Utah, Ascione (1998a) found that 18% of women reported they delayed seeking help and leaving the batterer out of concern for their pets.
• A study surveying domestic violence shelters across the U.S. (Ascione, et al., 1997b) found that 85.4% of women at shelters talk about incidents of animal abuse, 63% of children at the shelters talk about animal abuse, and 83.3% of domestic violence shelter professionals observed coexistence of domestic violence and companion animal abuse.
• Researching residents of a domestic violence shelter, 56.4% of children interviewed said they protected their pets, including putting themselves at risk to directly intervene when the batterer was trying to harm the pets (Ascione, et al., 1997a).
• Ascione and colleagues (1997a) conducted interviews with mothers seeking safety at a domestic violence shelter in Utah and found that approximately 25% of women said they delayed leaving the abuser out of concern for their animals, approximately 50% reported that their children had witnessed abuse of their pets and approximately 25% of women reported that their children had also either hurt or killed a family pet.
• Interviewing women at a domestic violence shelter in North Carolina, Flynn (2000b) found that 52% of women said their pets were still living with the abuser, 55% of those pets who had been abused were still living

with the batterer, and 40% of women reported they were still concerned about their pets, especially if the pets had been previously abused.

- In a study that surveyed women at a domestic violence shelter in Utah, Ascion (1998a) found that approximately 33% of women with children and pets revealed their children had hurt or killed a family pet.
- A FIREPAW study that surveyed women at domestic violence shelters found that 61% of female victims reported that their children had witnessed the batterer committing acts of abuse against their pets, and 43% of victims reported that their children had either been physically abused or threatened with physical abuse by their partners (Carlisle-Frank, et al., 2004a).
- With thousands of cases of animal cruelty reported every year and the majority of households with children also having pets, there is a chance that many violent homes have children who may be witnessing ongoing animal cruelty (Davidson, 1998).
- A FIREPAW study that surveyed women at domestic violence shelters in the Northeast (Carlisle-Frank, et al., 2004a) found that:
  - 48% of victims delayed seeking help and leaving the abusive home because of concerns about their pets
  - 65% of victims delayed leaving the abusive environment out of concern for their animals in cases where batterers had previously been abusive towards the family pet
  - 48% of victims had at least considered returning to the batterer due to concerns for the pets
  - 25% percent of victims stated they had at some previous time returned to the abuser out of concern for their companion animals
  - 35% of victims returned to the violence out of concern for their animals in cases where the batterer had previously abused the pet
  - 22% percent of victims reported they took their pets to a public shelter when they fled the abusive home
  - 20% of victims left their companion animals with the batterer when they fled to the shelter
- In the DeViney, et al. study (1983) pets were abused or neglected in 60% of families meeting the legal criteria in New Jersey for child abuse or neglect. Pet abuse was found in 88% of families displaying physical abuse of children. Veterinary services, pet sterilization and pet care were not significantly different in the abusive families from the norm in the general population. This means there is likelihood that veterinarians may well encounter victims of pet abuse. Arkow (1994b) has argued that veterinarians should begin to adopt responsibility, and in the interest of public health become reporters of animal abuse and suspected family violence, including suspected child abuse.

Reasons Why Animal Abuse May Occur in Violent Homes

There have been numerous studies examining the factors associated with animal abuse inside violent homes. For those professionals already working with perpetrators and victims of domestic violence, some of the findings will ring familiar bells while other findings may surprise even the most seasoned of veterans. . .

To Control, Intimidate, Silence Human Victims

Research has revealed that batterers (almost always male) sometimes threaten to harm or actually harm animals as a way to gain power, control, intimidate, terrorize, and silence partners, children, and pets (DeViney, et al., 1983; Gelles and Strauss, 1988; Walker, 1989; Muraski, 1992; Yllo, 1993; Adams, 1995; Arkow, 1996; Ascione, 1998a; Flynn, 2000b).

The American Humane Association and researchers tell us that animals are sometimes tortured, threatened and killed within violent homes in order to keep sexually abused children silent (Finkelhor, et al., 1988; Boat, 1995). The link between childhood sexual abuse and threats to pets is not uncommon (Adams, 1994). Violence against animals is also frequently a part of sexual exploitation of intimate partners in violent homes. Animal abuse may also occur as a way of sexually violating female partners as batterers may force their partners to have sex with the family pet to humiliate, coerce and control her. This is abusive to both women and their companion animals (Adams, 1994).

According to Adams (1995) male batterers harm and kill companion animals in order to demonstrate to the partner who is in control, to perpetuate the violence, to keep human victims terrorized, to teach human victims submission, to isolate the partner from others, to express rage, to punish the partner, to force the partner to be involved in the abuse, to threaten the partner not to leave, and to demonstrate power and domination over family members.

Adams (1995) has also argued that killing a pet reinforces isolation of the partner, deprives her of significant relationships and increases her dependence on the batterer. Killing a pet also eliminates competition of attention and affection from the partner and eliminates the support the pets give her. Death or harm of a pet causes profound physical reactions of grief to the woman (sleeplessness, headaches, etc.) making her weak and vulnerable, and threats to harm or kill a pet sends the ultimate message to human victims: You are next.

To Scapegoat/Blame the Animal for All Their Personal and Family Troubles

Research has demonstrated that companion animals living inside violent homes may be blamed for all the batterers' personal and family problems

(DeViney, et al., 1983; Kellert and Felthous, 1985; Vermeulen and Odendaal, 1993; Adams, 1994; Carlisle-Frank, et al, 2004a). DeViney and colleagues (1983) found that abusers of animals and children often report deep affection for their victims, but when they have more than one pet they tend to scapegoat one of the animals, splitting the animals into "good pets" and "bad pets" categories. At least one researcher who analyzed the role of pets in families has argued that one role pets have is to serve as "surrogate enemies" (Veevers, 1985). Research data indicate that violence against pets who held that role by family members was evident. Veevers argued that pets who were family scapegoats might be physically abused, threatened or killed in order to control or emotionally torture human family members.

To Boost Ego/Machismo

One researcher has found that batterers may abuse pets because, like abuse of women and children, he perceives himself as failing to meet traditional masculine expectations such as not being able to support his family (Flynn, 2000b).

Stress Combined with Poor Coping Skills

When stress and strain levels are elevated and coupled with poor or nonexistent coping skills batterers may abuse the family pet (Carlisle-Frank, et al., 2004a).

Beliefs that Abuse is Justified/to Retaliate or Punish an Animal for What the Animal Did

Research has demonstrated that animal abuse may occur when batterers hold the belief that abuse of animals is justified (the animal did something to "deserve" being abused), for revenge, or to retaliate against an animal or someone else (DeViney, et al., 1983; Zahn-Waxler, et al., 1984; Kellert and Felthous, 1985; Ascione, 1993, Adams, 1994; Carlisle-Frank, et al., 2004a).

Mastery Over the Animal is Satisfying

One researcher has found that animal abuse may occur because batterers achieve satisfaction from mastery and control of animals (Kellert, 1980).

Personality Traits

Individual personality traits may be another contributing factor to animal abuse. It has been argued that personality traits such as impulsivity, sensation seeking, irritability, low self-control, lack of concern for negative consequences for their actions (Agnew, 1998), and an inability to empathize (Zahn-Waxler, et al., 1984; Ascione, 1992; Agnew, 1998) are common among those batterers who abuse the family pet. One researcher has argued that animal cruelty is part of a collection of behaviors that indicate extreme personal dysfunction with poor impulse control (Lembke, 1994). It has also been suggested that animal cruelty is most often committed by lonely, isolated people. These people also have long-standing frustration and resentment about being denied acceptance, appreciation and recognition they feel they deserve (Robin, 1999).

Learned to Abuse Animals in Family of Origin

Batterers who abuse companion animals may have learned this behavior from witnessing parents or caretakers abusing their own pets in their family of origin (Carlisle-Frank, et al., 2004a).

To Prevent Future Torture

Children who are either physically or sexually abused sometimes kill their own pets rather than have the pet endure ongoing torture and abuse by the abusive parent or guardian.

To Discipline Children

According to the American Humane Association, pets are sometimes hurt or killed to punish a child for something the child did.

Dysfunctional Family Dynamics

According to a study done by DeViney, et al. (1983) animal abuse might occur because of "triangling". Common in dysfunctional, violent families, this is where aggression is directed against one family member indirectly through abusing a third family member. Since families so frequently become attached to pets, these animals can become targets of abuse intended to hurt another family member.

Jealousy of Bond Between Human Victims and Animals

Batterers may target animals because of the strong bonds between women and their pets (Flynn, 2000b). Breaking such bonds increases the batterer's control over the partner. Batterers may also hurt pets out of jealousy—the partner may be bonded to the pet more than to the batterer, causing the batterer to experience jealousy and rage at the pet (Flynn, 2000b).

Sense of Entitlement

Batterers' attitudes of entitlement and right to dominate may influence their tendency to abuse their pets. The "I-have-a-right-to-do-what-I-want-in-my-own-house" justification frequently extends to the batterer's belief he has a right to batter female partners, children and companion animals (Adams, 1994).

ATTITUDES, BELIEFS AND TREATMENT OF PETS IN VIOLENT VS. NON-VIOLENT HOUSEHOLDS

As we have seen, over the past two decades or so there have been a number of theories and studies conducted to uncover the possible reasons behind animal abuse within violent homes. At FIREPAW we hypothesized that animal abusers' attitudes, beliefs and behaviors regarding their pets might be among the many possible contributing factors for why companion animals are abused. We asked the question, "Aside from the actual animal cruelty directed toward animals, do animal abusers differ from non-animal abusers in their attitudes, beliefs, and treatment of pets in general?" In order to pursue the answer to this question we surveyed members of households with the highest likelihood for incidence of animal abuse—pet-owning women seeking assistance from domestic violence services. We also surveyed a comparison group of pet owner/guardians who visited veterinary offices and clinics in the same region. This second group was hypothesized to have a significantly lower incidence of ongoing animal cruelty to the family pets.

The Study

Do pet abusers differ from non-animal-abusers in what they expect from their pets? Do animal abusers differ from non-abusers in the way they interpret the animal's behavior? Is there a difference in the way these two groups interact with their pets? The FIREPAW study surveyed pet-owning respondents from domestic violence shelters and veterinary clients as to their partners' (1) perceptions of companion animals as sentient beings vs. property, (2) tendencies to "scapegoat" the family pet for personal and/or family problems, (3) sensitivity to hassles and stressors in the environment—particularly those perceived as being caused by the pets, (4) unrealistic expectations about animals.

All of the respondents analyzed in this study had companion animals. There were 52 respondents from the veterinary clients group and 34 respondents from domestic violence shelters used in the final results. Fifty-three percent of the domestic violence group respondents and 2.7% of the veterinary client respondents reported physical abuse to the family pet. The two populations were pooled together and then assigned either Animal Abuse (DV/VET-AA) or No Animal Abuse (DV/VET-NA) group status depending on their report of whether their partners had committed pet abuse within the previous 12 months. This resulted in 63 members of the Non-Animal-Abusing (NA) group and 23 members in the Animal-Abusing (AA) group. (See Table 1.) For the purpose of this study animal abuse was defined as socially unacceptable, deliberate and unnecessary suffering and harm inflicted on animals.

Perceptions of Companion Animals as Sentient Beings versus
Objects or Property

One goal of this study was to determine whether abusers of the family pets recognize their companion animals as sentient beings or whether they tend to view their pets primarily as property. At least one scholar has argued that many people are ignorant about animals experiencing adverse consequences of abuse and have difficulty empathizing with the pain felt by animals (Agnew, 1998). A lack of empathy, Agnew has hypothesized, is one of the key features associated with animal abuse. Researchers Herzog and Borghardt (1988) found that many people believe animals do not experience pain, therefore leading animal abusers to often deny or minimize the pain experienced by the animals they abuse. Additionally, researcher Clifton Flynn (2000a) found that pets might be victimized in violent families because they are considered "property." These findings support the hypothesis that animal abusers may tend to more frequently perceive their pets as objects/property as opposed to sentient beings.

Results: Believing Pets are Sentient Beings versus
Viewing Them as Objects/Property

In order to assess attitudes, perceptions and behaviors that might indicate a tendency towards either viewing the family pet as a sentient being with feelings and preferences or as an object (property), respondents were asked questions about how their partners interacted with the family pet. More specifically, respondents were asked to report how their partners typically reacted to the following: (a) Telling pets they love them; (b) Showing pets affection; (c) Daily care-taking of pets; (d) Speaking to/Interacting with pets; (e) Referring to pet as object/property vs. family member; (f) Celebrating pets' birthdays; (g) Taking pets on family outings and trips; (h) Permitting pets to live indoors with the rest of the family; (i) Including pets in family photo album.

Telling pets they love them. When asked how often their partners told the pets that they loved them respondents indicated that non-animal-abusing (NA) partners tend to more frequently tell their pets they love them than partners from the animal-abusing (AA) group. Forty-one percent of NA tell their pets they love them "daily", while only 4.8% of AA do so. Animal abusers were reported more frequently to "never" or "hardly ever" tell their pets they love them. Respondents reported that 90.5% of AA never or hardly ever tell their companion animals they love them. In comparison, only 37% of non-animal-abusers were reported to never or hardly ever tell their companion animals they love them. The difference between these two groups was highly statistically significant, meaning there is a very low likelihood that these differences occurred by random chance.

Showing pets affection. When asked how often their partners showed affection toward their pets, NA were reported to show more affection than AA. Respondents reported that animal abusers "never" or "hardly ever" show affection toward their pets. Many more (81.8%) animal abusers failed to show affection toward the family pet than NA (15.2%). Furthermore, respondents reported that NA show affection towards pets "daily" or "weekly". Respondents reported that far less companion animal abusers showed affection toward the family pet on a daily or weekly basis than non-animal abusers (84.8% of NA showed affection to animals on a regular basis while only 18.2% of AA did so). The difference between these two groups was highly statistically significant.

Daily care-taking of pets. When asked who was more likely to take part in the daily care-taking of the family pet respondents reported that 54% of NA were likely to take part in the daily care-taking and playing of the family pet, while only 13% of AA were reported to participate in the caring for or playing with the family pet. Again, the difference between the non-animal-abuser and animal-abuser groups was highly statistically significant with regard to this question.

Speaking to/Interacting with pets. Animal abusers and non-abusers were also reported to interact differently with their pets. Respondents reported animal abusers tend to talk to their pets primarily through "commands" or "threats" only (82.6% of AA do so while only 4.8% of NA talk to pets primarily through threats or commands). Non-animal-abusers were reported to most often talk to their pets "conversationally" (95.2% of NA talk to pets conversationally while only 17.4% of AA talk to pets conversationally). The differences between the two groups was highly statistically significant in this area and thought to represent the differences in overall attitudes and perceptions about the pets between these two groups.

Referring to pet as object/property vs. family member. When respondents were asked whether their partners tended to refer to the family pet as property or as a full-fledged family member the majority of non-animal-abusers were reported to refer to their pets as "full-fledged family members" (84.1%) while only 17.4% of animal abusers referred to pets as family members. Respondents from the animal abusing group most often reported that their partners referred to the family pets as "property" (60.9% of AA refer to pets as property while only 4.8% of NA do so). The results were again highly statistically significant. Additionally, respondents reported that animal abusers who believe their pets are sentient beings punished pets less often than animal abusers who reportedly believe their pets are property. Again, the differences between these two groups were highly statistically significant.

Celebrating pets' birthdays.   According to respondents the majority of non-animal-abusing households celebrate their pets' birthday. Animal abusing households, however, were far less likely to do so. When given several choices of possible family members—including pets—and asked to check all that apply for whose birthday was celebrated, AA households were less likely to celebrate their pet's birthday (only 8.7%) while NA households were more likely to celebrate their pets' birthday (55.6% of non-animal-abusing households celebrate their pets' birthdays). Additionally, non-animal-abusing households were reported to be much more likely to give gifts to their pets for their birthdays (71.4% of NA give pets birthday gifts) while households with animal abuse tend to be much less likely to do so (only 17.4% of AA give pets birthday gifts). The difference between these two groups was highly statistically significant for this question.

Taking pets on family outings and trips.   When given choices of several family members—including pets—and asked to check all that apply for who went along on family vacations or family outings such as picnics, walks, trips to the park, car rides, etc., non-animal-abusing households were reported to be just as likely to bring their pets along on family outings or vacations as to leave them behind (47.6% of NA take pets along on family outings). However, respondents reported that animal abusing households tended to be much less likely to bring their pets along on family outings or vacations (only 8.7% of AA take pets along on family outings and trips). The difference between these two groups was highly statistically significant for this question.

Pets living indoors with the rest of the family.   It was hypothesized that animal abusers might have a tendency to perceive their pets as objects or property and therefore would be less inclined to appreciate the animal's needs to be close to the other family members or to have preferences for comfort. As expected, according to respondents, non-animal-abusing households were significantly more likely (92.1%) than animal abusers' households (56.5%) to permit their pets to reside in the "living area" of their house (living room; bedroom; free-range to roam throughout the house). Likewise, animal abusers were reported to be more likely to require pets to live outside (with or without shelter); garage; or a cordoned-off "pet area" separate from the rest of the family. This question also indicated a highly significant statistical difference between the two groups.

Including pets' names along with other family members on greeting cards. It was hypothesized that animal abusers would be less inclined to consider pets as members of the family worthy of having their names listed with the other family members on greeting cards. As expected, when given a choice of several family members including the family pet and asked to check all that apply for whose names typically appear as signatures on family greeting cards, respondents reported that animal abusing households tended not to include their pets' names on greeting cards while non-animal-abusing households were reported to be just as likely as not to include the pet's name with other family members on greeting cards. (Respondents reported that 47.6% of NA included pets' names on greeting cards, while only 8.7% of AA did so.) Again, the difference between these two groups was highly statistically significant.

Including pets in family photo albums. The final question in determining attitudes about whether pets were viewed as sentient beings and members of the family or perceived as objects/property concerned whether the pet was included in the family photo album. Using the family photo album as yet one more marker of the types of attitudes and relationships people have with their animals (Ruby, 1982; Entin, 1983) it was hypothesized that the pets would not be included in anything that symbolized or portrayed the "family" for animal abusers. As it turns out the non-animal-abusing households who have family photo albums were far more likely to have their pets' pictures in the family photo album (NA = 79.4%). Animal-abusing households who keep family photo albums, on the other hand, were just as likely to exclude the pet's picture in the family photo album as include it (47.8% of AA include pets' photos in the family album). The results for this question indicated highly statistically significant differences between these two groups.

Objects/Property versus Sentient Beings. Independently these questions appear to support the hypothesis that animal abusers are indeed differentiated from non-animal-abusers with regard to certain attitudes, perceptions and behaviors regarding the family pet. If, as it was hypothesized, these questions are indeed measuring something akin to perceptions of animals as sentient beings versus objects/property we would expect to see statistically significant results when grouping these questions together in to a single measure. Indeed this is what occurred; further statistical analyses appear to indicate that animal abusers tend to perceive their pets as objects/property and are less likely to recognize them as sentient beings, while non-animal-abusers tend to be more likely to perceive their pets as sentient beings and less likely to view them as property. The results were highly statistically significant, which tells us there is a very low likelihood that the differences between the AA and NA groups occurred by random chance.

Unrealistic Expectations for Companion Animals

It has been suggested that animal abusers frequently believe their abuse of animals is justified (Agnew, 1998). In such cases the abuse is believed to be deserved because the animal has done something the abuser did not like. Researchers Kellert and Felthous (1985) found that self-reported animal abusers often said they abused animals to retaliate against animals they perceived had "wronged" them or to eliminate undesirable traits in an animal such as the tendency to damage property or make noise. It has been reported that some abusers refuse to let animals outside and then beat them when the animals eliminate in the house (Arkow, 1994b). Another goal of this study was to determine whether abusers of family pets tend to have more unrealistic expectations about their pets (that is, about the animals' ability to control natural behaviors such as barking and excreting) than non-animal-abusers, and whether there was more frequent and harsher punishment by animal abusers than non-animal-abusers of the family pets when these expectations went unmet.

Results: Unrealistic Expectations for Companion Animals

In order to determine whether animal abusers and non-animal-abusers had unrealistic expectations about their pets respondents were asked questions concerning what issues upset their partners most when the pet misbehaves. Choices included: (a) the disrespect the pet shows the partner; (b) partner believes s/he should be listened to by the pet because s/he is in charge; (c) safety of the pet or other family member is in jeopardy when pet disobeys; (d) property damage due to pet's bad behavior; (e) concern over others' perception of the family resulting from the pet's behavior; (f) upset because it is necessary to yell at/discipline the pet. Questions concerning the most common reasons the respondents' partners think the pet disobeys him/her included these choices: (a) the pet disobeys because the pet disrespects the partner; (b) pet disobeys because pet does not know any better; (c) pet disobeys to get attention (d) the pet disobeys because s/he is inherently bad (e) the pet lacks training to understand (f) the pet is just behaving as an animal naturally would.

Respondents were also asked about the type, intensity and frequency pets are routinely punished, as well as beliefs their partners may have expressed about companion animals such as cats should never scratch the furniture, dogs should not bark unless they are "watchdogs", cats should not kick litter outside of the litter box, and dogs should be able to "hold it" even if they have not been walked/let out all day.

It was believed that compared to NA, animal abusers would tend to more often have unrealistic expectations for the family pet such as believing the animal has more control over natural bodily occurrences than is actually true (e.g. believing companion animals ought to be able to "hold" excretion for long periods without "accidents") or that the family pet is doing things out of "disrespect" to the partner (e.g. the animal does not follow commands he/she was told the week before) or the family pet is doing things to "spite" the partner, or the partner has unrealistic expectations for the animal's ability to understand what is expected of them.

Respondents were asked seven questions in order to assess the expectations their partners have about their animals and to determine whether there were any significant differences in these expectations between AA and NA. According to the respondents, when asked about what types of issues upset their partners about their pets' misbehaviors, 87% of AA were reported to have unrealistic expectations about their pets (such as getting upset about the "disrespect" the pet shows by not recognizing that the partner is in charge). This is compared to 23.8% of NA reported as having unrealistic expectations about the family pet. The difference between these two groups was highly statistically significant.

Animal abusers were reported more often than non-abusers to believe "disrespect" was one of the primary reasons pets disobeyed them (73.9% of AA believed this to be true compared to only 22.2% of NA). The difference between these two groups for this question was again highly statistically significant.

Additionally, respondents reported that AA had more expectations about how their pets should behave than NA. Animal abusers were reported to believe their pets "shouldn't" do certain things such as make noise or have occasional "accidents" far more often than their non-animal-abusing counterparts (87% of AA held these beliefs while only 46% of NA did so). Again, the difference between these two groups was highly statistically significant.

Expectations about how pets should and should not behave appear to have translated in to the frequency and level of punishment the pets received. As previously discussed, animal abusers reportedly tended to punish their pets more frequently than non-animal-abusers for misbehaving. In addition, animal abusers were more frequently reported to use harsher, more severe methods of discipline than non-animal-abusers when punishing their pets for misbehaving (65.2% of AA used harsh punishments frequently compared to only 3.2% of NA). The difference between these two groups for the level of intensity of punishment was highly statistically significant.

Independently these questions appear to support the hypothesis that AA and NA are indeed differentiated with regard to certain attitudes, perceptions and behaviors regarding the family pet. If, as it was hypothesized, these questions are indeed measuring something akin to unrealistic expectations regarding pets, we would expect to see significant results when grouping these questions together in to a single measure. Indeed this is what occurred; additional statistical analyses appear to indicate that compared to their non-animal-abusing counterparts, animal abusers tend to have unrealistic expectations about how their animals should behave. Neither the unrealistic expectations—nor subsequent punishment behaviors when the expectations go unmet—were shared by non-abusers. The results were highly statistically significant, meaning that it is highly unlikely that the differences between these two groups happened by random chance.

Pets Made the Family Scapegoat

Previous research has indicated that family pets—especially those residing in angry and aggressive households such as those families with ongoing domestic violence—are often made the scapegoat for family and personal problems (DeViney, et al., 1983; Zahn-Waxler, et al., 1984; Kellert and Felthous, 1985; Veevers, 1985; Lockwood and Hodge, 1986; Vermeulen and Odendaal, 1993; Adams, 1994; Flynn, 2000b). It has also been argued that stressed and strained people may use animals as scapegoats because animals provide a safe target for the discharge of aggressive feelings (Agnew, 1998). Is it possible that animal abusers may be more inclined to scapegoat the family pet than non-animal-abusers? Another goal of the FIREPAW study was to determine just that.

Results: Pets as Scapegoats

It was hypothesized that animal abusers would be more likely than non-abusers to scapegoat pets for daily frustrations. More specifically, it was hypothesized that animal abusers might be more inclined than non-animal-abusers to unfairly blame the pets for their feelings of frustration and anger. It was also hypothesized that AA would be more likely to take their frustrations out on the pets than would their NA counterparts. This increase in frustrations, it was hypothesized, might take the form of more frequent punishments for the family pet.

The reports from respondents indicate that animal abusers tend to be far more likely than non-animal-abusers to use their pet as a scapegoat. When asked to choose from several family members, including the family pet, who, if anyone was a scapegoat for family or personal problems, the results indicating the level of differences between the AA and NA groups were highly statistically significant. A total of 29.2% of AA reportedly scapegoat the family pet, while only 1.6% of the NA were reported to do so.

Additionally, the results indicate that non-animal-abusers tend to punish their pets less frequently than animal abusers. When respondents were asked about the frequency with which the family pets were punished the most common response for non-animal-abusers was "never" or "hardly ever" (95%), while only 34.8% of AA never or hardly every punish the pets. The most common response for pet abusers for how often they punished their pets was "a few times a week" (56.5%). Only 3.3% of NA were reported to punish their pets that often. These results were again highly statistically significant.

Stress, Hassles and Pets

It has been suggested that those who engage in animal abuse tend to be more sensitive to stress and strain. According to Agnew (1998) animal abuse may function as a coping mechanism. People may abuse the family pets to reduce stress or to get revenge against the perceived "cause" of the stress. One of the primary perceived stressors for animal abusers may be the pet's own behavior. Research findings indicate that animal abusers frequently report the animals' "bad" behaviors as a reason for abusing them (DeViney, et al., 1983; Kellert and Felthous, 1985; Felthous and Kellert, 1987b). Another goal of the present study was to determine if animal abusers were adversely affected by more daily hassles or stressors than non-animal-abusers and in particular, whether animal abusers tended to be more frequently set off by the behavior of the family pet.

Results: Hassles and Stressors

It was hypothesized that AA would be more reactive to everyday life stressors and hassles than their NA counterparts and that pets would be viewed more frequently by animal abusers as one of the key stressors or hassles. Respondents were asked to choose all that apply from a 12-item list of everyday events that set their partners off. Included in this list were items such as "Pets misbehaving," "Messy house," "Lights left on in unoccupied rooms," "Problems with in-laws," "Money problems," "Dinner not on the table on time," and "Problems at work". As suspected, AA were reportedly set off by many more items than NA. According to respondents, non-animal-abusers were reported to be most frequently set off by only one item. Animal abusers, on the other hand, were reported most frequently as being set off by 8 items. The results were highly statistically significant with NA having a mean of 3.33 items setting them off and AA having a mean of 6.78 items that regularly upset them.

Additionally, animal abusers were reportedly set off by "pets misbehaving" significantly more often than NA. Respondents reported that 84% of non-animal-abusers were *not* regularly set off by the pets misbehaving, while 78 % of pet abusers reportedly *were* regularly set off by something their pets did. Again, the results were highly statistically significant, meaning the differences between these two groups were unlikely to have occurred simply by random chance.

WHAT THIS ALL MEANS

The results of this study indicated statistically significant differences between animal abusers' and non-animal abusers' general perceptions, attitudes and treatment of the family pet. The findings of the present study seem to indicate that like their human counterparts, violence directed toward animals appears to be embedded in a complex content of abusers' attitudes, perceptions and belief systems about the victims. More specifically, the key features separating animal abusers from non-animal-abusers in the present study were:

(1) perceptions of companion animals as sentient beings vs. property,
(2) tendencies to "scapegoat" the family pet for personal and/or family problems,
(3) sensitivity to hassles and stressors in the environment—particularly those perceived as being caused by the pets,
(4) unrealistic expectations about animals.

It is important to note that further research is needed to test these variables under a variety of conditions and settings to determine whether the findings in this study are consistent and applicable to other populations. Like all social science studies there are a variety of factors that may have affected the results: It is possible that the regional culture of the area surveyed in this study is unique enough as to prohibit applicability of the results to other communities.

Additionally, the small sample size could have affected the results. Age, income, and educational levels can also affect the results. Caution should be used therefore, when generalizing the results shown here to other populations until the findings have been further replicated under a variety of conditions.

Despite these disclaimers there remain a number of potential applications the results of this study can have for professionals working in the field:

Intervention: Those investigating cases of potential animal abuse can question possible abusers as to their beliefs and attitudes about their pets.

Table 1. Attitudes, Perceptions, Beliefs, and Treatment of the Family Pet

Domestic Violence Victims and Veterinary Clients: Animal-Abusing households (DV/VET-AA) vs. No-Animal Abuse households (DV/VET-NA)

Domestic Violence Group	Veterinary Clients Group
• 53% of DV group reported abuse to family pet in past 12 months	• 2.7% of veterinarian clients group reported abuse to family pet in past 12 months

Perceiving Animals as Sentient Beings vs. Viewing Pets as Property

Domestic Violence Group	Veterinary Clients Group
• 90.5% of DV/VET-AA partners reportedly *never or hardly ever* tell their pets they love them	• 41.3% of DV/VET-NA partners reportedly tell their pets they love them *daily*
• 81.8% of DV/VET-AA partners reportedly *never or hardly ever* show affection toward pets	• 84.8% of DV/VET-NA partners reportedly show affection to pets *daily or weekly*
• Only 8% of DV/VET-AA partners reportedly take part in daily care/play with pets	• 54% of DV/VET-NA partners reportedly take part in daily care-taking and playing with pets
• 82.6% of DV/VET-AA partners reportedly talk to pets primarily *through commands or threats*	• 95.2% of DV/VET-NA partners reportedly talk with their pets *conversationally*
• 60.9% of DV/VET-AA partners reportedly refer to pets as *property*	• 84.1% of DV/VET-NA partners reportedly refer to pets as *"full-fledged family members"*
• 91.3% of DV/VET-AA households do not celebrate their pet's birthday	• 44.4% DV/VET-NA households do not celebrate their pet's birthday
• Only 8.7% of DV/VET-AA partners take pets on family vacations and/or family outings	• 47.6% of DV/VET-NA partners take pets on family vacations and/or family outings
• 56.5% of DV/VET-AA partners prohibit pets to reside indoors in the "living area" of home w/ rest of family	• Only 7.9% of the DV/VET-NA partners prohibit pets to reside in "living area" of home w/ rest of family
• Only 8.7% of DV/VET-AA households include pets' names on greeting cards	• 47.6% of DV/VET-NA households include pets' names with other family members names on greeting cards

(continued)

Table 1. *(continued)*

Domestic Violence Group	Veterinary Clients Group
Pets as Scapegoats	
• 29.2% of DV/VET-AA partners reportedly tend to blame pets for their feelings of frustration and anger/scapegoat pets • 56.5% of DV/VET-AA partners reportedly tend to take frustrations out through *frequent punishing of pets (a few times each week)*	• Only 1.6% of DV/VET-NA partners were reported to blame pets for their feelings of frustration and anger/scapegoat the family pet • 95% of DV/VET-NA partners *reportedly never or hardly ever take out their frustrations by punishing pets*
Unrealistic Expectations for Animals	
• 87% of DV/VET-AA partners reportedly have unrealistic expectations of what pets "should" do / what pets are capable of • 87% of DV/VET-AA partners reportedly tend to become unreasonably upset about pet's behavior • 73.9% of DV/VET-AA partners reportedly tend to believe their pets "disrespect" them as the key reason their pets disobey • 65.2% DV/VET-AA partners reportedly tend to engage in frequent and harsh punishment of pets when their expectations for the animals go unmet	• 46% of DV/VET-NA partners reportedly have unrealistic expectations about what pets "should" do / what pets are capable of • 23.8% of DV/VET-NA partners tend to become unreasonably upset about pet's behaviors • 22.2% of DV/VET-NA partners reportedly tend to believe their pets "disrespect" them as the key reason their pets disobey • 3.2% of DV/VET-NA partners reportedly engage in frequent and harsh punishment of pets when their expectations for the animals go unmet
Hassles and Stressors	
• DV/VET-AA partners reportedly tend to be set off by *numerous* daily hassles and stressors (Avg. 6.8 items) • 78% of DV/VET-AA partners are reportedly frequently set off by pet's misbehavior	• DV/VET-NA partners reportedly tend to be set off by *fewer* daily hassles and stressors (Avg. 3.3 items) • 16% of DV/VET-NA partners are reportedly regularly set off by pet's misbehavior

When coupled with other red flags and identifiers of potential animal abuse the attitudes and perceptions people have about their companion animals and the way they interact with their pets may be revealing enough to put an intervention plan in to action.

Treatment: Therapists and counselors can use the findings of this study to develop questions that will reveal the attitudes, beliefs and perceptions people have about companion animals when working with perpetrators and family members who have been part of violent households.

Prevention: Family and child service professionals and caseworkers working with child survivors of family violence can use the findings of this study to probe clients as to their beliefs and perceptions about companion animals and the ways they treat their pets. Identifying how children coming from violent homes think about and act toward animals can be especially useful for identifying potential problematic behaviors before they actually surface. As the abuser's attitudes and actions may be imitated by the children, recognizing and understanding the perceptions, attitudes and behaviors children have about the family pet may have implications for those programs targeting at-risk children and adolescents.

RED FLAGS FOR OTHER PROBLEMS: WHY WE SHOULD CARE WHEN PETS ARE BEING ABUSED

Abuse to innocent companion animals within violent households is horrific in and of itself. But there are other reasons for professionals to care about cruelty to animals. Animal abuse within violent households can be an important red flag that other problems may be going on in the family. Let's take a look at what researchers have found. . .

- One of the key reasons it is critical to attend to animal cruelty is that it may be a marker for other forms of family violence (Flynn, 2000a). Research on animal abuse within domestic violent settings indicates that it is motivated almost entirely by a relationship with violence against humans. Coexistence of violence, power and control in violent situations with humans is likely operating in cases of animal abuse within domestic violence families as well. (Solot, 1997). Therefore, animal abuse is a key marker for professionals to attend to. Animal cruelty may be a symptom or red flag that child abuse, partner abuse, elder abuse or some other form of violence is going on within families (Boat, 1995; Arkow, 1996). Research indicates that animal abuse occurs where there is also partner abuse (physical abuse and/or sexual abuse against female partners) occurring in heterosexual relationships (Walker,

1979; Browne, 1987; Dutton, 1992) and homosexual relationships (Renzetti, 1992), child abuse (Fucini, 1978; DeViney, et al., 1983) and sibling abuse (Wiehe, 1990).

- Killing of a companion animal is frequently a sign of the escalation of violence directed toward women (Browne, 1987).
- Both child abuse and pet abuse may serve as markers for the other (Ascione, 1993; Boat, 1995; Arkow, 1996). Such a relationship has important implications for prevention and intervention for reducing violence directed at both human and non-human family members (Flynn, 2000a).
- Children may be seriously adversely affected by abuse to the family pet. Ascione and his colleagues (1997b) conducted interviews with the children staying at a domestic violence shelter and found that two-thirds of children reported witnessing pet abuse (including seeing their animals strangled, shot and poisoned); 46.4% of children said the perpetrator of the animal abuse was either a father, stepfather or boyfriend of their mother; 13.2% of children admitted to hurting pets including throwing the animal, hitting the animal, or stepping on the animal; 7.9% of children admitted to hurting or killing animals other than their own pets. There is ample evidence that those children who witness animal abuse of the family pet may be at an increased risk for going on to become aggressive individuals who use violence (both against animals and people) to problem solve (Arkow, 1996; Ascione and Lockwood, 1997; Quinn, 2000).
- Harming animals as well as describing abuse of animals when combined with physical symptoms and preoccupations may be a warning sign that a child has been a victim of ritual abuse within the family (Adams, 1994).
- Anecdotal evidence suggests child victims of sexual abuse injure animals as a sign that something is wrong (Boat, 1995).
- Animal abuse is often a component of the emotional abuse suffered by battered women. When physical abuse decreases, emotional abuse may increase. Animal abuse is a reminder to victimized partners and an effective control strategy of batterers (Jacobson and Gottman, 1998) that may have serious consequences for the emotional well-being of female victims.

CONSEQUENCES OF ANIMAL CRUELTY IN VIOLENT HOMES

There are numerous consequences of ongoing animal cruelty within violent homes. As we have already seen, research has indicated there is a tendency for victims of family violence to delay seeking help and leaving the batterer out of concern for the family pets (Ascione, at al., 1997b; Ascione 1998; Flynn 2000b; Carlisle-Frank, et al., 2004a). Additionally, research findings indicate that when the human victims flee the violent home about half of the animals are left behind with the batterer (Ascione 1998; Flynn 2000b; Carlisle-Frank, et al., 2004a). In one study of victims who fled the batterer, more than one-fifth of the pets were abandoned, taken to the animal shelter, or given away (Flynn, 2000b). Women whose companion animals had been abused were as likely to leave their pets behind with the animal abuser (55%) as with batterers who had never harmed the pets (50%). Let's take a look at some of the other consequences of animal abuse:

Animals suffer. Animals living within violent households who are stressed sometimes hide, cower, and become anxious or depressed. The ongoing tension, fear and conflict in the domestic violence atmosphere may cause pets to become fearful, aggressive and guarding. It may trigger an attack as the animal tries to protect family members.

Animals can become stressed simply from the ongoing screaming and yelling that is common in violent households. Stressed companion animals may shake, hide or urinate after being abused or witnessing their fellow family members being battered. Animals provide unconditional love for fellow victims and might become aggressive over time, sometimes trying to protect women and children from being battered (Flynn, 2000b). Animal abuse and ongoing violence in the household may create more aggressive animals who, unable to discern levels of threat, could hurt or even kill children and adults in the community. One study of violent families found that 69% of families with animal abuse reported a family pet had injured a person, compared to only 6% in non-abusive families (DeViney, et al., 1983).

In addition to the torture, emotional stress and pain they must endure, pet "turnover" may be higher in domestic violence families. Pets may more often run away, be killed, surrendered at shelters for their own safety or otherwise mysteriously disappear (Ascione, et al., 1997b). Research has also shown that pets of battered women may sometimes receive lower levels of regular and emergency veterinary care than non-abused family pets (Ascione, et al., 1997b), placing them at increased risk for sickness, disease, and complications resulting from injuries that have not been attended to.

Additionally, a lack of safe shelters and pet-friendly rental housing may cause victims to relinquish their beloved animals to public shelters. Unfortunately, there is a likelihood these innocent animals will be euthanized due to overpopulation of companion animals and the lack of available adoptive homes for pets (Adams, 1995; Carlisle-Frank, et al., 2004a). And of course, companion animals left behind with batterers are at an increased risk for being harmed, severely neglected, or even killed as well as suffering great stress because they miss the women and children who have fled (Flynn, 2000a).

Human victims risk future harm.   Researchers studying women at battered women's shelters have found that around one-fifth of women delay
seeking help and leaving the batterer due to concern for the safety of their pets
(Ascione, 1998a; Flynn, 2000b; Carlisle-Frank, et al., 2004a) but that is not
the only risk human victims face with regard to abuse of their animals.
Women and children who have fled the violent home may try to check up on
and visit their pets due to missing them and being so concerned about them
(Flynn, 2000a). This may put these women and children at serious risk should
the batterer return while they are visiting their pets. Additionally, children
have reported that they have tried to run interference and block the batterer
from harming their beloved pets. Such behavior is of course very risky.
Within the violent home pets may be the vehicle to coerce victims of elder
abuse to submit to abusers' wishes as well (Boat and Knight, 2000). Women
and children often remain at risk because they stay silent due to the abusers'
threats to their pets. These threats are used to maintain a "climate of terror"
(Adams, 1994) and place the women and children in a deleterious position.

Children may become abusive.   One scholar has reported that as many as
90% of children are aware of abuse to their parent and to their animals
(Adams, 1995). Children who witness parent and companion animal abuse
may be at risk for compromised psychological adjustment and have an increased risk to engage in interpersonal violence and cruelty to animals (Ascione, et al., 1997a). One reason is because children observing abuse of their
pets and their parent may adopt these behaviors and engage in imitative cruelty to animals (Ascione, 1998a). A study conducted by DeViney and colleagues (1983) revealed that in 37% of child-abusing households the children
were also involved in cruelty to the family pet.

There are other potential negative consequences to children witnessing animal abuse from their caretakers as well. Children may experience anger at
the mother or selves for not protecting their pets (Adams, 1995). The need to
maintain silence in response to the torture and cruelty of a beloved pet in
order to stay safe often causes the mother to not show grief. Children may
model this reaction to the harm and death of a loved one, learning it is unsafe
to vent feelings of despair and fear (Adams, 1995).

Attachment and separation causes deep emotional pain.   When a batterer destroys a pet he may be destroying the woman's only source of comfort and affection (Adams, 1994). Battered women have reported that their
pets serve as important sources of emotional support during their abusive relationships. This is particularly true if the pets have also been abused (Flynn,
2000c). Attachment to a pet may be profound. This is especially true if leaving the batterer means moving to a place that does not permit pets (Boat and
Knight, 2000). When pets must be left behind with the batterer or surrendered

to a public shelter this can be especially stressful for human victims. In addition to being victimized emotionally by watching their beloved pets tortured and being completely powerless to stop the abuse (Flynn, 2000b) victims also miss the emotional support of their pets during the difficult time of readjustment after leaving the batterer (Flynn, 2000c). Leaving animals behind, especially leaving them with the batterer, is extremely upsetting for most female victims of domestic violence (Flynn, 2000c).

Battered women mourn and grieve for abused/lost pets. When their pets' deaths occur within the context of control and violence these women may feel guilt, rage, and hopelessness for not being able to protect the beloved pet from the batterer (Adams, 1995). Additionally, women might feel the need to surrender their pets to a public shelter rather than risk torture of the pets by the batterer. In these situations women may still feel profound grief for the loss of a deeply felt close relationship with their companion animals. Making such a choice may also cause women to feel anger and disappointment. Women may need to hold back or control their grief in front of the abuser to avoid revealing how upset they are about giving up their pet so as not to increase their own risk with the batterer. Women may act like the pet did not matter and pretend not to care (Adams, 1995).

A final word about the findings.   A professional in the family violence field once wrote that given the solace so many victims receive from their companion animals and the fact that many victims delay leaving the violent home and even return to the batterer out of concern for their pets, having a better understanding of the factors associated with abuse of the family pets may have implications in helping the humans victims (Hutton, 1983). Two decades later, armed with the rich findings presented in this chapter professionals can now turn those implications in to directed, effective plans of action for investigation, intervention and protection of *all* the victims of family violence.

TALES FROM THE STREET:
COULD IT ALL HAVE BEEN PREVENTED?

The quiet of the early morning shift was shattered by the voice of the dispatcher calling our unit to respond to an address for a domestic dispute. The dispatcher informed us that an unidentified caller reported a disturbance going on inside a third floor apartment. We acknowledged the call and headed for the location. Within a minute we were re-called and informed that a second call had been received reporting the disturbance. Less than a minute later the dispatcher called over the air for an additional unit to assist us as multiple calls were now being received, all reporting screams coming from the apartment accompanied by the sounds of breaking glass and objects being thrown about. Within four minutes of our first notification we arrived and quickly observed a horrific scene unfolding. Household items were lying smashed on the sidewalk. Outside and hanging by his neck from the front third floor porch was the body of a tan-colored dog.

The voices of at least two children could be heard screaming from within the building. We quickly entered through the front door and proceeded to the third floor accompanied by officers from other arriving units. Reaching the third floor we observed the apartment door shattered into multiple sections with only remnants hanging from the hinges. The interior was total chaos; broken glass, smashed furniture, and clothing were strewn everywhere. Sitting on the floor of the front room, in the midst of the carnage, we observed two small children, partially dressed, screaming uncontrollably. One of the officers entered the room to approach the children and quickly stopped and stated, "Oh shit!" The source of his outburst was the observation of a woman's crumpled body lying behind an overturned couch in the far corner of the room.

The remaining officers now proceeded to search the rest of the apartment for any additional victims. The search was quickly concluded and no additional individuals were discovered. During this process a supervisor and detectives were requested to respond as well as an ambulance. In the interim the children were moved to another room and attempts were made to calm them down. The victim in the front room was beyond any help we could administer, as her death appeared to have occurred well before our dispatch.

Talking with the children it was slowly revealed that the live-in boyfriend of the mother had returned to the apartment in the early hours of the morning in a drunken rage and had started aggravating the dog which he had abused many times prior. The children's mother and he had become involved in an oral confrontation about his continued abuse of the dog and the affect it was having on her and the children. The argument proceeded to also include other issues that had been building to a boiling point over the last few months. The arguing had caused the children to awaken and the older one had proceeded to the bedroom door to observe the situation.

Suddenly the boyfriend rose from the bed, striking the mother with his fist as he did. He then grabbed the dog by the collar and attaching a stout leash around the dog's neck, dragged the dog down the hall and out to the front porch. The child watched him tie the leash to the porch railing and then drop the dog on the outside of the railing, leaving the dog to hang.

The boyfriend now came back into the apartment and the little boy ran back to his own bedroom and helped his younger brother hide under their bed.

As they hid under the bed they heard continued yelling and banging from the front of the apartment. After it was quiet for some time both boys came out from under the bed and eventually found their mother, dead, behind the couch in the front room. The police arrived quickly after their discovery.

A search of the entire building eventually revealed the boyfriend hiding in an unused coal bin in the basement. He was well known to the officers because of prior incidents. As a result of this latest incident two little boys were left without a mother and most likely emotionally scarred for life. Could this have all been avoided? A very good chance if someone had made the call when things were still at the early stages of animal abuse incidents and not waited until the lives of a human and animal were viciously taken.

* * *

A woman staying at a domestic violence safe house periodically called home to check on the condition of the animals she left behind. When she did, her husband would pull feathers out of her parrot so the woman could hear the bird scream.

* * *

During a domestic dispute one man killed his partner with a hammer, then shoved his partner's dead body in the closet. The murderer abandoned the couple's dog when he fled the scene. When the man's body was discovered the dog was in the closet with him, huddled next to the corpse. The dog was covered with cuts, scars, burns, and was emaciated. A new family later adopted the dog. The murderer's family discovered where the dog is and periodically calls the new adoptive family saying, "Thanks for taking care of the dog. He'll be back for *her* when he gets out!"

* * *

One batterer threw his wife against the wall, then followed up by throwing her tiny kitten against the wall as well. The woman and her children fled to a shelter with their pets, including the kitten. All charges against the abuser were dropped or pled down except for the animal abuse charge.

* * *

A woman undergoing an assessment at a domestic violence shelter sat emotionless throughout all of the questions about the physical, emotional and sexual abuse she and her children had suffered. When the questions moved to animal abuse however, she wept openly as she described the torture and killing of her dog. The abuser first shot the dog several times with a BB gun, then left her to suffer for several hours while he took the family on an outing. When they came home the abuser was angry because the dog was still alive. Making his family watch, he took a shovel, dug a hole in the backyard, and then beat the dog to death with the shovel and threw her body in the hole.

* * *

During an intake interview, a safe shelter resident was asked if her abuser had hurt any animals or pets. She replied that he hadn't, ". , , but my son used to hit the dog with a baseball bat. We were lucky it was a nice dog and didn't bite my son." When the caseworker looked at her in disbelief, she added, "It was only a plastic bat."

* * *

One caller to a domestic violence hotline refused to come into the shelter because there was no place for her to put her dog. The abuser had threatened on several occasions to kill the dog if the woman left him and since he had several weapons, she believed he would do it. After trying to troubleshoot with the hotline worker for over an hour, the caller ultimately decided to stay with the abuser rather than put her dog in danger.

* * *

One abuser gathered his family into the living room. Without a word, he lifted the family cat by her forepaws, disemboweled her with a hunting knife and dropped her body to the floor. Then he walked away.

Chapter Three

When the Perpetrator is a Batterer

When people think about what motivates perpetrators of family violence to batter they usually think about their need to control and manipulate their victims. It makes sense how such tactics might be effective with human victims but it becomes a little less clear how family pets might factor into this equation. Even more perplexing is why some batterers abuse their companion animals right along with the human family members (including emotional, physical and sexual abuse) while other batterers never lay a finger on their pets. As we have seen in the previous chapter, researchers have found that only about half of those batterers who have pets ever abuse or threaten to abuse them. So how can professionals who interact with perpetrators or victims of family violence ever determine whether animals in these homes are also at risk?

When FIREPAW set out to study domestic violence batterers who are also perpetrators of animal abuse we wanted to know just that. We hypothesized that perhaps there were some important differences between batterers who abused their pets and those batterers who did not abuse pets. More specifically, we set out with a research study designed to uncover the perceptions, attitudes and behaviors that might distinguish batterers who abuse only human family members from those batterers who also abuse the family pet. Recognizing such a distinction would be critical, we believed, because it might help explain why people choose to abuse animals and what potential remedies can be developed to guide treatment efforts. It might also help professionals who encounter perpetrators and victims of family violence to recognize and identify those companion animals most at risk for being abused.

AN IMPORTANT DISTINCTION

In Chapter Two we examined the results of the FIREPAW study comparing the attitudes, perceptions, and behaviors of pet abusers and non-pet-abusers. In that study we surveyed people from *non*-violent homes (respondents were all members of the pet-owning general public visiting veterinary offices and clinics) and compared their responses to people from violent homes (most all of whom were seeking assistance from domestic violence safe houses).

In the study we will discuss in this chapter, we only looked at domestic violence batterers. We examined the beliefs, perceptions and behaviors of those domestic violence batterers who abused the family pet in addition to abusing human family members and compared the findings to the beliefs, perceptions and behaviors of domestic violence batterers who never laid a finger on their family pets. In this study we wanted to see what, if any, factors might help determine or predict which batterers would also abuse their companion animals or whether the decision to batter, terrorize and sometimes kill the family pet was simply a matter of random chance.

ATTITUDES, BELIEFS AND BEHAVIORS
ASSOCIATED WITH PET ABUSE

Before discussing the results of the FIREPAW study that explored the differences between batterers who abuse the family pet and batterers who never touch or threaten their companion animals, it is important to look at some key findings about batterers that have been derived from previous research studies. There is a wealth of findings from empirical studies examining batterers and how they think about and act in their relationship to animals. These findings have been quite revealing and can serve as markers or red flags for professionals who may suspect potential animal abuse or who encounter victims or perpetrators of animal abuse.

What can Trigger Batterers to Abuse Pets?

One of the factors linked with batterers abusing the family pet is the way they perceive the animals. Chief among these perceptions is viewing the family pet as "property" that one can do with as he or she pleases. There has been a lot of talk these days about the campaign to change the language of pet "owner" to pet "guardian." Some people have argued that the 'guardian campaign' as it is commonly known, is nothing more than social engineering and political correctness. Proponents for changing the terminology argue that changes in the language will, over time, cause a shift in public perception and attitudes about companion animals. This shift in public attitudes will eventually lead to a change in behavior, proponents contend, and improved treatment of pets (Carlisle-Frank and Frank, 2005). The campaign aside, researchers studying animal abuse know that there tends to be a definite trend in batterers thinking of their pets as property, in the same way they think of their refrigerators or trucks. In 2000, Dr. Clifton Flynn reported that while studying human victims of family violence he found that pets might be victimized in violent families because they are considered "property." The FIREPAW study examined the "property" variable as well, in an attempt to determine whether batterers who abused the family pet tended to more often think of their pets as property and less often perceive the pets as sentient beings with feelings. These findings will be discussed later in this chapter. For now however, suffice it to say that Flynn's findings were supported.

Making the family pet the "scapegoat" and blaming the animal for all that goes wrong and all of one's personal problems and failures is another factor that is suspected to trigger the batterer to abuse the pet. Nearly two decades of empirical studies from numerous researchers have indicated that those animals most at risk for being abused have also become the family scapegoat for personal and family problems. This is especially true for those pets residing in angry and aggressive households such as those families with ongoing domestic violence. Researchers and scholars alike (among them, DeViney, Dickert and Lockwood, 1983; Zahn-Waxler, Hollenbeck, and Radke-Yarrow, 1984; Kellert and Felthous, 1985; Veevers, 1985; Lockwood and Hodge, 1986; Vermeulen and Odendaal, 1993; Adams, 1994; and Flynn, 1999a; 2000b) have all argued that when the pet has become the family scapegoat, the animal is at the greatest risk for being abused. Why would this happen? Agnew (1998) has argued that stressed and strained people may use animals as scapegoats because animals provide a safe target for the discharge of aggressive feelings. Pets cannot call the police, notify school officials, or file a complaint. Once again the silent victims are the easiest targets.

Despite the fact that many pet-abusing batterers believe their pets are property and do not have feelings, these batterers have also been found to hold beliefs that their pets intentionally do things to disobey or hurt them. Abusers who believe their pets intentionally do not listen, that they disobey on purpose or act out to aggravate the batterer are most at risk for abuse. Drs. Kellert and Felthous (1985) found that self-reported animal abusers often said they abused animals to retaliate against animals they perceived had "wronged" them.

Stress and strain have also been shown to trigger abuse of the family pet in violent homes. One well-known scholar has suggested that those batterers who engage in animal abuse tend to be more sensitive to stress and strain (Agnew, 1998). Batterers may abuse the family pets to reduce stress or to get revenge against the perceived "cause" of the stress. One of the primary stressors for abusers may be the pet's own behavior. Other researchers have reported that animal-abusing batterers said they abused their pets in order to eliminate undesirable traits in the animal such as damaging property or making noise (Kellert and Felthous, 1985). Animals who damage property, bark incessantly or make other types of disturbances can cause stress and strain in many non-violent homes. Violent households, however, may be more vulnerable to such behaviors. It would seem plausible that those animals who behaved in ways that batterers found annoying or disturbing would be more likely to raise the stress levels within the home and therefore more likely to be on the receiving end of violence. On a related point, several researchers (DeViney, et al. 1983; Kellert and Felthous 1985; Felthous and Kellert 1987a) have found that animal abusers frequently report the animals' "bad" behaviors as a reason for abusing them.

A final factor thought to be related to abuse of the family pet in violent households is hunting. It is important to note that hunting, like the other factors mentioned, does not "cause" abuse to companion animals. Most hunters do not abuse the family pet. So what is the link between hunting and abuse to companion animals? Some researchers and scholars have suggested that the attitudes and behaviors of those who engage in pet abuse may be similar to those who hunt. Dr. Agnew (1998) has argued that animal abusers— including some hunters—have a more dominionistic attitude toward animals believing they are distinct from and superior to animals and that they have been granted divine dominion over animals to use as they please. One researcher has stated that hunting combined with threatening or harming a pet are warning signs for identifying a batterer (Statman, 1990), and other researchers have pointed out that many abusers who are cruel to animals also kill them for sport (Pope-Lance and Engelsman, 1987). To further clarify the relationship, scholar and author Carol Adams (1994) has argued that battering incidents of human and non-human victims increase just prior to the hunting season.

While theoretical arguments have been persuasive, empirical evidence has been less than conclusive about the relationship between batterers who hunt and abuse of the family pet. While researchers Herzog and Borghardt (1988) found that some people intentionally expose their children to abuse of their companion animals to reinforce them for participation in what they term "other forms of abuse" like hunting, the results of a recent study conducted by Dr. Cliff Flynn (2002) indicate that while hunting appears to be related to harming stray or wild animals, hunting appears to be unrelated to the abuse of companion animals, other forms of animal abuse, or violence directed toward humans. It is important to note that the subjects in Flynn's study were college students with an average age of 20.3 years and therefore the results may not be indicative of the 'typical' hunter.

The FIREPAW study as we will see, compared the number of hunting batterers who abused their pets to the number of hunting batterers who never harm or threaten their pets. While the results are interesting, nonetheless hunting should in no way be thought of as a marker for pet abuse. Rather, in cases of suspected animal abuse hunting may be one possible factor that when taken in conjunction with *many other* factors, may be a possible red flag for professionals to probe further.

SELECTIVE BATTERING OF THE FAMILY PET: PET-ABUSING AND NON-PET-ABUSING DOMESTIC VIOLENCE BATTERERS

There appears that something curious is going on with batterers of domestic violence. Why do some of them avoid harming or threatening the family pet while others abuse their companion animals right along with the other family members? The FIREPAW study hypothesized that those domestic violence abusers who harm the family pets may tend to differ from non-pet-abusing batterers in their perceptions, attitudes, beliefs and behaviors with regard to their pets. More specifically, the FIREPAW study examined whether there were differences between abuser-types in terms of (1) their perceptions of companion animals as sentient beings versus property, (2) tendencies to "scapegoat" the family pet for personal and/or family problems, (3) sensitivity to hassles and stressors in the environment—particularly those perceived as being caused by the pets, (4) batterers' unrealistic expectations about companion animals, (5) batterers' previous relationships with pets in their families of origins. For the purpose of this study animal abuse was theoretically defined as socially unacceptable, deliberate and unnecessary suffering and harm inflicted on animals.

Background

Victims of domestic violence were questioned about their and their partners' attitudes, perceptions and behaviors with regard to their companion animals. Their partners included both batterers who were pet abusers and batterers who reportedly never abused the family pet. Why question the victims about pet abuse? Dr. Frank Ascione (1998a) has suggested that it is important to assess the batterers' perception of animal abuse as well as the victims'. An

important question he has proposed for study is "What is the victim's knowledge of the partner's history (as a child, adolescent and adult prior to the current relationship) of animal abuse?" Assessing the conditions surrounding the
batterers' attitudes, beliefs and actions surrounding abuse from the victim's
perspective was the primary approach of the FIREPAW study. Victims' perspectives were believed to be more reliable than those of the batterers in this
case. Why? Because victims have been shown to be more reliable than batterers when recounting types and frequency of violence within the home. Researchers Edleson and Brygger (1986) found that partners in domestic violence families tend not to agree about the different forms of violence the
batterer perpetuates. In fact, when victims and batterers who had undergone
intervention were asked about the previous violence and/or threats against
pets, the victims and batterers only had exact agreement 24% of the time
about the types and frequency of pet abuse that had occurred.

Given the potential for disagreement about the specifics surrounding pet
abuse, whose report should we trust—the victim or the perpetrator? The evidence seems to favor the victim. This is primarily because batterers frequently will not disclose their abusive behaviors directed toward pets, making their reports unreliable. And since they frequently do not admit to pet
abuse obtaining accurate reports regarding their attitudes, perceptions and actions surrounding pet abuse from pet abusers themselves would be useless.
Scholar and author Carol Adams (1995) has argued that batterers choose not
to disclose their abuse of animals because it exposes their controlled and cal-
culated reasons for violence. According to Adams, despite the fact that practitioners working with batterers have documentation of their deliberate harming or killing of the family pet, it is rare for batterers to ever disclose having
harmed their animals. This argument appears to have empirical support. Animal abuse expert Phil Arkow (1994a) has reported on a comprehensive assessment of the intake statistics of domestic violence perpetrators. And what
was the overall conclusion? Most batterers simply do not admit to pet abuse.

Given the potential unreliability of their responses, the FIREPAW study
utilized the responses of victims of domestic violence rather than the batterers themselves to report on the factors surrounding pet abuse within their
homes.

The Study

Domestic violence shelters in the Northeastern region of the United States
were contacted and asked to participate in the study. Shelter managers and
staff members placed the questionnaires in a prominent place and advised
victims seeking services that participation was voluntary and anonymous.

Out of the 48 respondents who participated in the study, 34 of them had pets. The majority of results presented in this chapter are based on only those respondents with pets, with all respondents included for comparison purposes for the 'hassles/stressors' items, the 'hunting' item, and the 'relationship with pets in family of origin' items.

In order to minimize interviewer bias and problems associated with the sensitive subject matter, data about batterers' perceptions and behaviors regarding the family pet were collected via questionnaires. The survey consisted of 78 items. Twenty-six of the questions were subdivided in to three scales: a Sentient Beings Scale (to measure the extent to which batterers view their companion animals as having feelings and preferences and therefore the ability to feel pain from the abuse), a Hassles and Stressors Scale (to measure the extent to which batterers are affected by daily stressful events and the extent to which the family pets are blamed for that stress) and an Unrealistic Expectations Scale (to measure what types of unrealistic ideas and expectations, if any, batterers have about companion animals' ability to behave in certain ways).

All of the results discussed in this chapter were tested statistically and found to be significant; most were found to be highly statistically significant.

General Findings about Pet Abuse and Batterers

Whether someone was designated as a pet-abusing batterer (PAB) or non-pet-abusing batterer (NPAB) was based on actual abuse only (as opposed to threats). The PAB and NPAB categories were defined by how participants responded to being queried whether their partners ever abused their pets. Respondents were then asked to specifically define what they meant by 'abuse.' Ninety percent of the types of pet abuse reported included 'physical' abuse items and 10% included 'neglect' items only. Eighty percent of pet-abusing batterers were reported to have both threatened and abused the family pet.

When asked to give specifics about the type of abuse directed towards their pets 43% of the respondents with pets reported that batterers did so through physical punishment described as "punching, hitting, choking, drowning, shooting, stabbing, throwing against the wall/down the stairs, etc." Thirty percent of respondents reported that abusers verbally threatened to either kill or hurt the pet. Twenty-six percent reported that the abusers denied food and/or water to the animal and another 26% denied the animal veterinary care. Of those families where pet abuse had occurred, 48% of respondents reported it occurred "often" during the past 12 months and another 30% reported that abuse to the family pet had occurred "almost always" during the past 12 months. Victims whose pets had been abused reported that abuse to the family pets occurred an average of 51% of the time violent outbursts had taken place over the past year. Finally, the findings indicated that hunting might be related in some way to violence directed toward the family pet. Respondents reported that 52% of pet abusing batterers also hunt, compared to only 11% of non-pet abusing batterers with pets.

PERCEPTIONS, ATTITUDES AND BEHAVIORS OF PET-ABUSING AND NON-PET-ABUSING BATTERERS

Fifty-three percent of respondents said their partners had physically harmed their pets. Given that previous research has supported the finding that not all batterers abuse their companion animals this begs the question, 'Do batterers with pets who abuse the animals differ in some way from those batterers who abuse human family members but never touch the pets'? The findings of the FIREPAW study seem to indicate they do. . .

Perceiving the Animal as a Sentient Being Versus Viewing the Pet as "Property"

Our perceptions are directly related to our behavior. In other words, people tend to behave in ways that are consistent with the perceptions they have about themselves and others in the world. It was believed that whether batterers recognized their pets as sentient beings who are capable of feelings and preferences or whether they view the pets merely as property they can do with as they please might be related to whether batterers behaved abusively toward their pets. If perceptions about the animals as sentient beings versus perceptions of the animals as mere property could be shown to be related to whether batterers abused the family pet, such perceptions could be red flags or markers for companion animals who may be at most risk of being abused.

The FIREPAW study hypothesized there may tend to be a difference between pet-abusing and non-pet-abusing batterers with regard to viewing companion animals as sentient beings versus viewing them as property. Respondents were asked fourteen questions in an effort to tease out those batterers who recognized that animals were sentient beings with feelings and preferences from those batterers who perceived their pets primarily as objects or property. Many of the differences were quite striking such as how rarely abusers told pets they loved them relative to the public at large. Pet abusers also rarely showed affection to their pets; ninety percent were reported as never doing so. Likewise, 95% of PAB talked only to their pets through commands and threats, while only 5% talked to their pets conversationally.

There was also a difference between the two types of batterers with regard to how they perceive their family pets. When asked directly whether batterers viewed their companion animals as property or as family members, 70% of PAB were reported to consider their pets as property. In sharp contrast, 64% of non-pet-abusing batterers were reported to believe their pets were full-fledged family members.

Pets as Scapegoats

Can there be any relationship between making the family pet a regular scapegoat for personal and family problems and violence directed toward that pet? It was hypothesized that those batterers who routinely make the family pet the scapegoat for their stress and problems might be more likely to abuse the pets right along with other family members than those batterers who do not make the family pet the scapegoat. If pet-abusing batterers were found to be more likely to scapegoat the family pet then this could be yet another marker professionals could use to probe further for pets suspected at risk for abuse. Another goal of the FIREPAW study therefore, was to determine whether pet-abusing batterers had a higher tendency to scapegoat the family pet than non-pet-abusing batterers.

When asked to identify the specific family members typically made the scapegoat for daily frustrations/family problems and the frequency at which this occurred, pet-abusing batterers were reported to scapegoat the family pet more often than non-pet-abusing batterers.

Hassles and Stressors

It was hypothesized that pet-abusing batterers and non-pet-abusing batterers might differ in the types and frequency of life events they got upset by. Additionally, it was believed that pets would be viewed more frequently as one of life's key stressors or hassles by PAB than NPAB. Responses were derived from a 12-item list of everyday events (e.g., work problems; messy house; lights on in unoccupied rooms). Pet-abusing batterers were reportedly set off by many more items than non-pet-abusing batterers. Remember, these were all batterers in the sample, regardless of whether they abused pets, so presumably, they all had a tendency to be set off by some life events. Interestingly, cleanliness of the house seemed to be an especially important issue for pet-abusing batterers, with batterers who were concerned about the cleanliness of the house significantly more likely to abuse the family pet. Of special note, pet-abusing batterers were reportedly set off by "pets misbehaving" significantly more often than non-pet-abusing batterers.

Having Unrealistic Expectations for Animals

Could batterers' expectations for their pets make those animals more likely to be abused? The FIREPAW study hypothesized that batterers who have unrealistic ideas and expectations about how animals "should" behave, unrealistic expectations about animals' ability to listen and follow the batterers' commands and orders, and unrealistic perceptions about the animals' ability to control or curtail natural behaviors may be more prone to abuse those animals when their expectations go unmet. Another goal of the FIREPAW study therefore, was to determine whether there was a difference between pet-abusing batterers and non-pet-abusing batterers with regard to unrealistic expectations about their pets (that is, about the animals' ability to control natural behaviors such as barking, clawing and excreting). We were also interested in trying to determine whether there was a difference between these two groups in the frequency and severity of punishment they gave the family pets when these expectations went unmet.

Again, in order to determine whether there were any significant differences between batterers who harmed both pets and humans and those batterers who never harmed the family pet, responses were analyzed for both abuser types. Ninety-five percent of pet-abusing batterers were reported to frequently get upset with the pet because the animal did not meet the batterers' unrealistic expectations about their animals. This was compared to 64% of non-pet-abusing batterers. The types of unrealistic expectations reported included the batterer getting upset over the disrespect the pet shows the batterer; the batterer's perception that the pet does not recognize that the batterer is in charge; the property damage the pet causes; others' poor perceptions of the family due to the pets' misbehavior.

Similarly, when respondents were asked questions concerning batterers' beliefs about statements such as 'Animals should never have "accidents",' 'Animals should not vocalize,' 'Cats should never scratch the furniture,' and 'Animals should always do as they are told,' the respondents reported that 90% of pet-abusing batterers have unrealistic expectations about their pets' behavior compared to only 57% of non-pet-abusing batterers. Such unrealistic expectations can serve as a marker to probe further into cases where professionals suspect possible animal abuse.

Pet Mistreatment in Family of Origin

If you don't know a horse, check his record, as the saying goes. There's also another saying: the best predictor of future behavior is past behavior. We wanted to know if the same were true for pet-abusing batterers. Would there be a tendency for pet-abusing batterers to have either been a witness of abuse

Table 2. Attitudes, Perceptions, Beliefs, and Treatment of the Family Pet: Pet-Abusing Batterers and Non-Pet-Abusing Batterers

Perceiving Pets as Sentient Beings vs. Viewing Animals as Objects/Property

Pet-Abusing Batterers (PAB)	Non-Pet-Abusing Batterers (NPAB)
• 63% Never tell pets they love them • None tell pets they love them on a daily basis • 90% Never show affection to pets • 95% Talk to pets only through commands or threats • 70% Consider pets "property"	• 21% Never tell pets they love them • 36% Tell pets they love them daily • 57% Show pets affection at least occasionally • 79% Talk to pets conversationally • 64% view pets as members of the family

Pets as Scapegoats

Pet-Abusing Batterers (PAB)	Non-Pet-Abusing Batterers (NPAB)
• More frequently scapegoat the family pet for personal and family frustrations • More frequently punish pets	• Less likely to scapegoat the family pet for frustrations and problems • Less frequently punish pets

Unrealistic Expectations

Pet-Abusing Batterers (PAB)	Non-Pet-Abusing Batterers (NPAB)
• 95% Have unrealistic expectations about their animals • 75% Punished pets harshly (physical punishment) • 68% Punished pets at least monthly	• 64% Have unrealistic expectations about their pets • Punishment of pets less harsh and less frequent

Hassles and Stressors

Pet-Abusing Batterers (PAB)	Non-Pet-Abusing Batterers (NPAB)
• Set off by multiple stressors daily • Tend to be concerned by cleanliness of house • 85% Set off by pet's behavior	• Set off by less daily stressors • Less concerned w/cleanliness of house. • 71% Not regularly upset by family pet

Adapted from: Carlisle-Frank, P., J. Frank, and L. Nielsen, L. "Selective Battering of the Family Pet." *Anthrozoös* 17, no.1 (2004a): 26-41.

of their family pet or engaged in animal abuse of their pets during childhood or adolescence? Another important question in the FIREPAW study therefore, concerned the type of relationship adult perpetrators of domestic violence had with their pets in their family of origin.

As it turned out there was a statistically significant difference between pet-abusing batterers and non-pet-abusing batterers with regard to their childhood relationships with the family pet. Of the 61% of respondents who reportedly knew about their partners' history with companion animals, the majority of respondents with non-pet-abusing partners ranked their partners' relationship with their family pets while growing up as "very" or "somewhat" close (63%). The majority of respondents with pet-abusing partners, however, ranked their partners' relationship with their family pets while growing up as "neutral" (77%). Only 21% of respondents with non-pet-abusing partners reported their partners abused their pets or witnessed abuse of their pet by a family member in childhood, while 50% of respondents with pet-abusing partners reported that their partners either abused the family pet or witnessed abuse of their pet by a family member during childhood.

WHAT THIS ALL MEANS

The findings of the FIREPAW study and previous studies indicate that when it comes to batterers, violence directed toward animals appears to be related to a number of key attitudes, perceptions and belief systems that are translated in to actions. Batterers, as the findings seem to indicate, are far from being a monolithic group. Some abusers appear unable to distinguish—or to care—that both their human and non-human victims experience great suffering at their hands, while others engage in a bizarre justification process for battering and terrorizing the human family members while protecting the non-human ones.

Once the findings of the FIREPAW study can be shown to be generalized, identifying potential trends in attitudes, perceptions and behaviors of pet abusers will not only increase our understanding of what drives those who abuse, but will also provide the variables necessary for creating profiles of potential animal abusers. Further research is needed of course, to test these variables under a variety of conditions and settings to determine whether the findings in the FIREPAW study are consistent and applicable to other regions. As with the study discussed earlier in Chapter Two, and all social science studies for that matter, it is possible that the regional culture of the area surveyed in this study is unique enough as to make the results not applicable to other communities or other conditions. The size of the sample of people studied, their ages, economic and educational backgrounds can all be variables that can potentially affect the results.

While caution should be used in generalizing these findings to other populations until the study has been further replicated, in the meantime there is some very useful information professionals can use when trying to assess suspected animal abuse. Perhaps the most useful information to take away from all of these studies are a number of red flags to alert those involved in identifying and/or stopping animal abuse. These red flags can be used to aid professionals in helping to determine if such suspicions merit further investigation or probing. . .

ARE THE ANIMALS BEING ABUSED IN THIS FAMILY?

Domestic violence can be a tricky thing to uncover. Sometimes it goes on for years without anyone other than the victims and the perpetrators knowing about it. When the victims are animals it can be even trickier to uncover. Chapters Eight and Nine offer strategies and tools for recognizing and problem solving suspected cases of animal abuse in your community. The following section offers professionals a number of markers for identifying potential pet-abusing batterers in cases where there are questions or suspicions that animal abuse may be occurring. It should be noted that if these attitudes, beliefs and behaviors do not appear to be present professionals should nonetheless still pursue any suspicions they may have about potential animal abuse. Remember, not everyone will be honest and forthcoming in cases where the possibility of abuse is being examined. This can be especially true for batterers. However, whether you are a veterinarian who has observed suspicious injuries to an animal, a law enforcement officer who has received a domestic violence call, a domestic violence or social service case worker or therapist working with victims or perpetrators, a teacher or counselor who has been alerted to abuse from a student, or an animal welfare worker or animal control officer working with a questionable situation, in cases where these attitudes, beliefs and behaviors are indicated it should serve to strengthen decisions to pursue further investigation and probing about suspicions of animal abuse. Here are some key signals to consider:

General Markers

The Batterer Appears Evasive or Uncomfortable When Asked Directly if S/He Abused the Family Pet

Those people whose professional work brings them in contact with domestic violence abusers know that batterers are not exactly the most truthful and forthcoming group of folks—especially when it comes to discussing their violent outbursts. Batterers may be well practiced in giving immediate, convincing responses to questions about their abusive actions so no matter what the response their answers should be set aside pending further questioning of victims or other witnesses. However, if a batterer clearly has difficulty giving a straightforward, consistent response when queried about pet abuse, this may be a signal that further investigation is needed.

A Family Member, Neighbor, Family Friend, etc. Has Stated They Witnessed the Batterer Abusing the Family Pet

Let's face it—speaking up about a batterer's abusive behavior is not without risk. Abusers can be scary people, especially when someone is giving a testimonial against them. Because of this risk professionals should weigh heavily witnesses' claims that they observed an animal being abused and act accordingly.

Victims or Others State the Batterer Has Made Threats to Harm or Kill the Family Pet

Again, people are at an increased risk for future retribution from the batterer for accusing him/her of threatening to engage in abusive activity. The fact that victims or others are taking these risks should not be dismissed until further investigation disproves their statements.

Obvious Suspicious Signs of Abuse and/or Neglect

As we have seen earlier, there have been some interesting studies conducted by veterinarian researchers indicating that a good portion of veterinarian practitioners encounter cases of injuries that appear suspicious. Frequently in such cases the animal's owner-guardian offers explanations that simply do not fit the injury. Of course there may be some reasonable explanation for an injury that is out of the ordinary. But if the owner's response seems inconsistent with the type of injury or there are obvious signs of what appear to be scars from a serious injury or signs that the animal may be malnourished or seriously sick, these are indicators that merit more probing. Likewise, a pet who has a long history of injuries, especially if it is discovered that previous pets have died or disappeared under mysterious circumstances, raises a red flag that the animal just might be at risk. If witnesses have given testimonials that the batterer has overtly refused food, water or veterinary care for the pet, further investigation should definitely be pursued.

Signs to look for:

- The pet has a suspicious injury (the explanation offered by family members does not seem right or is inconsistent) or a history of injuries

- The pet appears malnourished or has signs of serious illness, disease or scars/marking from injury (the explanation offered by family members does not seem right or is inconsistent) or a history of injuries
- The pet appears malnourished or has signs of serious illness, disease or scars/marking from previous injury
- History of injuries and/or deaths or mysterious disappearance of previous pets
- Family members, neighbors, friends, etc. have stated the batterer has refused food, water, medicine, or needed veterinary care for the pet

'Childhood Relationship with Pets' Markers

Batterer Was Not Especially Close with His/Her Pet During Childhood

In and of itself this little fun fact is not especially meaningful. Certainly many people were not always close with their childhood pets. When taken together with several of the other markers however, a pattern may begin to emerge that will make this yet one more indicator that pets may be at risk and further investigation is called for.

Batterer Either Abused the Family Pet or Witnessed Abuse of the Family Pet during Childhood

Now this one carries quite a bit more weight. As we will see in Chapter Four the findings are pretty clear about the cyclical trend for violence in children who have witnessed ongoing abuse to a loved one—including witnessing violence directed toward their pets. Equally powerful is the link between kids who torture and abuse their pets and future violent tendencies. But do such childhood experiences mean that batterers will abuse the family pet as adults? No, certainly not. What it does do, however, especially when other markers are found to exist, is to paint a picture of someone who may be putting the well-being and even the life of a defenseless creature at risk. Combined with other markers, this item might prompt further probing.

'Inability to Recognize Animals as Sentient Beings' Markers

This marker can be particularly revealing about the way the batterer views animals. When unable to recognize or acknowledge that animals have feelings, it increases the risk that the batterer has no concerns about the pet and therefore the animal may be at an increased risk for abuse when the batterer loses his temper. Signs to watch out for:

- Batterer does not think the pet has feelings or preferences
- Batterer only considers the pet an object/property and not a full-fledged member of the family

- Batterer rarely, if ever, shows affection to the pet
- Batterer rarely, if ever, tells the pet s/he loves the pet
- Batterer rarely, if ever, plays with, shows positive attention or takes care of pet's needs
- Batterer refuses to allow the pet to live indoors/spend time indoors with the rest of the family
- Batterer refuses to allow the family pet to be a part of family activities and outings
- Batterer or family member states the batterer believes the pet is his/hers to do with as s/he pleases
- Batterer talks to the family pet primarily through threats and commands, rarely using a conversational tone
- Batterer refuses/sees no need to allow the pet to have toys
- Batterer refuses/sees no need to include the pet in family celebrations, give the pet gifts, celebrate the pet's birthday, sign the pet's name on family cards, or include the pet's picture in the family photo album

'Tendency to Scapegoat the Family Pet' Markers

When anyone is singled out and blamed for all that is wrong in someone's life, be it the spouse, the children or the animals, they are at increased risk for being abused. This is especially true in angry or violent households. Companion animals are in a particularly dangerous position because they cannot speak out, they cannot report the abuser, and, unfortunately, too often their situation and condition goes unnoticed. Here are some signs to watch out for in suspected animal abuse cases:

- The batterer frequently blames the family pet for personal and/or family problems, or daily frustrations
- The batterer is reported to punish the pet frequently
- The batterer is reported to punish the pet for no reason/or for things pets should not be punished for/things the pet did not do

'Sensitivity to Hassles and Stress/Viewing the Pet as the Primary Source of Stress' Markers

It is possible that all domestic violence batterers are more sensitive to daily stressful events than non-batterers. However, those batterers who also abuse the family pet may be more sensitive to daily frustrations and hassles than non-pet-abusing batterers. This is especially true if the batterer views the pet and the pet's behavior (especially if the pet is seen as messing up the house) as the primary stressor. Here are some issues to probe in cases of suspected pet abuse:

- The batterer is frequently upset by the family pet's behavior
- The batterer frequently punishes the pet harshly for what the batterer perceives as "bad behavior"
- The batterer is sensitive to daily frustrations and stressors (such as work problems, money problems, problems with in-laws, messy house, dinner not ready on time, lights left on in unoccupied rooms, etc.) and is frequently set off by these events
- The batterer states the pet is his/her primary source of stress
- The batterer is particularly concerned about the cleanliness/tidiness of the house
- The batterer becomes upset with the animal if the house does not meet his/her cleanliness/tidiness standards

'Unrealistic Expectations for Pets' Markers

Batterers who have unrealistic expectations about what animals should and should not be able to do may be more likely to abuse those creatures when their expectations go unmet. For instance, the belief that animals should never have "accidents," even when they have not been let outdoors all day or when they have been placed in high-stress conditions (such as the stress of violent outbursts), is an unrealistic expectation. Likewise, batterers who believe that animals have the ability to always understand and follow their demands or that when the animals disobey the demands the animals are intentionally being disrespectful of the batterer's authority also have unrealistic expectations about animals. These erroneous beliefs about how animals can and should behave may put animals at an increased risk for being abused. This may be especially true in cases where the batterer frequently gets upset and/or harshly punishes the pet for not living up to the batterer's expectations. Here are some signs to look out for:

- Batterer tends to have unrealistic ideas and expectations about how animals "should" behave
- Batterer tends to have unrealistic expectations about animals' ability to listen and follow the batterers' commands and orders
- Batterer tends to have unrealistic perceptions about the animals' ability to control or curtail natural behaviors such as needing to eliminate urine/feces, barking/vocalizing, scratching, kicking litter out of the litter box, etc.
- Batterer frequently becomes upset with the pet over the perceived "disrespect" the pet shows the batterer

- Batterer frequently becomes upset with the pet because the batterer believes the pet does not recognize that the batterer is in charge
- Batterer frequently becomes upset with the pet because of the property damage the pet causes
- Batterer frequently becomes upset with the pet because of beliefs that others will have poor perceptions of the family due to the pet's misbehavior
- Batterer believes pets should always do as they are told
- Batterer tends to punish pet "harshly" (using physical punishment versus scolding or time-out) when the pet does not listen to the batterer's wishes
- Batterer believes that animals should never have "accidents" (even when they are not let out all day or when they are frightened)

Chapter Four

When the Perpetrator is a Child or Adolescent

Animal abuse committed by children and adolescents is surprisingly common (Miller and Knutson, 1997; Flynn, 2000a). It is also a tricky matter to identify. The reason is because animal abuse is often a secretive activity known only to the perpetrators and is therefore difficult to spot unless professionals know what other red flags to look for (Felthous and Kellert, 1987b). This chapter will highlight what experts currently know about animal cruelty committed by children and teenagers. Following this we will take a look at some of the challenges that professionals working in the trenches face when trying to recognize and intervene to rescue both the animals and the kids in cases of childhood animal cruelty.

WHAT TYPES OF ANIMAL ABUSE DO CHILDREN AND ADOLESCENTS TYPICALLY PERPETRATE?

Research results indicate that the most common acts of animal abuse committed by children and teenagers are killing a stray animal or hurting or torturing animals to cause it pain (Flynn, 1999a; 2000a). In one study the most common methods of committing cruelty to animals were shooting, hitting, beating, kicking and throwing the animal against a wall (Flynn, 2000a). Experts tell us that childhood animal abuse may vary in frequency and severity. It may range from developmentally immature teasing of animals by toddlers to serious torture. Chronic abuse of animals is seen as more significant than isolated incidents (Ascione, 2001).

One study asked violent criminals to recall their animal abuse histories as children. The results revealed a host of horrific acts. Respondents reported that as children they had deliberately inflicted pain and torture on pets, skinned trapped animals alive, stoned and beat animals, exploded animals, thrown animals off of high places, pulled the wings off of birds, wounded animals on purpose, tied animals' tails together, electrocuted, burned, blinded, and dismembered animals, broke animals' bones, poured chemicals on animals, snapped their necks and exploded animals in a microwave oven (Kellert and Felthous, 1985).

Another study revealed that the most common victims of childhood animal abuse were small animals (rodents, birds, reptiles), dogs, and cats. The most common type of animals deliberately killed were small animals such as mice, gerbils, rabbits, hamsters, birds, reptiles, etc. The most common animals to be tortured or deliberately hurt were small animals (50%) and dogs (44.4%) (Flynn, 1999a).

Group Versus Solitary Animal Abuse

Children and adolescents who abuse animals may do so in one of two ways: (1) as a solitary activity (abusing animals while alone) or as a group activity (with others in their peer group). Animal abuse done in a group is frequently done on a dare, to prove masculinity or one's worthiness to be a part of a gang, fraternity or club, or as a form of "recreation" in that torturing and/or killing animals is done to obtain a break from boredom. As you might imagine, there are some distinct differences between those children and teens who abuse animals within a group and those who torture and kill animals while alone.

One researcher recently examined the differences between those children and adolescents who perpetrated animal cruelty while alone and those children and adolescents who participated in animal cruelty as a group (Henry, 2004a). The study surveyed college students about their previous exposure to and participation in animal abuse as children and adolescents. It was expected that solitary animal abusers would be (1) less sensitive to the treatment of animals as adults and (2) have a more extensive history of delinquent behavior than those who abused animals as part of a group activity. It was also expected that solitary animal abusers were more likely to have been exposed to animal abuse at an earlier age than group participants of animal abuse.

The results suggest that those children who engage in solitary as opposed to group acts of animal cruelty appear to be at higher risk for a lack of sensitization for other living beings and for future delinquency—including future acts of animal cruelty. They may also be at greater risk for psychopathology. This is in contrast to those children and teens who participate in group activities of animal abuse who may be responding to peer pressure or "group think" (when independent judgment and thinking is replaced by the will of the group).

The researcher's final conclusion was that children and adolescents who are solitary animal abusers might be at an increased risk for antisocial tendencies and a diagnosis of conduct disorder. Additionally, insensitivity to animal suffering, callousness and actually deriving pleasure from torturing animals may be more common among those children or teens who engage in animal cruelty while alone as opposed to those who participate in animal cruelty within a group (Henry, 2004a).

HOW COMMON IS CHILDHOOD ANIMAL ABUSE?

As researchers have discovered, evidence of animal abuse in childhood is alarmingly high (Miller and Knutson, 1997; Flynn, 2000a). You may recall from Chapter Two that surveys of women and children staying at domestic violence shelters revealed that violent homes had a high percentage of children who had witnessed—and participated—in abuse of the family pet. A brief review of these figures is worth reiterating here:

In a study of women staying at a domestic violence shelter in Utah approximately 50% of women reported that their children had witnessed abuse of their pets and approximately 25% of women reported that their children had also either hurt or killed a family pet (Ascione, Thompson and Black, 1997). Another study found that approximately 33% of women with children and pets revealed their children had hurt or killed a family pet (Ascione, 1998) and in a different survey abuse to the family pet had been done in the presence of children in 75.5% of the cases (Quinlisk, 1995).

Sixty-one percent of women seeking assistance from domestic violence services who responded to a survey about pet abuse reported that their children had witnessed the batterer committing acts of abuse against their pets (Carlisle-Frank, Frank, and Nielsen, 2004). Ascione (1996) found that 32% of women in a domestic violence shelter in the Northwest said their children had hurt or killed their pets, often to imitate the behaviors they had witnessed in the home. And a study conducted by DeViney and colleagues (1983) revealed that in 37% of child-abusing households the children were also involved in perpetrating cruelty to the family pet.

Ascione and his colleagues (1997) conducted interviews with the children staying at a domestic violence shelter and found that two-thirds of children reported witnessing pet abuse (including seeing their animals strangled, shot and poisoned); 46.4% of children said the perpetrator of the animal abuse was either a father, step-father or boyfriend of their mother; 13.2% of children admitted to hurting pets including throwing the animal, hitting the animal, or stepping on the animal; 7.9% of children admitted to hurting or killing animals other than their own pets.

As alarming as those figures are, families with partner and child battering are not the only environments in which child and teen animal abusers come from. Let's take a look at some of the research findings on child and teen animal abuse. . .

Flynn (1999a; 2000a) surveyed college students about their experience with animal cruelty. Nearly half of them (49%) had either observed or perpetrated animal cruelty. A surprising 17.6% had actually perpetrated animal abuse. The majority who had perpetrated animal abuse had also witnessed it. Approximately one-third had observed someone hurt or torture an animal and more than 25% had witnessed the killing of an animal. (An alarming 40% who killed or hurt or tortured animals claimed they were not bothered by the abusive act.)

For those children and teens witnessing animal abuse by others the perpetrators were most frequently friends/neighbors, followed by fathers and step-fathers. Within families, fathers were more likely to have abused animals than other family members.

The results indicated that more males than females witnessed and/or perpetrated animal abuse during childhood. Approximately 66% of males had either witnessed or perpetrated animal abuse compared to 40% of females who reported experiencing animal abuse during childhood. When it came to actually perpetrating animal abuse 34.5% of males had inflicted cruelty compared to only 9.3% of females. Males were 6 times more likely to have killed a stray animal, 3 times more likely to have hurt or tortured an animal and almost 6 times more likely to have killed a pet than females.

Of those people who said they had either witnessed or perpetrated animal cruelty, respondents were most likely to first witness animal abuse between the ages of 6–12. (Approximately 30% of those respondents first witnessed animal abuse during their teenage years.) Most perpetrators who hurt or tortured an animal or killed a pet did so between the ages of 6–12, and most perpetrators who had killed a stray animal did so as a teenager. A total of 29.4% of respondents had killed an animal between the ages of 6–12, 50% tortured an animal between the age of 6–12, and 33% tortured an animal as teenagers.

The most common acts of animal abuse reported included killing stray animals (13.1%), hurting and torturing animals (6.7%) and killing a pet (2.6%). Males were 4 times more likely than females to have abused animals in childhood. More than 33% of males admitted to harming or killing animals and 10% of females did.

Almost all perpetrators of childhood animal abuse had abused animals on more than one occasion. Approximately 25% of respondents reported having killed stray or wild animals as children on 3 or more separate incidents. An additional 27.8% reported torturing or hurting an animal on 6 or more separate occasions. According to the results of this study approximately 50% of all children and 66% of male children are exposed to animal cruelty. Approximately 20% of all children and approximately 33% of male children may perpetrate animal cruelty (Flynn, 1999a; 2000a).

Unfortunately, the results of the previous study are not unique. Other studies have also revealed a large proportion of children and teenagers who have witnessed and/or perpetrated animal abuse. . .

- In another study approximately 50% of college students reported either perpetrating or witnessing animal cruelty when younger. Out of these, 20% of respondents had actually abused animals as children, one in seven had killed a stray animal, 10% had hurt or tortured animals as children and 3.2% had killed their own pets. Males were twice as likely as females to have observed or perpetrated animal abuse (Miller and Knutson, 1997).
- A recent study surveying college students revealed that 51% of participants said they had observed at least one act of animal cruelty. Males were more likely to have observed animal cruelty than females. Of those reporting they had witnessed animal cruelty in childhood, a surprising 63% had observed animal cruelty more than once. A total of 18% reported actually engaging in animal abuse at least once and 12.4% reported *more* than one incident in which they engaged in animal cruelty. Again, far more males than females engaged in animal abuse (Henry, 2004b).

Other Findings Have Included:

- A study examining the self-reports of animal abuse during childhood of 299 inmates with felony offenses and college students (Miller and Knutson, 1997) found that: For inmates 16.4% had hurt animals as children. Of these, 32.8% had killed a stray animal, and 12% had killed a pet. For students 9.7% had hurt animals as children. Of these, 14.3% had killed a stray animal, and 3.2% had killed a pet.
- A report created by the Humane Society of the United States revealed that of more than 1,000 cruelty cases examined for the year 2001, 20% of intentional, malicious acts were committed by teenagers—95% of whom were males (Crary, 2002).
- As many as 45% of the perpetrators in nine school shootings from 1996 to 1999 allegedly had histories of animal abuse according to research done by Verlinden (2000) as reported by Ascione (2001).
- Researchers studying incarcerated sexual homicide perpetrators' self-reports of animal cruelty during childhood and adolescence found that 36%

of perpetrators abused animals as children and 46% did so as teenagers (Douglas, Burgess and Ressler, 1995).

- A study asked 64 convicted male sex offenders about their animal abuse in childhood and adolescence. Results revealed that 48% of rapists and 30% of child molesters had abused animals as children (Tingle, Barnard, Robbins, Newman, and Hutchinson, 1986).

- Results of a study asking college students about their childhood animal abuse revealed that 87% had observed animal abuse—64% did so at age 12 or younger. Another 17% actually engaged in animal abuse (24.8% males and 6.7% females). Of those who engaged in animal abuse, 57% acted alone on at least one occasion. A total of 35.6% reported they were not bothered by having participated in animal cruelty as children, 31% were bothered somewhat, and 33.3% were bothered a lot. A total of 73% of the participants currently own a pet (Henry, 2004a).

WHY KIDS ARE CRUEL TO ANIMALS: KEY FACTORS RELATED TO CHILDHOOD ANIMAL ABUSE

Law enforcement, clinicians, and other professionals working in the field have identified a number of key markers related to childhood animal cruelty. Researchers have come along in recent years to determine the extent to which these factors hold up over different populations and conditions. We will take a look at the highlights of their findings. The primary factors include:

1. Conduct Disorder
2. Domestic violence in child's family
3. Child/teen victims of sexual and/or physical abuse
4. Corporal punishment
5. Other antisocial behaviors/Triad behaviors
6. Peer pressure
7. Witnessing abuse to animals
8. Gender of child
9. Age child is first exposed to animal cruelty

Conduct Disorder

Animal cruelty is most often reported for younger boys who have been referred for mental health services, especially for Conduct Disorder (CD). In fact, animal abuse may be one of the first signs of CD symptoms to appear in younger children (Ascione, 2001). It is thought that animal cruelty may be exhibited by as much as 25% of children diagnosed with Conduct Disorder (Arluke, Levin, Luke and Ascione, 1999). In a review of the research on childhood animal cruelty Miller (2001) reported that childhood animal abuse has been found to be a reliable diagnostic criterion for CD. According to parents' reports of the median age for onset of "hurting animals" in these children is 6.5 years old (Ascione, 2001).

So what is Conduct Disorder (CD) exactly? The American Psychiatric Association's most recent version of the Diagnostic and Statistical Manual of Mental Disorders (DSM-IV) describes Conduct Disorder (CD) as being characterized as a persistent pattern of antisocial behavior and callous disregard for others. Animal abuse is one of the features of CD. Conduct Disorder is one of the most frequently diagnosed conditions for children according to the American Psychiatric Association. Conduct Disorder affects between 2% and 9% of children in the U.S. Symptoms usually surface in late childhood to early adolescence and may continue into adulthood. A substantial number of those people whose conduct disorder continues on into adulthood show symptoms of Antisocial Personality Disorder. Children and adolescents with Conduct Disorder typically show the following symptoms: a persistent pattern of violating and ignoring the rights and feelings of others, little ability for empathy and little concern for the feelings, wishes or well-being of others, a tendency to destroy property, lie and steal, and a tendency to be aggressive.

Children with CD may display bullying, threatening, intimidating behaviors and a lack of appropriate feelings of guilt and remorse. Violence, aggression and destructive behaviors predominate. Experts tell us that cruel or abusive behavior directed toward animals may be a serious indicator of child psychopathology. In children with CD, physical violence and cruelty are commonly directed toward both animals and people.

Domestic Violence in Child's Family

Does growing up with domestic violence and witnessing parental abuse of your pets make it more likely that you will go on to abuse animals? It may well increase the likelihood. One research study found that childhood socialization about companion animals in the home affects adulthood attitudes and behaviors toward pets. The study revealed that kids who grew up in homes where pets were neglected or abused were more likely to perceive such treatment as acceptable. Children were also found to be more likely to imitate the abusive patterns of their parents/caretakers (Raupp, 1999).

Practitioners and researchers alike have been alerted to the issue of children who witness parental abuse to the family pet. The reason is because esearch results appear to stack the odds against both the children and the animals. One study revealed that children residing in a domestic violence shelter were twenty times more likely to have witnessed pet abuse than children from a control group (Ascione, et al., 1997). This is troubling, considering the findings that suggest that the chaotic home with aggressive role models is one of the most common factors for animal cruelty later in childhood (Tapia, 1971). Additionally, children have been found to mimic the behavior of parents who scapegoat and abuse the family pet. One study found 32% of the children in households with ongoing domestic violence had imitated the abuser by hurting or killing the family pet (Ascione, et al., 1997). Other research findings have revealed that some parents find their children's aggressive, abusive behavior towards the family pet "cute" (Zahn-Waxler, Hollenbeck, and Radke-Yarrow, 1984). Such reactions can have a significant impact on a child's future attitude and behavior toward animals.

When a child witnesses combined parent and companion animal abuse, it may compromise that child's psychological adjustment even further and increase their propensity for interpersonal violence (Felthous, 1980), thereby increasing the likelihood of their own cruelty to animals (Ascione, 1998a). Children who witness violence directed at both their parent and their pet may go on to abuse their pets, using the animals as scapegoats for their own anger (DeViney, et al. 1983; Arkow, 1996). It is also possible that some children from chaotic and violent families begin to abuse animals to convince themselves they do not care about the things they often lose (Lockwood and Hodge, 1986). They may also mimic their families' abusive behaviors toward animals because it is the only thing that seems normal to them (Lockwood and Hodge, 1986). As we have already seen, there have been numerous studies demonstrating a link between abusive behavior directed towards animals in childhood and subsequent violence during adulthood (Kellert and Felthous, 1985; Lockwood and Hodge, 1986; Felthous and Kellert, 1987b; Ascione, 1993; Boat, 1995; Arkow, 1996; Flynn, 1999a; Miller, 2001).

What is the likelihood that witnessing or perpetrating abuse to the family pet during childhood will continue into adulthood? Research findings have suggested that pet abuse may be cyclical. Focusing on the childhood of domestic violence batterers, a FIREPAW study examined the relationship batterers had with their pets in their family of origin. One-half (50%) of respondents living with pet-abusing batterers reported that during childhood their partners had also abused the family pet or witnessed abuse of their pet by a family member. This is compared to only 21% of respondents with *non*-pet-abusing batterers (Carlisle-Frank, et al., 2004).

Common features of children who abuse animals include violent, chaotic homes where paternal abuse and alcoholism are also frequently present (Felthous, 1980; Kellert and Felthous, 1985; Flynn, 2000a). Identifying childhood animal cruelty may not only help predict those individuals who are engaging in violence now, but who may do so later on in adulthood (Flynn, 2000a).

Child/Teen Victims of Sexual and/or Physical Abuse

Research indicates that child victims of both physical abuse and sexual abuse may abuse animals (DeViney, et al., 1983; Douglas, et al., 1995; Ascione, 2001). These children may be acting out their pain or may kill the animal who has been repeatedly threatened or tortured by the abuser in order to end the animal's suffering (Urban, 2002). Even if adult family members do not abuse animals some children may express the pain of their own victimization by abusing vulnerable pets (Ascione, 2001).

Corporal Punishment

At least one study indicates that perpetrators of animal cruelty are more likely to have received corporal punishment during childhood and are more tolerant of family violence than non-perpetrators (Flynn, 1999a). Research results indicated that among boys, being frequently spanked by fathers is related to those boys perpetrating childhood animal abuse. Sixty percent of teenagers who were physically punished by their father's perpetrated animal abuse compared to only 23% of teenagers who did not get physically punished by their fathers (Flynn, 1999b).

Other Antisocial Behaviors/Triad Behaviors

Animal abuse has been correlated with other violent and antisocial behaviors (Offord, Boyle and Racine, 1991; Ascione, 1993). Animal cruelty is seen as one of several signs of an aggressive lack of impulse control during childhood (Felthous, 1980). Some researchers have found that a connection exists between enuresis (bed-wetting), fire-setting and cruelty to animals (Hellman and Blackman, 1966). A combination of animal cruelty, fire-setting and bed-wetting are a triad of symptoms in childhood that has been correlated with delinquency and antisocial and aggressive behavior later in adulthood (Felthous, 1980). A clinical review (as opposed to empirical research) conducted by Tapia (1971) examined this issue. Though not tested empirically the results were nonetheless revealing. Studying 18 cases of males 5–15 years old where animal cruelty was the main issue, she found that bullying, fighting and other aggressive symptoms such as destructiveness, fire-setting, theft and poor impulse control were all evident. It should be noted that while some have argued that this triad of behaviors has value for predicting future criminal behavior, other researchers have argued that the results have been inconsistent.

Peer Pressure

Peer reinforcement for showing off or daring may result within group acts of animal cruelty that would not occur if the child were alone (Boat, 1995). In this way, peer groups may actually reward animal cruelty. Animal cruelty may be an especially rewarding experience for male adolescents attempting to develop and prove their masculinity—one-half of all teens have been found to commit their crimes in groups (Arluke and Luke, 1997).

Witnessing Abuse to Animals

The results of recent research suggest that a child's exposure to animal abuse is associated with an increased likelihood of that child's own participation in animal abuse (Henry, 2004a). In fact, the results of one study suggest that observing animal abuse made children on average 3 times more likely to participate in animal abuse than those who never observed animal cruelty (Henry, 2004b). Of those respondents who reported they observed animal cruelty as children, 26% also reported participating in animal cruelty, compared to only 10% who never observed animal cruelty. Additionally, 30% of those who observed animal cruelty more than once actually participated in animal abuse, compared to 10% of those who never observed animal cruelty or observed animal abuse only once. In this study a friend or neighbor was the most common perpetrator (71%) of animal cruelty who respondents observed abusing animals. A father or stepfather was reported 16.3% of the time. No participants reported observing animal abuse perpetrated by their mother or stepmother. Of those who reported observing a father or stepfather committing animal abuse, almost 43% of the respondents indicated that they too had participated in acts of animal cruelty.

The same appears to hold true for teenagers. Baldry (2003) studied the relationship between observing acts of animal cruelty and actually participating in acts of animal abuse. The results indicate that for adolescents, observing animal abuse by a family member or peer significantly increased the risk for their own participation in animal abuse.

Gender of Child

Animal cruelty is more common in boys (Flynn, 1999a; 2000a; Miller, 2001; Henry, 2004ab) and in children referred for treatment for behavioral issues (Ascione and Lockwood, 2001).

Age Child is First Exposed to Animal Cruelty

Results from a recent study indicate that the age at which a child is first exposed to animal abuse may be an important risk factor associated with future negative behaviors. More specifically, the results suggest that males who witness acts of animal abuse at an early age (12 years or younger) may be more likely to engage in future animal abuse themselves. Approximately 32% of respondents who first observed animal cruelty at an early age (12 years old or younger) participated in animal cruelty themselves, compared to only 11.5% of those who observed animal cruelty over 12 years of age (Henry, 2004b). Children who witness animal abuse at an early age may also have an increased likelihood of greater involvement in other delinquent behaviors (Henry, 2004a).

Other Possible Factors Influencing Childhood Animal Abuse

In addition to the key factors listed above, researchers have also identified some additional conditions that may motivate children and teenagers to abuse animals. . .

Emotionally and physically unavailable fathers may be a contributing factor to children abusing animals (Felthous, 1980). Other motivations for children and teenagers to abuse animals may include to control an animal; to retaliate against an animal or to seek revenge against an animal or punish an animal; prejudice against a specific animal breed or species (such as cats); to express aggression through animals/to enhance one's own aggressiveness; to shock people for amusement; to retaliate against another person; to displace hostility from some person to the animal (especially when children are from chaotic and violent families); sadism—they enjoy watching animals suffer (Kellert and Felthous, 1985).

And finally, Ascione (2001) has identified the following items as potential motivations for children and adolescents to abuse animals:

- curiosity/exploration . . . usually by young children
- peer pressure
- mood enhancement (to relieve boredom or depression)
- sexual gratification
- forced abuse (child is coerced to abuse animals by a more powerful person)
- attachment to an animal (child kills an animal to prevent its torture by another person)
- animal phobias
- identification with child's own abuser (child-abuse victims mimic their batterers)

- post-traumatic play (victims of child abuse reenact violent episodes with an animal)
- imitation (copy parent/adult's abusive "discipline" of animals)
- self-injury (using animals to inflict self-injuries)
- rehearsal of violence against humans
- emotional abuse tool (injures a sibling's pet in order to frighten sibling)

When Does Childhood Animal Abuse Typically Occur?

Animal abuse can begin as early as when children are toddlers and appear throughout childhood on into adolescence. Research suggests cruelty to animals during childhood is most prevalent among preschoolers, then decreases over childhood until mid-adolescence (age 16) (Achenbach, Howell, Quay, and Conners, 1991). It is possible however that animal cruelty itself does not decrease over this time period but that children can begin to engage in cruel acts more covertly as they age—older children may have an easier time hiding what they are up to (Ascione and Lockwood, 2001).

Types and Stages of Childhood Animal Abuse

The following types and stages have been created to help professionals explain, understand and predict animal abuse in childhood. . .

Types of Child and Teen Animal Abuse (Ascione, 2001):

Exploratory/Curious Animal Abuse: Age can vary but children in this category are likely to be preschool or early elementary school age. These children are typically poorly supervised and lack training in humane treatment of animals.

Pathological Animal Abuse: These animal abusers are more likely (though not necessarily) older children than the previous category. In this category children's animal abuse is symptomatic of psychological disturbances. The child's abuse of animals in this category may be linked to their own physical or sexual abuse or to witnessing ongoing domestic violence of a parent and/or pet.

Delinquent Animal Abuse: Children in this category are most likely adolescents and animal abuse is likely just one of several antisocial activities they are engaged in. Animal abuse in this category may be linked with gang/cult-related activities or group violence with friends.

Developmental Stages of Animal Abuse in Childhood (Ascione, and Lockwood, 2001)

There are several developmental models that have been created to help explain the scenarios under which children and adolescents might commit acts of cruelty against animals. The following briefly highlights four such models:

Maintenance model proposes that animal abuse may be maintained both at early and later stages of development. Animal abuse may be accompanied by other symptoms of antisocial personality disorder such as fire-setting and vandalism.

Desistence model says that animal abuse may be present in earlier developmental stages but then ceases to occur in later developmental stages. (Animal abuse stops completely and is not replaced by other deviant behaviors.)

Emergence model proposes that animal abuse may be absent during early stages of development and emerges later on in the child's development. With this model other antisocial behaviors (such as bullying other children) may precede abusive behaviors directed toward animals.

Escalation model states that animal abuse may be present in early childhood but then ceases to occur in later developmental stages. When animal cruelty behaviors cease they may be replaced by other antisocial behaviors such as assaulting people. This model states that animal cruelty during earlier developmental stages predicts interpersonal violence during later developmental stages. This final model has been argued by some researchers to be more the exception than the rule.

What are The Consequences of Children and Teenagers Abusing Animals?

There are a number of potentially serious social and personal consequences to children and adolescents witnessing and participating in animal abuse. Let's take a look at the highlights of some of the findings. . .

Developmental Problems in Childhood and Adolescence

There is the potential for numerous negative social and psychological developmental outcomes that may result from children's observing or perpetrating animal cruelty: Among them are the potential for the child to inhibit or distort empathy and to learn to disregard the feelings of others, both animals' and people's. In violent home scenarios this compromised ability to empathize may result because children are often deeply attached to their pets and observing violent abuse or death of a pet at the hands of others can be emotionally devastating (Ascione, 2001). Whether the child is from a violent home or not the result of witnessing or perpetrating animal abuse can be uncaring disregard for others, and a complete lack of regret or remorse from hurting animals and people. In short, observing or participating in animal cruelty, especially for young children, may result in callous, insensitive attitudes toward the suffering of others (Ascione, 1992; 1993).

According to one researcher children and adolescents who are solitary animal abusers may be at an increased risk for antisocial tendencies and a diagnosis of conduct disorder (Henry, 2004a). Results from his study indicate that young adults with the least concern for the treatment of animals were found to be those males who had both observed and participated in animal cruelty on multiple occasions as children (Henry, 2004b).

Flynn (2000a) has argued that there may be serious negative psychological and physical risks to children engaging in animal cruelty, especially when guns are involved. Additionally, witnessing animal abuse, particularly on multiple occasions, may desensitize children to violence in general.

There are other potential negative consequences to children witnessing animal abuse, especially from their caretakers. In domestic violence situations children may experience anger at the mother or selves for not protecting their pets (Adams, 1995). The need to maintain silence in response to the torture and cruelty inflicted on a beloved pet in order to stay safe often causes the mother to not express grief. Children may model this reaction to the harm and death of a loved one, learning it is unsafe to vent feelings of despair and fear (Adams, 1995).

Delinquency and Antisocial Behavior in Adolescence and Adulthood

Early exposure to animal abuse may impair a child's sensitivity to the treatment of living beings thus increasing the likelihood that the child may engage in antisocial behavior directed at people and/or animals (Ascione, 1993). A recent study examined the relationship between animal cruelty and other forms of antisocial behavior. The results showed that respondents who participated in acts of animal cruelty had higher scores on self-reported delinquency than individuals who had never observed or participated in acts of animal cruelty. The highest delinquency scores were for those males who had both observed and participated in animal cruelty on multiple occasions (Henry, 2004b).

Future Aggressive, Violent an/or Criminal Behavior

- As we saw in Chapter One, there have been numerous studies demonstrating a link between aggressive, violent criminals and childhood animal cruelty (Kellert and Felthous, 1985; Felthous and Kellert, 1987b; Merz-Perez, Heide, and Silverman, 2001; Merz-Perez and Heide, 2004). The literature suggests an association between a pattern of animal cruelty in childhood or adolescence and a pattern of dangerous and recurrent aggression against people later on in adulthood. According to psychologist and expert in the treatment of childhood cruelty to animals Mary Lou Randour, Ph.D., animal cruelty in childhood is one of the first warning signals of future aggressive behavior and violence (Crary, 2002).

- The results of one study demonstrated that childhood animal abusers were three times more likely than non-abusers to have a history of criminal behavior. This was particularly true with violent offences. Animal abusers were five times more likely to have committed at least one violent crime than non-abusers (Arluke, et al., 1999).

- There is ample evidence that those children who witness abuse of the family pet may be at an increased risk for going on to become aggressive individuals who use violence (both against animals and people) to problem solve (Arkow, 1996; Ascione and Lockwood, 1997; Quinn, 2000).

- According to Arkow (1996) childhood cruelty to animals is a symptom of psychopathology particularly when it is accompanied by other symptoms and a family history of chaos and violence. Children with repeated acts of animal cruelty tend to show other abnormal aggressive and antisocial tendencies.

- Flynn (1999a) surveyed college students to determine whether their animal abuse during childhood was related to current approval of interpersonal violence against children and women in families. Respondents who had abused an animal as a child or as an adolescent were significantly more likely to support corporal punishment and to approve of husbands slapping their wives. The author suggests that engaging in childhood violence against less powerful beings may generalize to acceptance of aggressive acts directed toward others less powerful within the family.

- While the triad has not been shown to be consistently predictive of violent behavior in adulthood across all populations, Hellman and Blackman (1966) found that the triad of behaviors (animal cruelty/fire-setting/bed-wetting) is common in the backgrounds of violent criminals. A total of 74% of criminals who committed aggressive crimes had triad behaviors as children.

- Kellert and Felthous (1985) examined the relationship between abusing animals in childhood and aggression in adulthood. They interviewed criminals and non-criminals. Aggressive criminals revealed significantly more childhood incidents of animal cruelty than any other group. Approximately 25% of aggressive criminals reported abusing animals on 5 or more occasions as a child (none of the non-criminals had this occur). Aggressive criminals committed more animal cruelty in childhood and significantly more severe acts of torture. Felthous and Kellert (1986) tested the same population as above. All aggressive criminals with a history of substantial animal abuse reported fighting during childhood. The majority also fought as adults.

- Studies show a link of sexually aggressive crimes in adulthood and animal cruelty during childhood. In one study approximately 50% of rapists and 25% of pedophiles were animal abusers as children (Tingle, et al., 1986).
- FBI profiles of serial killers feature childhood animal abuse as a key factor. Previous studies have shown that 36% of serial murders tortured and killed animals as children; 46% of serial murderers tortured and killed animals as adolescents (Lockwood and Church, 1998).
- Felthous and Kellert (1987b) found that some of the most notorious mass and multiple murderers have perpetrated excessive animal cruelty during their childhood. This, the authors argued, is indicative of poorly controlled aggression.
- Interpersonal violence is associated with repeated acts of animal cruelty in childhood (Lockwood and Ascione, 1998a). Studies have revealed a relationship between childhood animal cruelty and later violence directed toward people in adulthood (Kellert and Felthous, 1985; Felthous and Kellert, 1986; Tingle, et al., 1986).

Some Thoughts for Professionals Concerning Children who are Cruel to Animals

As we have seen throughout this chapter, beyond the obvious issue of cruel, painful torture inflicted on innocent creatures, the phenomenon of child perpetrators of animal abuse comes with its own unique set of problems for the child, family, community and society in general. Childhood perpetrators of animal cruelty require the attention and action of a number of professionals within the community. Law enforcement, animal control officers, family therapists, family and child service professionals, domestic violence caseworkers, fire officials, teachers, and child psychologists all may interface with child perpetrators of animal abuse—and they are all needed to intervene and assist in helping to stop the violence.

As we have already seen, children may imitate animal cruelty they have witnessed from adults (Boat, 1995). Therefore, parents who trivialize or fail to punish animal mistreatment (or worse—encourage or model it) such as kicking the family dog or shooting strays, promote violence, ignore psychological problems and actually end up condoning violent behavior (Flynn, 2000a).

According to one researcher, animal control officers and law enforcement professionals can be instrumental in helping parents recognize the seriousness of children's acts of animal cruelty. Parents may dismiss even horrific acts of cruelty until an ACO or other law enforcement professional explains and educates them about the reasons they need to be concerned and the need for them to seek help for their children (Boat, 1995).

In addition to identifying whether the child's animal abuse behavior occurred as a solitary act (the child abused animals while alone) or as part of a group/peer activity, there are three other points for professionals to keep in mind when coming across children and teenagers who have abused animals: (1) Animal abuse perpetrated by children may identify (a) those who currently live in violent homes, and (b) those who may engage in future antisocial behaviors (Arkow, 1996); (2) Assessing whether animal abuse is chronic (a pattern of such behaviors) or an acute problem is essential for its predictive value of future problems (Ascione and Lockwood, 2001); (3) Child animal abuse requires examining the child's family, social and community environments in order to understand this type of violent behavior (Ascione, 2001).

Among the programs that are now offered to assist professionals working with child and adolescent animal abusers is the AniChild program offered by Society and Animals Forum (a.k.a. Animals and Society Institute; previously Psychologists for the Ethical Treatment of Animals—PsyETA). Based on the techniques used to treat batterers, this cognitive-behavioral intervention approach is tailored to specifically treat children and adolescents who have abused animals. There are also a number of assessment tools now available to screen children for animal cruelty. Among them are the Animal-Related Experiences Inventory (Boat, 1995) and the Cruelty to Animals Assessment Instrument (CAAI) for obtaining information on animal maltreatment— intended for children aged 4 and older (Ascione, et al., 1997). Additionally, major animal welfare organizations now offer information and training materials for identifying and treating childhood animal cruelty: The American Humane Association (AHA), the Doris Day Animal League, and the Humane Society of the United States (HSUS) are among those organizations offering training and educational materials in this area. See Chapter Ten for contact information.

TALES FROM THE STREET: THE A B C'S OF VIOLENCE

I am going to simply write about the facts uncovered while working on the street at actual incidents involving childhood animal cruelty. Don't expect too many intricate explanations using highly confusing technical or scientific terms, as they have no place in this discussion. First I want provide you with my interpretation of the simplified A B C's of Violence. . .

What are the A B C's of violence and where do they come from? For many years certain individuals felt that they consisted of the big three indicators, Arson, Bedwetting (Enuresis), and Cruelty to Animals. Other learned individuals in the field of child development and crisis intervention had some doubts about the second segment, Bedwetting, as a truly reliable signal. Much effort was put into proving or disproving this theory and to some the question is still unanswered.

While this dilemma may be argued for years to come without ever reaching a conclusive answer, some additional information may assist you in forming an opinion. One very well known and widely acknowledged fact is that children are strongly influenced by their environment. A second sad fact is that children living in a violent setting have an overwhelming tendency toward violent behavior in later life. Does this mean that every child from a home in which domestic tranquility is missing will grow up to be a vicious individual? No, not by any stretch of the imagination. The significance arises from the fact that "left unchecked" those children will definitely have a propensity towards violence. This is where we, as professionals, fit into the overall picture: LEFT UNCHECKED . . . it is our job not to let this happen.

So where are we at this point? We know the theories of the A B C's of violence, the pros and cons, and a possible forming place for the triggering mechanism. We are also aware of another well-known fact concerning children and constant exposure to a violent environment. It will take its toll on all of these children eventually, but what is it called and where does it fit? What is this indicator that replaces Bedwetting?

The answer is a phenomenon best described as "Battering Reaction Syndrome." The major source for this is a child being constantly exposed to a violent surrounding, whether it be from a domestic violence home setting, a victim of bullying at school or in the home neighborhood, or threats from potential gang violence. So now it is time for you, the reader, to make your own decision. Bedwetting vs. Battering Reaction Syndrome, one is a well-known medical condition, the other, a major occurrence in today's society.

Whatever your decision, please remember a very important rule concerning this entire premise: any of these signs by themselves do NOT offer a positive indication of future potential violence on the part of the child. They are extremely reliable warning signs that the individual may need help in the future. The signs may emerge in a preschool child as antisocial behavior when interacting with other children, cruelty to an animal (real or stuffed toy version) or a fascination with fires. Older children may show additional signs including alcohol and drug use, gang affiliation, seclusion, discontinuance of long-standing friendships and involvement in high-risk sexual activities.

Before we go any further I want to acknowledge any readers who may suffer from the same tendency for an unchangeable mindset that I have. Any time I attend a training session, listen to a speaker, or read a printed article I always question the speaker's credentials: what gives them the authority to make the statements they do and expect me to believe them? I find it very easy to read a book or paper and then recite it to others, taking a bow when I'm done, but is it my work? Have I stood in the middle of these situations and made my own first-hand observations? Have I listened to the anguish of victims and seen the actual problem? Have I made a difference in their lives with what I did and the services I provided to them? I have a major problem accepting words from those that have never done the actual work. That said I feel it is my time to justify my own words. . .

When you work as a police officer for thirty-two years in a major city you get to see and do a lot—some nice things, some not so nice. Another benefit is that you receive an awful lot of training along the way both in informal and formal settings. I was also able to do some additional training as time went by that other officers never got. So where do I get my expertise to make the statements I've made about the "A B C's of Violence"? I will cover each aspect one by one starting with A—Arson.

A IS FOR ARSON

Arson, long an interest to me because of the ways I have seen it used over the years. There have been so many varied reasons, but all illegal, and they have always made me look twice at the situation. Sitting at my desk, in the district station one day I received a phone call. It was Elaine Mesiti, a good friend from the Boston Fire Department who had worked with me often on numerous children's safety programs we had conducted. She made an offer to me that I could not refuse, a chance to attend a training seminar about children and fire-setting. I could not get the paperwork filled out quickly enough. This would be a great tool for me as the district I worked in at that time had sixty-five percent of the school-age children attending the public schools living within its boundaries. Another fact I was to learn soon after was that the prior year Boston had had a higher number of fires and fire alarms in its schools than anywhere else in the nation. The training I was going to attend was being conducted by the Massachusetts Coalition for Juvenile Fire-setter Intervention Programs, Inc. and held at the Boston Fire Department Training Academy. The main purpose of the training was to establish and educate members of Boston Fire's own in-house program. The fact that I would be attending on my own time and at my own expense was of no matter to me as it was the opportunity of a lifetime. The entire training process was conducted over a ten-week period and each class was better than the week before. The first five weeks we learned the how's and why's related to the juvenile offenders, how to conduct pre-screening interviews of the individuals and their families, and how to assess them after the interview process was completed.

The second five-week segment taught us how to design and conduct teaching programs for the children. The programs ranged in length from up to fourteen weeks, so much preparation was needed to properly develop appropriate programs for the different age groups. At times it seemed like an overwhelming task, especially when the multiple cultural groups involved were considered. This is where I really came to appreciate the knowledge of Ms. Irene Pinsonneault, Coordinator of the Statewide Coalition for Juvenile Fire-setter Programs. If it wasn't for Irene and Sgt. Paul Zipper from the Massachusetts State Police and the excellent instructors they provided, we would have completed only half the process. A truly remarkable job completed by highly capable people left me with the confidence to take the next step, application of the training at field level. It was time for Elaine Mesiti, Inspector Eugene Anderson, and myself to put our learning to the test. It was time to hit the streets and do some interviews and investigations about our potential students of the program.

The first time is always the most difficult. Even with many years of law enforcement behind me it was still a challenge to conduct that first home visit. New questions were being asked of people. We were not building a criminal case; we were doing more background-oriented interviews, a little different from the usual procedure. But the more we did, the more comfortable we became. Little ideas and changes started to be implemented to make the questions flow and keep people at ease. Many, many times we were most thankful for the thoughts and ideas provided by Irene, Paul and the instructors who had done these interviews before us. It certainly is easier to not be the first one trying to make things come out right. Luckily, a lot of the bumps had already been removed from our road making for a pretty smooth trip overall.

Pretty soon we had completed the pre-screening interviews and our first list of students was finalized. They came from three categories of fire-setters: curious, crisis, and delinquent. The pathological fire-setter was always referred to professional programs designed to deal with deep-seated psychological motivators.

Enjoying interaction with older kids I chose to teach the thirteen- to sixteen-year-old age group. I assure you that planning a twelve-week program is most appropriate when dealing with this age group. The first four weeks was spent establishing communication with the students. Usually teenagers don't talk much to start with in these sorts of situations, but in this setting conversation was all but absent. There is no standard pattern for opening discussions with youth groups, and the key is sometimes hard to find. My first group started their conversation slowly between each other and by careful listening we found the items of importance to them, then we used these same subjects to slowly open the door. By the time week five arrived we actually spoke back and forth in meaningful conversations. I was surprised to learn that what had been shown in videos and what I had discussed during the first four weeks had in fact been heard and retained by all of them. They just hadn't been ready to participate.

Now that the door was open and communication was increasing by leaps and bounds, interaction was ongoing and so was learning. I won't go into the entire process other than to say that it covered such subjects as fire safety, fire science, fire knowledge, and the fire service itself. One important aspect was that during each twelve-week program the instructor got a chance to sit at some point with each of the students individually and have a chance to talk about the initial incident that brought them to the program. The majority of my students arrived as a result of incidents in school such as false alarms, setting off sprinklers, and lighting small fires in bathrooms and trash containers. My two most serious cases, a boy and a girl, were both there for setting actual building fires. The interesting thing was that these two individuals seemed to be getting the most out of the classes and participated in class quicker than the other students. I did some additional background research looking for a possible reason for this and found one common denominator: they had both been sexually abused. Certainly not a reason to become an eager student, but interesting to know.

Eventually we opened up with each other enough to ask some serious questions, one of them being about animal involvement and animal cruelty issues. My male student with the serious fire-setting background opened up about something I had never heard before, nor had any of my colleagues. He told a story about how he and his very close friend, also a young male, got revenge on adults they felt had done wrong by them, in a twofold manner. He would find their cars or other personal property and set them on fire. I asked him if he ever hurt any animals to get even, but he said he liked animals and wouldn't hurt them. I asked him what he would do if the people didn't have a car or something else to burn but they did own an animal. It seems this is where his close friend would fit into the picture, as he would be more than eager to kill the animal. Of course he wasn't really a bad guy, the student explained, because he would never light a fire that could hurt someone. My student was open about this entire process and a quick review of fire department logs for his neighborhood confirmed his statements. We were able to meet with the other child and his parents shortly thereafter and as a result, a counseling program was arranged for him.

This same student provided me with another unique situation later on during the classes. One of the assignments was to draw three pictures of good fires, such as a stove, heater, engine, etc. and three pictures of bad fires. My new friend handed me a group of pictures that were of excellent quality and we sat down to talk about them. The three pictures of good fires were very original but bare minimum. The pictures of the three bad fires were just short of masterpieces, even the smallest details were included, and an entire picture was presented of each incident. I asked him why these were so all encompassing and the others just met the cut-off. His reply was that he knew the bad fires, because they were ones he lit, and if I wanted to see more, he would draw them for me. Quickly I advised him that the assignment was completed but I may want to see more pictures at a later time.

The Big Picture

The A B C's of violence appear in many different ways and I had never given any prior thought to children engaging in both fire-setting and animal abuse, but I certainly did after that class. You are never too old or too smart to learn something new so keep your eyes and ears open. Of the sixteen children in the thirteen- to sixteen-year-old groups I worked with, three had animal cruelty incidents in their past to go along with their fire-setting problems. Twelve of these kids, including two of the three animal abusers, came from homes that provided nowhere near a stable environment in which to live, the third abuser was residing in a special setting foster home. His situation required that the foster parents have a house in which no one smoked, be equipped with an electric stove only, have a smoke detector in his bedroom, have someone awake in the house at all times, and he was to never be left alone in the building. A tough set of requirements to meet but luckily they had found people willing to do it. The young girl who had been a serious fire threat and previously sexually abused had no known history of animal abuse, but did have a history of running away from home and most often ended up involved with more than one older man at a time when located. Elaine Mesiti, Gene Anderson and I handled quite a number of cases before agendas changed and staffing was reduced due to budgetary changes. Elaine and I still communicate on a regular basis and try to follow up on things that come to our attention. I still get to work with Irene Pinsonneault and her staff, as it is a major component in my Link-UP Program as well as one of my more talked-about subjects.

B is for Battering Reaction Syndrome

B—Battering Reaction Syndrome, the second letter of the A B C's of Violence, and replacement for Bedwetting, is growing rapidly in today's society. Where did I learn all of that? Education, research, and working on the streets. Let's cover the education aspect first. It was 1992 and the captain of the district I was assigned to informed me that I had won a scholarship to attend a training seminar called the "Child Witness to Violence Project" being conducted at Boston Medical Center. I told the captain I didn't remember applying for any scholarship and he replied, "I did it for you, be there Tuesday at 1:00 P.M." End of story.

Tuesday arrived and ten lucky cops got to go to Boston Medical Center and listen to a bunch of social workers tell us how to save the world. We sat in a conference room at a long table, cops on one side and the social workers on the other, kind of like the Korean Truce talks of the early 1950's, lots of looking not much talking. Finally a female officer said, "Are you social workers?" One of them said, "Yes, we are," and held her breath. The female officer stated, "What do you want to tell us?" which sounded more like an interrogation of a suspect than an opening comment. The lead social worker, later to be identified as Betsy McAlister Groves, Director of the program, stated her intentions about the proposed training and its target. Violence was on the increase in Boston at a rapid rate and many children were becoming eyewitnesses to these incidents on a daily basis. The Child Witness to Violence Program was aimed at finding these children, through collaboration with the Boston Police Department, and providing counseling. Betsy went on to say that all they wanted to do was teach police officers to be more aware when children were present and pass that information on to the Child Witness staff. I guess you might say that they wanted us to really "see" the children that were at so many of the calls we responded to.

After giving it some thought I said to Betsy, "Where have you been? We've been bringing kids to the Pediatric Nurses here for years, and they had no training but never turned us away when there was nowhere else to go. This sounds like something I needed years ago, tell me more."

The program was to run for ten weeks and during that time we would have instruction about P.T.S. in children, domestic violence programs, abused children, court procedures with the District Attorney's Office, and how the Department of Social Services (Children's Services) functions. When the course was completed we would be expected to see children that witnessed violent incidents in an entirely different frame of mind and make notifications to the Child Witness Program by use of simple one-page referral forms.

The next ten weeks seemed to pass by fairly quickly and I was actually beginning to enjoy some of the classes. Around the eighth week the entire concept was pulled together when Rick Weissbourd of the Kennedy School of Government at Harvard University came in and spoke about the resiliency of children and how they can survive when given a chance to do so. He put it all into focus and left a room full of experienced street cops with an entirely new attitude about helping children found in these situations. The last two sessions of the training process involved a wonderful round-table discussion with Boston Medical Center Pediatric Staff, a final exam and an opportunity to make suggestions as to possible curriculum changes for future classes.

The week following our last session I was working as the street supervisor and responded to a shooting during the 12:00 P.M. to 8:00 A.M. shift. Upon arrival I learned that a sixteen-year-old male involved in the local drug trade had been shot by three individuals, all armed with handguns. The individuals had arrived in a van, later found to be stolen, and forced their way into the victim's front hallway where he was shot repeatedly before they fled the scene in the vehicle. One of the most important items that immediately came to my mind was the fact that this entire incident had occurred in front of the victim's five younger brothers and sisters. I was instantly grateful for my recently completed Child Witness to Violence training.

Not to extend discussion of the Program and its success I will end my story by saying that as time went on I became an instructor for the Child Witness to Violence Program to both Boston Police Officers, Firefighters, Emergency Medical Technicians, and Law Enforcement Officers from local humane organizations. I continue my work with the Project today by using its staff as a very vital part of the Link-UP Program as well as continuing to teach various agencies about it throughout New England.

C is for Cruelty

C—Cruelty to Animals, last of the three, but far from the least. In fact, it's probably the most important of all the indicators, and for a very simple reason. Having been in law enforcement for a number of years I was well aware that cruelty to an animal was a crime, but other than seeing it in conjunction with other crimes, I had never dealt with it specifically. All of that was to change abruptly during the early summer of 1995. Suddenly the district I was working in was flooded with calls about dogs being used as weapons and tools of intimidation. It seems that the bad guys were not stupid, you can go to jail for a mandatory year for carrying a gun, but how much time do you get for having a violent dog on the end of your leash? Time to do something about the problem and do it fast as things were quickly getting out of hand. I quickly found out one very important fact: cops do gangs not dogs, and humane law enforcement officers do dogs not gangs.

Many people have said I was not the brightest light on the string but I do have some electricity flowing through my brain. I thought: let's bring the cops, animal control, and the humane agencies together. Presto, there you go ladies and gentlemen . . . the birth of what would later be known as the Northeast Animal Control/Humane Task Force. One requirement though, if you want something to be a success, know what you are doing. Time for more training.

The Animal Rescue League of Boston was my savior from the very first step. They always took time to listen to my ideas, provide as much support as possible, and most of all to allow me to get that all-important training in the field of humane law enforcement. I was quickly enrolled in some basic training programs being held throughout the area and in short order had my feet very wet. I was also lucky enough to spend many hours working along side Lt. Alan Borgal of ARL 's Law Enforcement Dept. Alan has spent his entire life in the humane field serving in many roles including his present position as the Director of the Law Enforcement Department. To say that he has a wealth of knowledge would be an understatement, and he continues to amaze me with his facts, figures, and telephone skills daily.

Finally I was ready to go, loaded with training, plenty of time in the field, and research on-going looking for some answers to that age-old question, "There has to be a better way!" We were not at any loss for cases to investigate; we had them by the hundreds. There were more twists and turns than a roller coaster, characters with more unique personal indicators than the cast of an English mystery movie.

In the beginning of this section I made the statement that the C—Cruelty to Animals, could be the most important indicator and now I'll explain why. When you attempt something new and it works, the normal reaction is to try and make it better. This is done by looking over your successes. When we, The Task Force, had been operating for about six months it was time to give it a closer look. To do this I took twenty-five random cases, out of the over one hundred we had completed, and went through each one looking for common denominators. Three very interesting facts came to light quite quickly. Number one was that the suspects in each case had prior involvement with the courts as a defendant in some type of criminal proceeding. Number two was that over ninety percent of these individuals had been involved in crimes of violence, a much higher percentage than I ever expected or had seen listed in other surveys. Number three was without a doubt the most important fact I found, and the basis for just about everything that followed: the link between abused children and animal cruelty.

People call 911 about a mistreated dog or cat that they see or hear at an overwhelming pace, but the same cannot be said about neglected or abused children, wives, or girlfriends living at the same locations. So what does the prudent person do? Let's utilize our Child Witness to Violence training and see the children while we check out the animal, and to take it one step further, don't forget to observe the other people present. So our new focus was expanded to respond to all calls concerning animals possibly being mistreated or neglected and make sure we saw everyone else as well. In short order we had found senior abuse, domestic abuse, and child abuse at a very high number of visited locations. Link-UP was now working more than ever making sure we had all our needed agencies up to speed and that open communication was ongoing on a daily basis. At this point I would like to describe just one incident in which most all the Link-UP agencies were involved. . .

Boston Animal Control received a call from the Boston Police Department's Anti-Gang Violence Unit requesting assistance in serving a search warrant with the Boston Police Special Entry Team. The Animal Control Office was notified because of information that violent dogs may be present at the location. Animal Control was well aware of the location, as the Task Force had visited the address on more than one prior time. As a result, Task Force members met the other agencies at the local district station before the warrant's service. All information available was pooled so that everyone understood the situation fully.

The Entry Team and Gang Unit affected the entry to the house with the assistance of one Animal Control Officer who secured the dogs in an empty room. The individual wanted for a homicide was arrested and removed from the scene. The premises were now searched for the weapon used in the crime and while doing so the officers found a number of other compounding problems. The Link-UP agencies were then utilized to render assistance for the following problems: The Department of Social Services, (children's services) removed three children from the location to foster care. Emergency Medical Services removed an elderly male (in his 80's) from a urine- and feces-encrusted bed in which he was found lying. He had been placed in this home as a type of foster setting and the occupants were being paid to provide care and services to him. The mother of the children who were removed by D.S.S. was arrested on outstanding drug-trafficking warrants and removed to the women's detention unit. The four dogs were removed from the building and taken to the City Animal Shelter by Animal Control. The mummified body of a cat was found in a back bedroom, and the remains of shredded cats were found scattered in the backyard area where the dogs were kept. Inspectional Services Response Team (building inspectors) arrived and inspected the building. The building was found to be unfit for occupation and secured after the last person was removed. Additional agencies such as the District Attorney's Office, local media, and local utility companies also responded before the scene was secured. The original incident that brought forth much of the background information made available to the authorities before making their first move? It all started with a call about an animal incident!

The individual arrested for the homicide had a long history of prior restraining orders sought by a number of different women and involvement with animal cruelty issues earlier in his life. The most regrettable part of this entire incident is that the suspect had been a student in an area school for troubled youths when younger, and I had often talked with him when interacting with the students. He was always respectful and seemed to get along well with the other students.

What has all of this attempted to do for you, the reader? I hope that we have clarified a few things concerning the "street version" of the A B C's of Violence. What they look like to the practitioner who is standing at the crime scene at 2:00 A.M. under a falling rain, when you have ten seconds to make a decision and it has to be the right decision. I am not talking about a conference where highly trained academics and medical experts are gathered to exchange their latest discoveries. I am certainly not talking about a judge's decision that is all too often controlled by prior case law decisions that must be followed. I am gearing all of this to you, the professional doing fieldwork, the person like me, out there in the middle of all of this craziness.

Remember what was stated in the beginning and if you find an individual displaying one of the characteristics discussed in this chapter you have probably not encountered a potential mass murderer, but do give them a little better look. If you find someone showing two out of the three symptoms, it is time to make sure a properly trained individual in addition to yourself is informed. (Remember, it may very well be beyond your training.) If you are unlucky enough to find all three indicators in one person, don't turn your back, as this is someone that needs a lot of very specialized professional help—and quickly.

So there it is, simple as A B C, all you have to do is take a good look the next time you get that call about the dog or cat in trouble. Oh, and you may want to keep a copy of this book close at hand, it makes a great field reference!

Chapter Five

The Neglected Animal

Snoopy was just a tiny puppy when his caretakers went through a bitter divorce. The wife was granted custody of the children and after a long, contentious battle over property, she maintained she should have the puppies as well. Still holding out, the husband agreed to a settlement only if he could have Snoopy, one of the puppies.

On the day following the final court hearing the husband, we'll call him Bruno, built a cage in the back of the restaurant he owned, dumped Snoopy in it, and never looked back. Not when Snoopy cried because he was afraid and lonely. Not when Snoopy was drenched from downpour rains and frightened from the lightning and thunder. Not when he whimpered in pain from the blaring sun beating down on him. Not when he cried out from the freezing temperatures of winter. Not when he needed someone to play with him and something—anything—to play with and to do. Not even when he cried out each day from no food and no water. Sometimes the employees of the restaurant would hear Snoopy's cries when they went to empty the trash and once in awhile if Bruno wasn't around they would throw Snoopy some stale, hard crusts of bread. Unable to eat much of the rock hard bread it at least gave Snoopy something to play with and he would toss the bread chunks up in the air over and over again and try to catch it in his mouth just to pass the time.

One day an animal rescuer caught wind of Snoopy and his condition and went over to the restaurant to have a look. It had been a full year since Snoopy was thrown in the cage and forgotten about. He was less than half the weight he should have been and his ribs protruded from his tiny body. When the rescuer saw the conditions Snoopy was forced to live in and how thin and malnourished Snoopy was he started asking around to get the full story. The next day he went to have a talk with Bruno. He told Bruno he could no longer refuse to give Snoopy food and water. He told him that it was cruel treatment to keep an animal locked up around the clock. He educated him about the need for dogs to be with their family members. And then, after asking Bruno how *he* would like to be locked up in a cage for his entire life and slowly starved to death, he told Bruno to consider the meeting as a warning. If he did not start to immediately care for Snoopy the dog would be taken from him. He returned and gave two more such warnings. Bruno ignored all of them.

Shortly afterward Snoopy was taken to a new family who adopted him. Humans might not have been so forgiving. Even after all he had been through in his short life Snoopy was filled with love and he gave kisses and wagged his tail mightily inside his new home with his new family. After a lot of love and care Snoopy began putting on weight and gaining muscle strength and within six months he received a clean bill of health from his veterinarian. Every once in awhile Snoopy's family members will see him tossing one of his balls up in the air to himself, a habit that will likely never go away, but these days Snoopy gets around the clock attention and love, sleeps at the foot of his family members' bed, and today is a healthy, happy creature.

Snoopy's story had a happy ending. Most neglected animals are not so lucky.

A CLEAR PROBLEM THAT OFTEN APPEARS FUZZY

While there are some data available on neglect of companion animals it is sparse. Research studies have typically combined neglect along with abuse so it is often difficult to tease these figures apart to determine how widespread neglect of companion animals actually is. In addition, neglect is a gray area and often difficult to identify and pin down. Frequently neglect is not so clear-cut as overt abuse and oftentimes does not come to the attention of authorities. We do know animal neglect exists, of course. Law enforcement, animal control officers, humane officers and animal welfare organizations have seen it first hand for decades. A well-known study of animal abuse mentioned earlier in this book that was conducted in South Africa examined nearly two thousand cases reported to local SPCAs over the course of a year (Vermeulen and Odendaal, 1993). The vast majority of the cases involved general neglect, such as dogs being tied out without shelter, unsanitary conditions, and lack of necessary veterinary care. According to researcher and veterinarian Gary Patronek, VMD, Ph.D. (1997) these conditions are similar to what is reported anecdotally within the U.S. Additionally, women seeking assistance from domestic violence shelters have reported that 26% of batterers denied food and/or water to their companion animals and 26% denied the animals veterinary care (Carlisle-Frank, Frank and Nielsen, 2004). But as we have seen from the opening story about Snoopy, domestic violence households are not the only place in which companion animals face long-term, slow but sure cruelty through neglect.

Environments and Conditions Neglected Animals Can Be Found:

Anecdotal evidence stemming from reports from professionals working in the field tell us that the primary environments and conditions neglected animals can be found include:

- chaotic homes/homes with ongoing alcohol and/or other substance abuse
- homes where people are ignorant about the needs of companion animals
- homes where owners/guardians have mental illnesses
- abusive homes
- homes of animal hoarders
- chained/caged animals forced to live outdoors full-time
- homes where people are overwhelmed or otherwise ill-equipped to take care of even the most basic, fundamental needs of family members

Key factors associated with neglected animals:

- sickly animals
- malnourished animals
- anxious, lonely, depressed animals
- aggressive, fearful animals prone to attack/bite to defend their territory (chained dogs become excessively territorial and can become highly aggressive, bite and even kill those who encroach)
- animals who are suffering physically and emotionally

Range of neglectful actions that result in cruelty to companion animals:

- denial of food
- denial of water
- denial of needed veterinary care
- denial of mental stimulation—toys/play
- isolation: denial of affection and ability to interact with family, other animals
- full time chaining/tethering
- denial of full range of motion—full time caging

- forcing animal to live in unhygienic conditions resulting in illness, disease, infestation of parasites, etc.
- forcing animal to eat, urinate and defecate in the same limited space
- forcing animal to live outdoors in inclement weather conditions without adequate protection

Types of Animal Victims of Neglect

Humane investigators have responded to calls of neglect to animals ranging from horses to dogs to cats to rabbits and birds and everything in between. The fact is that any type of companion animal living with people may be a victim of neglect. Unfortunately most of these animals are hidden from view from the general public and so years can go by before authorities are alerted. Small animals such as rabbits, birds and gerbils are frequently kept indoors and neglected cats either live inside the home where they are unseen by others or prowl about the neighborhood in search of food, either missing the attention of neighbors or mistaken for a feral animal. Neglected cats who live outdoors at least part of the time run the added risk of getting hit by a car or suffering from serious illnesses brought about by parasites and malnutrition combined with lack of adequate shelter in extreme weather conditions.

Perhaps the most common and obvious of neglected animals is the tethered dog forced to live outdoors full time. The issue of tethered dogs has made the headlines in newspapers across the country in recent times and has caught the attention of municipal leaders, prosecutors and lawmakers. This form of long-term cruelty has potentially serious outcomes for the children and adults who live in the community where tethered dogs are kept. The next section will examine the factors involved in long-term chaining of dogs and why this can be one of the most serious types of animal neglect for animals and people alike.

When the Neglected Animal is a Tethered/Caged and Isolated Dog

Experts tell us that animal control and humane agencies receive countless calls every day from citizens concerned about animals in cruel tethering and isolation conditions. Animal control officers frequently spend many hours trying to educate pet owners about the dangers and cruelty involved in tethering, chaining, full-time caging or otherwise isolating their dogs.

Like humans who are social beings and can suffer extreme emotional disturbances with prolonged isolation from human contact, dogs are hard-wired to be pack animals. They need to be with their pack . . . their family members. When they are isolated this is extremely stressful for these animals. Their loneliness and isolation may cause them to become depressed or anxious—or neurotically anxious and dangerous. Researchers studying dog bites in Denver, Colorado found that chained dogs were 2.4 times as likely to bite than non-tethered dogs (Gershman, Sacks, and Wright, 1994), and a study of human deaths resulting from dog attacks found that 17% had resulted from dogs restrained on their own property (Sacks, Sinclair, Gilchrist, Golab, and Lockwood, 2000).

Neglect through Tethering: Harmful Effects to Dogs

A recent newspaper story in the northeast reported the case of a German Shepherd left outside tethered and unattended for so long that his dead body was actually frozen to the ground. According to Tammy Grimes, founder of the nonprofit organization devoted to stopping the practice of dog tethering, Dogs Deserve Better (DDB), dogs have been found with collars actually embedded in their necks, the result of years of neglect at the end of a chain. In addition to the psychological damage wrought by continuous chaining, dogs forced to live on a chain make easy targets for other animals, humans, and biting insects. Chained dogs are also easy targets for thieves looking to steal animals to sell to research institutions or to be used as training fodder for organized animal fights. Additionally, dogs' tethers can become entangled with other objects, which can choke or strangle the dogs to death. Neglect prevails with tethered, chained, caged and otherwise isolated dogs. Rarely does a tethered dog receive sufficient care, says Grimes. Additionally, because their frequently neurotic behavior makes them difficult to approach, chained dogs are rarely given even minimal affection.

Tethered dogs suffer from sporadic feedings, overturned water bowls, inadequate veterinary care, and extreme temperatures. Additionally, the dogs often must eat, sleep, urinate, and defecate in a single confined area. Owners who chain their dogs are also less likely to clean the area. Although there may have once been grass in an area of confinement, Grimes reports that it is usually so beaten down by the dog's frantic and repeated pacing that the ground consists of nothing but dirt or mud.

According to the Humane Society of the United States (HSUS) leaving a dog tethered, chained or otherwise isolated outside for extended periods of time can be physically, emotionally, and behaviorally detrimental. Isolated dogs are prevented from getting the attention, compassion and care they need. The U.S. Department of Agriculture agrees. Their position is that continuous confinement of dogs by a tether is inhumane. A USDA-issued statement in the July 2, 1996, Federal Register against tethering states, "Our experience in enforcing the Animal Welfare Act has led us to conclude that continuous confinement of dogs by a tether is inhumane. A tether significantly restricts a dog's movement. A tether can also become tangled around or hooked on the dog's shelter structure or other objects, further restricting the dog's movement and potentially causing injury."

Neglect through Tethering: Harmful Effects to Humans

Deprived of their basic needs tethered, chained and isolated dogs will invariably become adversely affected. A chained dog becomes hyper-territorial, and when a person invades its space, the dog, unable to flee, may automatically move into fight-or-flight mode and attack. Most experts in the animal welfare arena agree that chaining dogs is both cruel to the dogs and dangerous to children and adults in the community. According to Dogs Deserve Better founder Tammy Grimes, chained by the neck, tethered dogs live as prisoners, yet long to be pets living inside with love and attention from their family members. As a result of the dangerous emotional state tethering puts dogs in, chaining has taken a severe toll on this nation's children. According to Grimes, in the period from October 2003 until October 2004, there were at least 20 children across the country killed or seriously injured by chained dogs.

In addition to humans who can be viscously attacked by chained dogs, small animals may also fall victim. According to animal care experts, pet cats, rabbits, smaller dogs, and other animals are also at risk. Those animals that unknowingly enter the area where a tethered dog may be sleeping may be savagely attacked when the dog awakes and discovers another animal threatening his limited space. For these reasons the HSUS strongly recommends that all pets be kept indoors with the family—keeping an animal tethered for long periods is never acceptable.

Solutions for Putting an End to Tethered and Isolated, Neglected Dogs

Creating the law to make changes. In recent years, animal cruelty and public safety issues have inspired new regulations about dog tethering/chaining across the country. A recent newspaper report quoted Stephanie Shain of the Humane Society of the United States as stating that laws limiting or prohibiting dog tethering have now become a national trend (Hirschauer, 2005). A growing number of anti-cruelty laws and ordinances now include "adequate care standards" that make it illegal to keep a dog outside without proper shelter in inclement weather. A few communities have even enacted ordinances actually prohibiting the tethering of dogs. The number of cities and counties with dog tethering laws increased nationwide from 41 in 2002 to 68 in early 2005 (Hirschauer, 2005).

If you are interested in getting a law enacted to ban the practice of tethering in your community, or if you would like to strengthen other animal protection laws already in place, The Humane Society of the United States (HSUS) can help. Please see the contact information available in Chapter Ten.

According to Dogs Deserve Better (DDB), "A chained animal is caught in a vicious cycle; frustrated by long periods of boredom and social isolation, he becomes a neurotic shell of his former self—further deterring human interaction and kindness. In the end, the helpless dog can only suffer the frustration of watching the world go by in isolation—a cruel fate for what is by nature a highly social animal. Any city, county, or state that bans this practice is a safer, more humane community." Visit the Dogs Deserve Better web site for information on learning about, developing and changing laws prohibiting chained dogs in your community: Contact information is available in Chapter Ten.

Using education and persuasion.   According to HSUS, even if the dog's owner is not violating any laws, animal control officers and cruelty investigators may be able to persuade and empower the dog owner to take steps to improve the situation. As humane professionals know, in some instances persuading the animal's owner to voluntarily give up the dog is the best solution for the animal. Professionals working outside the humane investigation and enforcement arenas can locate their local humane society or animal control agency online at www.Pets911.com.

In certain situations—particularly in small communities where everyone knows one another—non-law enforcement professionals and members of the general public may assess a situation and determine that approaching the dog's owner directly may be detrimental to the animal and other less-empowered members of the household. In these circumstances an alternative educational-persuasive option may be to allow an outside organization to send the message to the dog's owner. Dogs Deserve Better (DDB), the 2003 First Place Winner of the ASPCA/Chase Pet Protector Award, is a non-profit organization dedicated to freeing the chained dog. DDB has a pre-written, non-aggressive letter for the caretakers of dogs chained in your community. If you have determined it is the best approach, they will even sign and send the letter for you. Their goal is to educate people about the need to stop the long-term tethering/chaining/confining of dogs. DDB volunteers have even built fences and doghouses to make the lives of these animals better.

ISOLATION AND COMPANION ANIMALS

While the neglect of chained dogs is frequently out in full view of the public many more neglected animals are suffering behind closed doors. It is important to remember what we said earlier: many cats, rabbits, gerbils, birds, and other companion animals commonly kept indoors are also suffering slow, silent, protracted deaths due to neglect. Still other companion animals like horses, pigs and goats may endure tremendous suffering, hidden in plain view of passersby. In addition to starvation, dehydration, and unattended illnesses and injuries these animals also suffer tremendously from a lack of social contact. In recent years scientists have become keenly aware of animal intelligence and animals' need for social contact. They are also aware of the serious negative consequences that occur when animals are deprived of that contact. Animals are sentient beings. Those of you who have lived with pets are probably aware that like human animals, non-human animals have feelings, preferences and a profound need to be close to their human family members. Companion animals who are isolated and denied social contact can suffer from depression and loneliness—conditions that can have serious consequences for exacerbating the physical ailments they are experiencing as a result of neglect. If you have ever heard the statement, "That animal died of a broken heart," remember that in the case of forced, prolonged social isolation and neglect this can literally be true.

THE VETERINARIAN'S ROLE IN IDENTIFYING NEGLECTED ANIMALS

Not only does the vast majority of animal cruelty arise from neglect, but it is also the form of abuse most likely to be encountered by veterinarians. According to a report created by researcher and veterinarian Gary Patronek (1997) the American Veterinary Medical Association (AVMA) recognizes that veterinarians may have occasions to identify cases of animal neglect as defined by state or local law. When cases of animal neglect are identified the AVMA considers it the responsibility of the veterinarian to report such cases to the appropriate authorities.

Patronek (1997) has argued that veterinarians are in a position to make a strong case to help neglected animals; especially in situations such as the effect isolation has on the well-being of a social animal like a dog who is denied interaction with other dogs and humans. As Patronek points out, while the category of mental abuse is not specifically identified in any U.S. animal cruelty statute, many veterinarians and other professionals would agree that dogs tethered and isolated long-term and deprived of attention and companionship do suffer. Isolation and tethering may be red flags for other forms of neglect that may be easier to take action against (such as inadequate shelter or poor nutrition). Therefore, he argues, the operational definitions that focus more on the *consequences* of the human acts of omissions of food, water, shelter or needed veterinary care may be more useful when attempting to define neglect (Patronek, 1997).

Problems Taking Action

One problem with identifying and taking action in suspected cases of animal abuse is the fact that some state animal cruelty laws are inconsistent in their language or scope (Patronek, 1997). Additionally, training and instruction regarding animal neglect is limited in veterinary curricula. Nearly all of the animals treated in the teaching hospitals where the vast majority of students receive their clinical experience are valued family companion animals. Thus, veterinary students are unlikely to encounter cases of animal neglect during their training, and they are even less likely to be exposed to the procedures for reporting a neglect case (Patronek, 1997).

Solutions

Patronek (1997) has suggested that when evaluating any animal for the possibility of neglect, it is useful for veterinarians to consider three general areas: (1) the severity of problems present; (2) the total number of problems; and (3) the duration of the problems. In many cases of neglect, he argues, it is possible and much more productive to educate and work with the owner to improve the standard of animal care. This can be done with the support and assistance of the proper enforcement agency. As we will discuss in Chapter Nine, an important aspect to meeting this objective is for veterinarians to join in community partnerships with law enforcement, humane investigators, animal control, and other professionals.

OTHER PROFESSIONS' ROLE IN
IDENTIFYING NEGLECTED ANIMALS

Neglected Animals as Red Flags for Other Serious Problems

Like animal abuse, animal neglect may be a red flag for other problems going on inside the home. Those symptoms of neglected animals that are visible (e.g., the underweight, barking dog tied on a chain) may serve as red flags for child or elder neglect, or chaotic, unhealthy home environments such as those that occur in the case of animal collectors or "hoarders" (Patronek, 1997). Veterinarians are trained to readily identify even subtle symptoms of neglect but unless the neglect has gone so far as to cause animals clear adverse symptoms, other professionals often have to look for other red flags to substantiate neglect. Indicators of potentially neglected animals include neglected children and/or elderly family members. Child and family service professionals should remember that children who lack appropriate hygiene and clothing corresponding for weather conditions, nutrition, and so on may be a red flag for generalized neglect within the home — including the family pets.

As researchers have suggested, all social service professionals should remember that pets sharing their client's environment frequently also share the risks. This may be especially true for the elderly. It is not uncommon for a neglected adult to have a neglected pet (Boat and Knight, 2000). In fact, neglect of pets was the most common finding among adult protective services clients in the Boat and Knight study (2000). Neglect rarely, if ever, involved only the companion animals. Rather, neglect of pets tended to be a pervasive symptom for an adult who was also unable to care for him-or herself. Boat and Knight recommend humane societies and animal welfare groups collaborating to develop informative brochures for adult protective service professionals, law enforcement and domestic violence case workers and shelter managers. They recommend that the brochure should include a listing of local animal control, animal welfare groups, volunteer veterinarians, a pet loss support hotline and group, and possible resources for emergency pet food and shelters.

A Final Word about Neglected Animals

According to the AnimalAwareness.org website, neglect is not easily defined because it can take different forms — from blatant cruelty to subtle, unintentional indifference. Unfortunately, even the most obvious neglect can be hard to see at times. And even if neighbors notice something seems wrong they are often afraid to get involved. That is why it is crucial for humane officers, animal control officers, animal welfare advocates, law enforcement, veterinarians and other professionals to take a proactive lead within their communities to rescue animal victims from the cruelty of ongoing neglect.

In addition to education about animals as sentient beings with feelings and needs, caretakers should be made aware that actions such as tethering their dogs runs a far greater risk of hurting them and their family than protecting them. According to animal welfare advocate Judith Fish, contrary to popular opinion, chained dogs do not make good watchdogs. Dogs instinctively protect their own territory, which in the case of the chained or tethered dog is their yard, not the house where they are never invited.

And finally, research has demonstrated that animals experience emotions such as jealousy, loneliness, boredom, and resentment (www.animalawareness.org). According to Judith Fish, because animals experience the same feelings that humans do such as pain, fear, joy and sadness, dogs chained for extended periods of time suffer from immense psychological damage. As we have seen, some bark incessantly out of frustration, loneliness and boredom. Others become depressed, sad or withdrawn. And still others become dangerously aggressive.

Whether it is a tethered and isolated dog, a horse deprived of necessary veterinary care, or a bird, rabbit, gerbil or cat being slowly starved to death, the feelings and well-being of animals should be taken very seriously. Law enforcement, domestic violence and child and family services professionals need to be alert and ask questions in cases where animals are present in families with problems. Likewise, humane investigators, animal control officers, veterinarians, and animal welfare advocates need to communicate their findings of animal neglect to their colleagues in the social service professions in cases where children and the elderly are living in the home. Neglect is the mute, vile cousin of abuse. If professionals do not take action to investigate and intervene the reality is that no one else likely will.

TALES FROM THE STREET: ANIMAL NEGLECT COMES IN STRANGE AND CRUEL FORMS

It was a nice warm day in the city. Summer was starting to really show its heat, but it still felt good after the exceptionally tough winter we just went through. My boss hangs up the phone and says that we have to go and meet the police at an address in a very well-to-do town just outside the city. "What's going on?" I ask. He says he'll fill me in on the way, but the short version is we are going to meet other staff from the Animal Rescue League and local town agencies.

As we leave the city behind my boss fills me in on the details. We are going to a possible animal neglect situation of someone who has landed in the hospital as a result of malnourishment. As we drive along I occupy my time by looking at all the beautiful homes with their backyard in-ground pools, three-car garages, and well cared-for lawns and shrubs. It's a great place to bring up a family, best of schools, clean environment, plenty of organized activities to keep the kids busy. I think to myself, all you need is the money to pay the bills.

I'm suddenly brought back to my present objective as the boss announces, "Here we are." I see a heavy outcropping of thick bushes along the side of the road. Closer inspection reveals a driveway almost covered over by large shrubs and in the driveway I see a number of different vehicles and people milling around. From the looks of it we've arrived at our destination all right, and it looks like there will plenty to do before we are finished. I can now make out the roofline of a small house through the overgrown trees and bushes surrounding it, located to our right at the end of the driveway. One of our ambulances has arrived and my boss is telling the driver he needs to don a protective suit and heavy gloves before entering the house. The situation seems to be deteriorating quickly. The boss comes over to me and says, "Get your camera. I'll meet you near the door on the side through those bushes."

I return to the vehicle and get my camera and then head back to he house. Another of our ambulances has arrived along with a local police cruiser. Upon my return to the yard I now see the boss pulling a protective suit over his clothes, and the sweat is already running down his face from the combination of heat and exertion. I follow the suited workers around the corner to the back door of the building and stand by as they enter the interior. To enter you have to go through a porch and take a sharp left turn through a rear door of the house. From my location I am limited to only seeing the porch but what I see gives me a pretty good idea of what is going on. The porch is jammed with junk, rubbish, old food jars, milk jugs, gardening supplies, newspapers, some old wooden benches and approximately five crates or cages that look like they are half-filled with dirt.

I can hear sounds like birds cooing coming from somewhere on the porch, but now my attention is drawn to someone coming out of the house. It is one of our ambulance drivers and he is holding a small dog in his arms. Taking a closer look it appears to be a young greyhound that is barely moving. The ambulance driver stops so I can get a picture of the animal before it is placed in the air-conditioned ambulance. I turn back to the porch area and a second ambulance driver appears carrying another similar dog that is also barely moving. This animal is also photographed before being placed in the ambulance. The process is completed three additional times before the boss comes out of the building and tells me that the last of the dogs has been removed and he is now going to retrieve the birds from the porch. I watch as he removes the first of the cages from the back porch and out into the yard. Looking inside I am amazed at what the cage contains.

Inside is a beautiful bird of magnificent colors jammed into a carrier that is filled halfway to the top with packed bird droppings. The other four cages removed from the rear porch also contain a bird jammed into a half-filled carrier. All of these items are photographed as they are removed from the porch and then carried to the waiting ambulances for transport. I am now allowed to enter the interior of the house to continue photographing the scene. The house is jammed clear to the ceiling with newspapers, books, clothes, food containers, all types and manner of furnishings. Nothing had ever been thrown away from the looks of it. Narrow passageways or aisles, that twisted and turned through the trash-filled rooms was the only means of traveling around the inside of the dwelling. The most startling revelation is that this house had been occupied until the day before our arrival.

The occupant had been living in these conditions for an unknown amount of time and had kept it hidden in one of the richest towns in the area. This situation had not developed overnight, during the previous week, month, or most likely even the prior year. It took quite a bit of time for this situation to arrive at its present level but no one found out. Or did they, and just looked the other way rather than rock the boat? Whatever the reason it was a pretty sad state of affairs for the occupant and everyone around him.

The animals, found later to be former prize-winning Whippets, had to be, with one exception, humanely euthanized due to the illnesses brought on by the living conditions they endured for who knows how long. As for the occupant and former owner of the animals, he is now living in a nursing home after having one of his legs amputated as a result of medical problems and prolonged lack of care. The house was condemned by the town as unfit for habitation and torn down before the year was over.

Could all of this been avoided? Most likely none of this would have occurred if someone had focused a little more attention on what was going on in the occupant's life. Someone had to have noticed at some time that things were not right. Some individual had to have driven in that driveway for one reason or another. A meter reader? Someone delivering groceries? A mail carrier? An adult services caseworker? There is no way they could not have realized that something was amiss at that location. Did the owner of the animals intend to commit acts of animal neglect and cruelty? It does not seem that was his plan. Did the situation get away from the owner over a period of time? I would say that was a definite possibility.

It turns out the occupant was an eighty-two year old retired schoolteacher with a good retirement income, living in a house that had been worth some substantial money at one point. The number of neglected animals totaled five dogs and four birds. And of course, let's not forget about the self-neglect of the animals' elderly owner.

The person was all alone in the world, but he didn't need to be. If the public were educated about the link between adult self-neglect and animal neglect perhaps someone would have taken the time to see what was going on and maybe just picked up the phone and made a call . . . a call that could have made a big difference for all victims involved, human and animals alike.

The first information I ever received about a location with a rather bizarre report involving animals came from the staff of a group home in which individuals with mental disabilities lived. The house was a stopping point along the road to recovery for the residents as they acclimated themselves back into coping with the general struggles of every day life. To say that they didn't need any additional outside pressures was an understatement. The staff was at wits end as they had tried a number of different approaches to address their residents' problems and the animal situation and had thus far met with total failure. One day it was suggested that I meet with the staff and residents to hopefully be able to find a way to restore some peace to their current situation.

Arriving for the meeting I observed the house in question, which was located to the right of the group home. I did not observe anything out of the ordinary. The meeting was conducted over a two-hour period and to be honest, by the time it ended I had some serious doubts as to the veracity of some of the complaints. They seemed so outlandish it was difficult to find any of them credible. At the conclusion of the meeting I assured the staff that I would check out the alleged "problem house" and render what assistance I could.

Leaving the group home it was now dark and I immediately noticed the area suffered from a lack of working streetlights. I felt that this condition was quite possibly a major contributor to the situation. Things don't look that bad, I thought. With some assistance from the city lighting department a lot of the problems could be cured quickly simply by repairing some streetlights.

Arriving at the house next door I observed what appeared to be large, dark objects on the front porch. Not knowing what or who they were I called out who I was, and receiving no response, felt that they were inanimate objects not to be feared. Opening the gate at the top of the steps I proceeded up a narrow walkway to the front porch entrance, all the while observing the absence of any lighting in the building's interior. Maybe we are dealing with an abandoned building or occupants just out for the evening. I knocked on the front door and waited an appropriate amount of time for a response. Not receiving any answer to my initial knock I proceeded to knock again, but this time much louder in case any occupants suffered from any hearing obstructions.

This was without any doubt the wrong move on my part as I suddenly had activated a wake up call to what sounded like the "Hounds from Hell." It seemed as though barking, snarling, growling, whining, baying, beasts had suddenly come out of thin air and appeared all around me. Being alone and not wanting to initiate a gunfight with unseen wild beasts in a heavily populated neighborhood I hastily retreated to the other side of the front gate. "What the Hell was that?" was my first thought as I sought to regain my badly rattled composure and still appear somewhat of a professional.

I turned and looked back at the house and saw nothing. Where were all the gargoyles that had just attacked me? Not only didn't I hear a sound, not a single solitary sound, but also everything was now as quiet as a cemetery. I don't believe in most things I can't see, feel or hear, but I must tell you that my views were beginning to change while standing on that sidewalk and looking back at that house.

After a long evaluation and much self-doubt about my present mental processes I decided my best move was to leave and return when the sun was up as I had read that vampires, etc. usually stayed inside during the daytime. I got in my car and drove back to the station, keeping my thoughts to myself upon my arrival. The next morning my first call was to animal control asking if they had any dogs licensed to the address or any prior calls reporting problems. The answer was a "no" to both parts of my question, which did not make me feel any better, either about myself, or the night before. Early that afternoon I decided to head back over to the house with the mystery animals. This time I would take a witness with me when I made my return visit. One of the officers working in my office was the lucky guy to accompany me on visit number two. As we drove to the location he also stated that he had never received any calls about the location nor ever heard of any problems associated with it.

Upon arrival I did everything exactly as I had the night before. I opened the gate, walked up the narrow walkway and approached the front door. So far so good, no sign of any monsters and the large objects on the front porch were found to be old floor model televisions placed on their ends as if forming a protective curtain. Feeling a little better in the daylight I once again knocked on the front door, no response. I knocked a second time, louder, just the same as I had the prior evening. Suddenly the monsters returned. They seemed to be everywhere. Once again we were surrounded by large numbers of wild beasts snarling, growling, barking, yipping and whining. They were everywhere.

But wait a minute . . . I don't see a thing. Where are they? Have I really lost it? No, I don't think so because the officer with me is hearing the same things. I can see it all over his face and he is just as unnerved as I am. It is time for both of us to head back through the gate and to the safety of the street. Making it back to the friendly feel of the city sidewalk we both look back at the house.

Suddenly there is an 'Ah-Ha'-moment! We have found the wild beasts; we are not crazy, after all! We look up and realize they are on the porch roof, which runs along the entire side of the house and across its front. The roof area seems to be covered with them . . . dogs, *wild* dogs like you would see on a National Geographic Special. They look in terrible shape and they are all running back and forth across the roof now, barking, snarling, whining, and baying. We stood and watched in amazement. Here we were in the middle of a very congested residential neighborhood and no one had ever called to complain. Suddenly, as if responding to a signal, however, the barking stops and the animals all disappear near the rear of the house on the porch roof. The area is now dead quiet once again; everything has returned to normal. The officer and I look at each other and both exclaim, "Did you *see* that? What the Hell is going on?" We have both been around a long time but this is a first for both of us.

I decide to leave a notice on the front door for the occupant, asking for a call to my number at the station. I would really like to meet this individual and hear what he has to say. A few seconds later the notice is posted, without the return of the beasts overhead, and we return to the station.

I wait a week and no call is received from anyone claiming connection to the address in question. The staff at the home next door also reports no activity or problems since our last visit. Possibly the occupant only needed the notice to be urged into making some changes. But I have to be certain. Time for a return visit to the set of the "Howling." Again I take an assistant. We pull up and get out. House looks the same, television sets still acting as sentries along the first floor porch, no beasts observed on the porch roof. Up to the front door we go, and I see that the notice is nowhere in sight. Obviously someone must have been here. Do I dare take the chance and knock on the door again? I guess one fairly subdued knock won't hurt. This time the door opens after a few moments and a face appears. "What do you want?" is my greeting from the person inside.

"Hi, I left a notice on the door last week about the dogs, are they yours?" I ask.

"Nope, they're Sam's," the person says.

"Is Sam here?" I ask.

"Nope, out."

"Do you know when he will be back?" I press.

"Nope, didn't say," is the response.

Quickly assessing that we were going nowhere fast I ask one last question. "Does Sam drive a car?"

"Nope," is all I hear as he closes the door.

Well that got us a whole lot of useless information in a hurry. Might have gotten more information from the dogs if they were able to speak, I think to myself. And by the way, where are they? We haven't heard a peep. I step back off the porch and look up at the infamous porch roof. Not a thing in sight. Time to go next door and update the staff as to our progress as well as to see if they know what Sam drives for a vehicle.

The staff at the group home says that everything has been quiet and they are not quite sure what Sam drives as he appears in many different vehicles but never as the operator. My business card is posted on the kitchen bulletin board so they can call me when Sam next appears. It's starting to get dark so I am thinking I had better get out of the area before I set the dogs off once more.

Two days later I am sitting at my desk when the phone rings. The voice on the other end says, "Sam is out front of the house now. He just pulled up in an old beat up station-wagon." Quickly out the door of the station I go and head for Sam's house. When I arrive at the house with the mystery dogs I see there is an old and very beat up station wagon parked at the curb out front. Two guys and a woman are sitting inside. The hood is open so steam from the radiator can slowly dissipate into the atmosphere. Walking up to the passenger side of the vehicle I ask if any of the occupants goes by the name of Sam. "No," is the answer received in unison from the three occupants.

"Do you know where Sam is?" I ask.

"I think he's in there," says the front passenger as he motions toward the house.

"Do you know Sam's last name?" I ask.

"Nope, just call him Sam," they all respond in unison again.

Time to go up to the house and seek out Sam. I knock on the front door and the same face as the last visit opens the door after a few moments.

"Can I talk to Sam, please?"

"I don't know if he's home, let me go look."

After a wait of a good five minutes the unknown occupant returns to the door and states,

"Can't find him. He must not be home," and then closes the door.

So much for that exchange of high-level information. Returning to the car I present the occupants with my business card and tell them that it is very important for Sam to call me right away, as he doesn't seem to be at home. I am assured that they will be more than happy to convey the message if they ever see Sam again. I am tempted to ask about the "ever" part but decide to bite my tongue. It's time for another approach to finding Sam.

The next morning I call the local utility company's security department and ask for information regarding the listing for services at Sam's address. Success! Within five minutes of my request, Sam has a last name. Time to go back to the house and give Sam one last chance before I head for the district court and seek some criminal complaints regarding the dogs and their care.

Arriving back at the house we find once again there is no one home, or at least no one willing to answer the door. I leave a note on the front door informing Sam of my intentions to seek complaints in the local court the next day. I am careful to spell Sam's first and last names on the notice in large letters so that they won't be missed. To better prepare for my court proceeding I now go into the adjoining yard and photograph the condition of Sam's yard.

It is filled with feces, torn rubbish bags, sharp cans, broken glass, old car parts, dirty water in old dishes, and plenty of television parts. No wonder the dogs were up on the roof.

After a short while I have pretty much all the evidence I need to present in court along with the dates of all the efforts we made to contact him. Applications are presented to the Clerk's Office the next day and Sam is given seven days to appear at the court. I personally deliver the notice to appear at the court to Sam's tenant, who doesn't make any promises that Sam will get it in time. My message to him is that for Sam's own good he should get down to the courthouse by the time designated.

By this point the ongoing pursuit of Sam and the mysterious, obviously neglected howling dogs case has become well-known around the station and often the focus of conversation with fellow officers. Two days after delivering the court notice I receive a call on my radio to contact the court. I call the Supervisor's room and one of the officers states that my friend Sam is at the courthouse trying to get the dog case dismissed. I immediately drive to the courthouse and go to the Clerk's Office where I ask if Sam is still in the building. I am told that he is in the waiting room hoping to speak with the Clerk Magistrate. I ask what he is wearing, and armed with a description, head down the hall to the waiting room. Entering the room I see one individual wearing the correct description of clothing sitting on a bench reading a newspaper that is covering his face. I approach and say, "Hi Sam, how are you?" The paper slowly comes down and behind it is the smiling face of my friend, Sam. Interestingly enough I now realize that Sam has an identical twin brother that just happened to answer the door the last few times I was at Sam's house and could never find him at home. What a small world, and it's getting smaller by the minute, especially for Sam!

"Well Sam, what a coincidence that we should meet here in the courthouse. Maybe we should just go upstairs and have some quality time talking with one of the judges," I suggest. Sam thinks it over for a few moments and then says he does not think it will be necessary.

I believe Sam has arrived at just the point we want him to be. He is well aware that he is cornered and we hold all the aces for this hand. It is time to play let's make a deal, and I have a deal Sam just can't pass up. My offer is for Sam and I to go back to the house and have Animal Control meet us there. We can then make arrangements to have all the dogs removed to the city shelter. They look in bad physical shape and a check of the records indicates that none of them have ever been licensed nor had any veterinary care or shots of any kind. Sam is a little reluctant at first but when he becomes aware of the large amount of fines he will incur his mindset changes. Animal Control is contacted and two vehicles are dispatched to meet us at Sam's house.

As Sam and I returned to the house I asked him about the dogs' amazing appearing and disappearing acts on the roof. Sam laughed and said that he always left a back window open when he went out, and the dogs stayed inside until someone entered his property at which time they would run up and down along the entire length of the porch roof. They always went back inside when the people left. When he is home he always keeps the window closed and the dogs inside. I asked him why he didn't take care of the dogs like he should have and he answers that they wouldn't be nasty and scare people away if they were pets. A simple answer but certainly not the way to do things.

Sam couldn't be made to see my way of thinking, but at this point I was not going to argue as we were going to get the dogs out of there and that was today's only objective. Within the hour Animal Control removed all seven dogs from the property. Before the job was completed, some of them were found to be in serious need of veterinary care. All of them were in need of some good feeding and cleaning. A Code Enforcement Officer was requested to the scene to issue a citation for the trash violations and storage of hazardous materials on the property.

A subsequent visit to the home next door was greeted with sighs of relief from the staff as things had recently deteriorated to the point that the residents were afraid to use the side driveway for getting in and out of the van for transportation. Being reassured that the animals had all been removed put the residents at ease.

I now walked over to the house located on the other side of Sam's house and knocked on the door. A middle-aged woman opened the door and I asked her if she had had any trouble with the dogs next door. She pulled back into her doorway and said in a very low voice, "They're evil animals, sent by the Devil!" The woman seemed clearly frightened by the presence of the animals and I asked her why she had never called anyone. Her response was, "You can't complain about the Devil. If you do you will suffer forever." I informed her that the Devil's dogs had been removed and she shouldn't have any more fears about them. She thanked me by saying that she would "Pray for me as the Devil would be angry." If the Devil was going to be angry with me, I thought, he would sure have to get in line and wait his turn as a lot of other people were ahead of him.

Returning to my car I was approached by my new friend Sam who asked, "Now that you have my dogs I don't have to go to court, right?"

"Sorry Sam," was my reply, "But you're wrong. You still have a lot of cleaning up to do and just because the dogs are gone does not make your neglect of them disappear." Sam appeared in court on the appointed date, and the court was informed that the dogs had been removed. Sam was sentenced to pay all bills and fines outstanding from the City. Furthermore, he was to have no more dogs as long as he lived within the city limits.

As roundabout and crazy as this entire case was, the bottom line was that the dogs were being terribly neglected. The situation had risen to the point of needing to approach the court and ask for warrants to seize the animals. Some people have questioned why Sam only had to pay some of the bills incurred from the severe neglect of his dogs. To seek a jail term or high monetary fine would have accomplished nothing. Jail would have made no difference to Sam; he had been in and out for minor problems many times over the years. And he certainly didn't have the money to pay any stiff fines. In this situation we reached the best conclusion for all involved. Mostly for the dogs who were removed from the neglectful situation and taken to the shelter to be cared for, receive behavioral training, and adopted.

So bottom line, how do you accomplish your task in these types of situations? Look over all the surrounding circumstances. In the current story we have to ask 'What would best punish Sam?' No dogs to guard his house would probably force him to stay around a little more, kind of like a mild form of house arrest. A second punishment was that he had to clean up his yard. If he failed to do so, Code Enforcement would be more than happy to issue more violation notices. In the city if you fail to pay those types of fines a lien is put on your property and Sam sure did not want to lose his house.

The moral of this story? Animal neglect frequently appears in many different shapes and forms. While it may or may not be easy to spot, once you do the real problem may be in determining the proper way to administer punishment and problem solving. Do you severely punish a senior citizen living on next to nothing for failing to feed and care for their animals properly? I wouldn't suggest that route, but something has to be done to enforce your message. Would you slap a puppy-mill operator on the wrist when he pulls the physically defective runts of the litter aside and leaves them to slowly starve to death? Certainly not. That is a case that calls for strong measures to be taken.

The point to remember is that when dealing with animal neglect, a long hard look has to be taken at the entirety of the circumstances before the best solution for *all* involved is finalized. Stay with the objective of helping the animal victims without making a bad situation worse and you will be successful.

Chapter Six

When it Stops Being Love and Starts Being Hoarding

Animal hoarding is a statistically rare occurrence but when it happens on *your* watch it seems as though it ought to be grabbing the headlines on the national news. Animal hoarding is a particularly insidious type of animal abuse. Those we interviewed who have experienced it firsthand tell us it is often far worse than any overt animal abuse case. That is because in animal hoarding cases the suffering has usually gone on for far longer and there are frequently many more animals involved.

While animal hoarding is not a new phenomenon the research field on the topic is still in its infancy. Nonetheless, there has been enough information gathered from fieldwork interviews, practitioners and researchers to give us some revealing and useful information on the topic. This chapter will offer an overview of what hoarding is, who hoarders are and how to recognize them, what is thought to make hoarders tick, the extent of the problem of animal hoarding and what happens to the animal victims of hoarding. We will end with some real-life tales from the street involving dealing with animal hoarding cases firsthand. The next chapter will offer strategies and techniques for dealing with hoarding cases. For now let's begin by looking at just what an animal hoarder is.

WHAT IS ANIMAL HOARDING?

At its most basic level, animal hoarding is the collection of unusually large numbers of animals (or at least more animals than the person can adequately care for) that results in extreme levels of animal neglect. As someone who has seen the ugliness firsthand has said, "Animal hoarding cases are cruelty cases.

Whether one animal or 100 suffer there is no valid excuse for it. . ." (Crosetti, 1999).

WHAT IS AN ANIMAL HOARDER?

According to the Humane Society of the United States (HSUS) an animal hoarder is someone who collects more animals than s/he can care for. Animal hoarders frequently fail to recognize (or refuse to acknowledge) when the animals have become victims of gross neglect.

According to the Hoarding Animals Research Consortium (HARC) in their 2002 report entitled, "Animal Hoarding Recommendations for Intervention by Family and Friends" an animal hoarder is a person who accumulates a large number of animals, fails to provide minimal standards of care (nutrition, sanitation and veterinary), fails to act on deteriorating conditions of the animals (disease, starvation and/or death) or the animals' environment (severe overcrowding or unsanitary conditions), and fails to attend to the adverse effects the animal hoarding is having on his/her own health and well-being (Allen, 2004).

OVERVIEW OF ANIMAL HOARDING

Hoarders are in almost every community; urban, suburban and rural areas have all experienced it (HARC/Frost, 2000). An estimated 700 to 2,000 hoarding cases surface every year across the United States (Patronek, 1999). Many of these cases may be committed by repeat offenders—a study of animal shelter personnel reported that 60% of animal hoarding cases they handled were from hoarders who had committed the same offense previously (Patronek, 1999).

For those involved in animal cruelty and neglect investigations, hoarding cases are often among the most horrific cases they will encounter. This is because there is long-term suffering of many—sometimes hundreds—of animals. There is often disease, illness, injury, malnutrition and parasites afflicting many, if not all animals. The conditions where the animals are kept are frequently horrific as well. Hoarders' homes are frequently filthy, unsanitary, cluttered with trash, and filled with feces and urine, requiring protective gear to be worn by professionals entering the home to investigate and remove the animals (HSUS/Simmons). Many of these homes are declared unfit for human habitation by housing code authorities according to HARC. In a survey of animal investigators across the country, 11% of hoarders' homes had been condemned (Patronek, 1999).

Newspaper reports of hoarding cases appear nearly every week some place in the country. Many times the organizations and agencies called to respond are unprepared for the extent—or the costs—involved in resolving the crisis situation. The costs associated with labor, overtime, veterinary care, euthanasia, arranging for adoptions, and items such as food, litter, and other supplies could run into the tens of thousands of dollars for a single hoarding case. This is especially true when there are hundreds of neglected animals involved (Podger, 2004; Associated Press, 2004a).

If they do not receive psychological counseling and strong boundaries and limits placed on their behavior, animal hoarders tend to repeat the cycle of their compulsive collecting and cruel neglect of animals. One hoarding case in Minnesota took a team of law enforcement, fire department officials, animal welfare professionals and health department officials more than seven hours to remove more than 400 rabbits. Twenty-five percent of the animals inside the home were dead. Five years later the hoarder was discovered with 160 rabbits inside her home and the seizure of sick, diseased, suffering animals began all over again. The home was so squalid and filthy officials deemed it uninhabitable. Two years previous to the incident with 400 rabbits, officials had busted this same hoarder (Associated Press, 2004b).

What Research and Data Gathering Have Taught us About Animal Hoarders So Far

Researchers in a pioneering case study conducted in New York City two and a half decades ago examined animal hoarders identified from animal control and city health department records. The results indicated that many hoarders believed themselves to be rescuers of animals who were unwanted and would otherwise die. Hoarders reported they received unconditional love from their animals, refusing to acknowledge the suffering they themselves had inflicted on the animals through neglect. Animal hoarders were usually resistant to the idea of allowing any of their animals to be removed. A large portion of animal hoarders in this study was socially isolated and living without utilities and plumbing. They frequently had collected inanimate objects as well as animals. The majority of the animal hoarders were female and unmarried. Dogs and cats were the most commonly hoarded animals in this study with males tending to collect dogs and females tending to collect cats (Worth and Beck, 1981).

More recently another researcher interviewed animal cruelty investigators about their experiences with animal hoarders (Patronek, 1999). Based on 54 case reports submitted by 10 animal cruelty investigative agencies the results of this study mirrored the earlier one conducted by Worth and Beck (1981).

Again most hoarders were found to be females (76%), nearly half of whom were 60 years or older, most were single and lived alone. The most common animals collected by hoarders were cats (65%) and dogs (60%). Farmed animals and birds were both hoarded in 11% of cases. Sickly and dead animals were discovered in 80% of the cases reported by shelter officials. Animal feces and urine were found to be present in the living areas of 69% of the hoarders' homes and in some cases on the hoarders' beds. Most of the hoarders were reported by shelter officials as failing to recognize the seriousness of the suffering of the animals under their care or of the living environment.

Animal People News, a publication that follows the latest trends within the animal welfare and animal rights arenas, examined news reports of 668 alleged animal hoarding cases in the U.S. The publication reported they found that females were the alleged perpetrators of animal hoarding in 59% of the cases. Females and males were joint alleged perpetrators in animal hoarding in 15% of the cases. Nearly two-thirds of alleged animal hoarders lived alone. Males who were alleged animal hoarders were almost twice as likely as females to be under the age of 30 when they were caught hoarding animals. The majority of both male and female alleged animal hoarders in the news reports were 40 years of age and older. Twenty-four percent of alleged animal hoarders were or had been pet breeders and 55% of these were female. Twenty-four percent of alleged animal hoarders claimed to be animal rescuers and of these 77% were female. Of those news reports that mentioned occupation, 4% of alleged animal hoarders owned pet stores, 19% were farmers. A disturbing 17% of alleged animal hoarders kept dead animals in their homes. Four percent of alleged animal hoarders had children who they kept living in the same filthy conditions as the animals and 2% kept elderly persons that way. Thirty-seven percent of alleged animal hoarders had previous convictions for similar offenses (Clifton, 1999).

Features of Animal Hoarding

If you do fieldwork and have never encountered the inside of a hoarder's home, prepare yourself: animal hoarders' homes have frequently been referred to as a "house of horrors." In addition to possibly hundreds of animals forced to live among their feces and urine, there may be dead animals stacked in closets or right alongside the ones who are still alive. There have even been dead human corpses discovered inside animal hoarders' homes. Frequently animal hoarders may also collect inanimate objects right along with their collection of innocent, sentient beings. Objects that hoarders have been found collecting along with animals have included excessive amounts of newspapers, batteries, light bulbs, soda bottles, magazines, trash (including the trash of their neighbors), used sanitary napkins, safety pins, paperclips, and human hair. The houses of hoarders may be extremely cluttered and filthy and teeming with noxious smells.

This section will take a look at some of the other features of animal hoarders and animal hoarding that professionals working in the field should be aware of. Some of the features come from the applied experiences of professionals who work directly with animal hoarding cases such as animal cruelty investigators and animal shelter officials while other features of note stem from trends and tendencies of animal hoarders and animal hoarding cases gathered by researchers, psychologists and other practitioners.

- Due to a combination of the difficulty treating animal hoarders' psychological problems, their ability to relocate, and inadequate laws governing their punishment and psychological treatment, animal hoarders almost always start hoarding again. The recidivism rate for hoarders who do not receive counseling and monitoring is estimated to be around 100% (Allen, 2004).
- Some hoarded animals are kept in makeshift cages 24 hours a day. The confinement and lack of emotional contact often causes them to go "kennel crazy." The hoarder may stash the overflow of animals in garages, sheds, trailers, or abandoned vehicles on the property and then simply forget about them (Myers).
- The fact that many if not most hoarded animals are unsocialized is particularly problematic. Even when previously hoarded animals are examined and found to be healthy, animal shelters have great difficulty retraining these animals to make them fit for adoption.
- Animal hoarders often claim to love their animals but their affection is actually obsessive possessiveness. They do not want to ever part with their possessions (the animals) under any circumstance, not even death (Crosetti, 1999).
- Animal hoarders tend to believe that life is always better than death—even when that life is filled with misery (Crosetti, 1999).
- Approximately 20% of hoarding cases involve dead animals hoarded right along with the living animals. Animal hoarders have kept dead cats and dogs stacked in the closet or even in their beds (Crosetti, 1999).
- Frequently animals seized in hoarding cases have gone without proper socialization or veterinary care for so long they suffer from diseases and major behavioral problems. The victimized animals frequently must be euthanized (Allen, 2004).
- Animal hoarding differs from other types of animal abuse in one important way: most hoarders do not intend to harm the animals (Allen, 2004).

- Quoting a director of animal control, Allen (2004) reports that an animal hoarding case is actually a cruelty case. This is because the animals are truly victims of cruelty and neglect. Allen argues that if hoarders do not have intent then we also have a human victim in need of intervention and services. If agencies only rescue the animal victims and do nothing for the human perpetrator of hoarding, then the hoarding is likely to recur again and again.
- Animal hoarders typically do not spay or neuter their animals—one of the key factors that separate them from legitimate animal rescuers. Therefore hoarders typically have many pregnant animals (Crosetti, 1999).
- Animal hoarders are often very secretive. Their houses may be far from the road or other neighbors. They often have heavy curtains or coverings blocking their windows, high shrubs and fences around their property and other types of blockades concealing their homes. For this reason prosecutors can cite hoarders' furtive behavior that indicate those guilty of mass animal neglect *know* their behavior is wrong—thus demonstrating that there was an intentional willingness and knowledge to commit cruelty to animals (Crosetti, 1999).
- Animal hoarding cases frequently involve homes mired in filth, sickening smells, clutter, animal feces and urine and dead animal carcasses (Allen, 2004).
- Animal hoarding cases are frequently the most disturbing of all the types of animal cruelty cases professionals must deal with. While intent is frequently not there, the condition of the animals and the environment they are kept in, and the magnitude of animals involved can make a hoarding case worse than those animals hurt by deliberate abusers (Allen, 2004).
- Hoarders are addicts and will do and say anything to justify and continue their compulsion to collect animals (Crosetti, 1999).

Getting Inside the Head of Animal Hoarders

The two faces of animal hoarders.   According to Rebecca Simmons, the Outreach Communications Coordinator for the Companion Animals section of the Humane Society of the United States (HSUS), hoarding and mental illness go hand and hand. In her article on animal hoarding she quotes Randall Lockwood, Ph.D., vice president for HSUS Research and Educational Outreach as saying that most hoarders are pathological even though they are still able to function quite well in society. Because hoarders may appear to be living normal lives it can make their compulsive need to collect animals difficult to spot. According to Simmons, this is compounded by the fact that animal hoarders are usually well-educated and highly articulate, allowing them to garner sympathy and manipulate others into believing the situation is actually under control.

Reasons animal hoarders give to justify their behavior. Animal shelter officials have reported the most common reasons hoarders give for the excessive amount of animals they keep include the fact that the animals are like their children, the belief that the animals are unwanted by everyone else, the belief that the animals would die if not for the hoarder, and the hoarder's love for the animals (Patronek, 1999).

Common beliefs of animal hoarders. Animal hoarders believe that they are "saving" animals from certain death (Allen, 2004). The Hoarding Animals Research Consortium (HARC) has interviewed people who have met the definition of animal hoarding. The findings to date reveal that animal hoarders may tend to believe they have special abilities to communicate with animals, special abilities to empathize with animals, or that saving animals is their life's mission.

Interviews with professionals who have worked with animal hoarders tell us the animals they collect may help to temporarily fill a compulsive need to control. Many hoarders view their animals as family members and believe they are doing the best thing possible for the animals. Animal hoarders may be fixed and rigid in their beliefs and are frequently resistant to receiving psychological treatment.

Backgrounds of animal hoarders. According to hoarding expert Randy Frost, Ph.D. and other experts in the field, animal hoarding may be linked to growing up in a stressful, chaotic home environment with poor, inconsistent or nonexistent boundaries (HARC/Frost, 2000; Allen, 2004). Many schizophrenics become hoarders. Other types of hoarders include elderly, isolated people unable to care for themselves and hundreds of animals—there is often self-neglect in addition to animal neglect (Allen, 2004).

The psychology of animal hoarders. For animal hoarders the animals may be instrumental in helping the hoarder to develop and keep self-esteem and a sense of identity. When officials get involved and make claims that the animals are in terrible shape this can be seen by the hoarder as an attack of their ability to do their job properly. This can be especially damaging to the hoarder's self-esteem and self-identity. In order to defend themselves hoarders will often go to great lengths to explain away the situation (Patronek, 2003).

According to Jane Nathanson, a licensed clinical social worker working with the Hoarding Animals Research Consortium (HARC), most hoarders have an intense need to save and care for animals as well as an overriding mistrust and contempt of people. They consider themselves to be doing humane acts and are often shocked when charged with neglect of the animals under their care. The key difference between animal hoarders and those individuals who rescue but do not hoard animals is in the hoarder's inability to stop the compulsion to take in more animals no matter how much suffering and neglect is occurring to the current animals under their care (Allen, 2004).

Many of the people who compulsively collect animals have the same skittishness, the same wildness and fear of people as feral cats (Allen, 2004). Randy Frost suspects a "nesting instinct" in some animal hoarders . . . the drive to create a home the hoarder feels safe and protected in where they are surrounded by unconditional, unquestioning love and affection.

And finally, according to researcher and founder of the Hoarding Animals Research Consortium (HARC) Gary Patronek, humane workers should remember that research is suggesting that there is no one single psychological diagnosis for hoarders. There appear to be differences in what motivates different hoarders, in the types of delusions they may have and in their capacity to recognize what is wrong and to respond to treatment. For this reason there is not one single approach that will work for all hoarders. Additionally, prosecution may be the best way to handle the situation in some, but not all, hoarding cases (Allen, 2004).

Models That May Help Explain Animal Hoarding

Animal hoarders appear to have an inability to resist the urge to collect animals, even when doing so will create serious problems. To date there are several models that may help explain animal hoarders' behavior (HARC/Frost, 2000):

- Delusional Model: This model says that an animal hoarder may have a problem with being out of touch with reality and engaging in fantasy thinking when it comes to the animals and their relationship to them. Interestingly, these same hoarders may be highly functional in their career/ professional lives.
- Dementia Model: This model says that animal hoarders may have problems understanding when their collection of animals is out of control due to cognitive impairment. (Thus far the data has not confirmed this model.)
- Addiction Model: This model says that animal hoarders may have problems similar to those addicted to alcohol or other substances. S/he may have impulse control problems, a preoccupation with their addiction of choice (in this case, animals), isolation from their social world, neglect of personal/ environmental circumstances, and a denial that there is a problem.
- Attachment Model: This model says that animal hoarders may have suffered from deprivation early in their childhood due to absent, neglectful or

abusive parents. Unable to thrive from a close parental attachment hoarders grow up without the skills or ability to form close, loving relationships with other adults. Animals then become a substitute for loving human relationships.

- Obsessive-Compulsive Model: This model says animal hoarders may experience an overwhelming sense of responsibility to prevent perceived harm from coming to animals and go to excessive measures to control the situation/prevent the perceived harm from occurring. Like those people diagnosed with OCD the animal hoarder may block out the reality of the situation (they often cause more harm to the animals themselves) even when it is pointed out to them.

What Therapists and Counselors Should Know about Animal Hoarders

According to the Hoarding Animals Research Consortium (HARC) therapists and counselors should know that animal hoarders like other types of hoarders may present with a variety of diagnosable psychological disorders including Borderline Personality Disorder, Obsessive-Compulsive Personality Disorder, Anxiety, Social Phobia, and Schizoaffective Disorder. Treating these diagnosable disorders may help in reducing the animal hoarder's tendency to collect animals. One treatment technique recommended by HARC for treating animal hoarders is "Motivational interviewing." Please see the resources listed in Chapter 10 for contact information to learn about this therapeutic technique.

DISTINGUISHING THE ANIMAL HOARDER FROM AN ANIMAL RESCUER OR SHELTER

We will talk more about this topic in Chapter Seven as we offer some specific red flags to help professionals distinguish a suspected animal hoarder from a legitimate animal rescuer. For now, however, it is important to note the following:

According to Crosetti (1999) and others working directly with animal hoarding cases, animal hoarders who claim to be running a "no kill shelter" can only be challenged if professionals outside the animal welfare arena understand what a legitimate animal rescuer or shelter is and does: a shelter is a safe haven where all animals are treated kindly and humanely. There is no starving, animals are not put in to positions where they kill one another in fights, animals do not live in filth, they do not breed and they are not left to suffer with untreated illnesses, disease or injury.

Animal Hoarders Can Be Those You Least Expect

While writing this chapter a media report was posted on the FIREPAW online magazine entitled, "165 Pets Taken from Ex-Mayor's Home." The report detailed how the former mayor of Beverly Hills, California had allegedly been discovered with a urine- and feces-soaked home that was so bad the neighbors had called in a complaint about the overwhelming stench detectable from outside the house. The rotting corpse of a dog was found in a broken freezer. A few months earlier, before a city inspection of her property from a previous complaint, she had allegedly loaded 2,000 pounds of dead animals into a rental van and parked it on an adjacent street. The former mayor had been "rescuing" animals for three years. Prior to the recent seizure officials had been conducting periodic inspections of the former mayor's home since the previous complaint. The former mayor maintains she is running a legitimate animal rescue for companion animals and that the police chief is persecuting her (Associated Press, 2005).

And what is the moral of this story? Understanding the trends and tendencies of the types of people animal-hoarders are is practical but being guided by the stereotypes can be dangerous. As the allegations in this little anecdote demonstrate, animal hoarders can be those you least expect.

TALES FROM THE STREET: UP CLOSE AND PERSONAL WITH HOARDING

In this section I will talk about some of my experiences and observations involving hoarding over the last thirty-plus years of working in the law enforcement field. The goal of this section is to offer a look at hoarding from someone who has seen it from actual fieldwork—a look at hoarding from inside the trenches, so to speak.

To most laypersons a hoarder is usually an older, single female who lives in a dirty house with a lot of cats or dogs. Sorry folks, not always the case. Hoarders are not always female, not always single, and a hoarding situation may involve rabbits, gerbils, or any manner of species.

Okay then, tell me, what is hoarding or collecting? My co-author has already talked about the definitions of hoarding in the previous section, including animal hoarding as defined by the Hoarding of Animals Research Consortium (HARC) in Massachusetts. HARC is part of the Tufts Center for Animals and Public Policy and was headed by my good friend Dr. Gary Patronek at the time of its development. So we already know that a hoarder is defined as someone who: 1) accumulates a large number of animals; 2) fails to provide minimal standards of nutrition, sanitation, and veterinary care; 3) fails to act on the deteriorating condition of these animals (including disease, starvation, and even death), or the environment (severely overcrowded and unsanitary conditions); and 4) fails to act on or recognize the negative impact of the collection on their own health and well-being. Of course many professionals in the mental health, law enforcement, and humane investigation fields would provide you with a far more graphic and crude definition of hoarding, especially after they have just visited a local hoarder on a hot summer day. But no matter how you describe it, the key point to remember is that it is a situation that is seriously out of control and that both the animals and the people living in the house are suffering. As professionals it is our responsibility to do something to alleviate the suffering of these animals and to assist the humans in the situation when we are notified of the problem.

One of the saddest statements I have heard is, "Why should we care about hoarding?" Folks, the plain truth of the matter is that when we become aware of a potential hoarding/collecting situation we are also being informed of a human who needs our help. And then there is the fact that if we do not become involved early on by trying to alleviate the situation it may very well end up getting to the point of needing to euthanize the animals. My feeling is that if we knew about it early on and didn't become involved we have also contributed to that inevitable animal cruelty that is sure to occur at some point.

What are the telltale signs of a hoarding/collecting situation? There may be many noticeable signs around the property, but it could also be very low key and hard to detect. If you live in a congested urban setting it won't take long before someone spots the problem: animals constantly seen wandering in close proximity to a certain location, the number of animals seeming to steadily increase week by week. Increased barking problems stemming from one yard or house on the block. Trash bags left out on rubbish collection day that produce strong odors week after week. No trash left out on trash days but increasing odors coming from a certain location as you pass by, especially in the warmer weather. Large numbers of cats observed in the windows of the location, lots of dogs running in the yard where all the grass has been torn up and only dirt remains. There may be multiple, high-volume (25–50 lb) bags of dog or cat food stored on the porch, or multiple empty bags thrown out weekly. These are just some of the things that *may* indicate a possible animal hoarding/collecting location. Remember that legitimate animal rescuers and people who breed cats or dogs as a business may display these same signs, so don't go accusing your local breeder of being an "animal hoarder" until you have investigated the situation or you may be sorry. Remember also that you may not see any food bags as the person may have reached a point where they cannot afford to buy the food needed. Have I confused you enough? Okay here's the best rule of thumb, if you have any doubts about a potential hoarder, call your local animal control officer or humane society and talk it over with them to determine the best way to proceed.

How about those of you who live in rural areas? Most of the signs are the same except they may be harder to observe. This is where the postal delivery person, the paper delivery person, and the utility worker play a big part. They may be going to the location day after day, seeing things and not knowing what they are seeing. I have had many people say after a hoarding situation has been uncovered that they saw the same thing day after day and never knew what they were looking at. The trained eye of the professional sees many more things but doesn't always get the opportunity to go up close and have a look-see. Team up with and educate the people in the community and let them be your eyes and ears every so often. And don't forget to take a good, close look around your neighborhood yourself once in awhile. You may be in for some surprises.

These are certainly not the "be all and end all" indicators or red flags of animal hoarding. But I hope they will provide you with some direction to start your investigation when it comes to concerns you may have about a potential animal hoarding case in your city or town.

This next point is a trickier one to determine; you may feel you need a crystal ball to reach a conclusive answer: How do you distinguish hoarding from an innocent love of animals? Excellent question. I don't know of anyone who ended up being defined as an animal hoarder who didn't view themselves as a lover of animals. I have never worked on a hoarding/collecting situation in which the person in question had used anything other than loving words when describing the animals in and around their house, barn, shed, or wherever the animals were being kept.

The biggest point here is distinguishing between a legitimate animal rescuer and an animal hoarder. The primary difference between an animal rescuer and a hoarder is that the rescuer knows his or her limitations and can set and maintain appropriate boundaries for limiting the number of animals in their care. Legitimate animal rescuers are constantly monitoring their own situation and willing to reach out to others when needing assistance with placement of animals so that their numbers will remain workable. They remain aware of factors such as care, feeding needs, veterinary requirements such as shots, and proper housing for the animals. At the same time they are also aware of their own personal needs and requirements to maintain a happy and healthy lifestyle for themselves and their family members.

Hoarders/collectors may start taking in animals in much the same way but rather than setting appropriate boundaries and focusing on the well-being of the animals they become all consumed with the *collecting* of animals. Slowly but surely the collecting of more and more animals takes precedence over their own personal needs—or the needs of the existing animals. Left unchecked these situations slowly deteriorate to that point all too vividly described in the media as a "house of horrors."

Many times I respond to a call about a "possible" hoarding/collecting situation and to my relief find someone with an abundant number of cats that are well taken care of and loved dearly by the owner. Finding this type of situation never bothers me, nor do I mind using my time to investigate the complaint as I now can leave my information in case I *am* ever needed in the future. More importantly, I have investigated and found that the animals are not suffering.

A frequently heard statement when I first knock on a door is, "I'm not an animal hoarder. I'm operating an animal rescue." Here is where you have to be able to communicate and do it well. Say the wrong thing and the door gets slammed in your face and you're in for a bad day. A major item of importance here is for you to *know* what a rescue does and to have already have dealt with legitimate animal rescuers in your area. You can't debate a claim without knowing the fine points of that statement. What does an animal rescue do, exactly? Don't guess what they do—go and speak to someone who works for a legitimate rescue and find out.

My professional observations have revealed good rescues, okay rescues, not so good rescues, and make-believe rescues. It's just like everything else in life. Some people are better at certain things than others. I know of rescues that help transport dogs from one area of the country to others due to shortages of adoptable dogs in that area. I have worked with breed-specific rescues that have been of tremendous help in some tough situations. I have also met less than honorable people that have claimed to operate rescues. So right from the start the claim of operating a rescue can have many implications.

Looking around at your surroundings should provide some indication of the legitimacy of the claim that the person is running a legitimate rescue. Rescues provide a proper environment for *all* animals in their care and custody, not just for certain ones. Do you have that evidence in this particular location? What kind of shelter are the animals being provided? Is it clean? Is there enough room considering the number of animals present? What are the plans for the animals? Are they going to be kept at the rescue, transported somewhere else, adopted out to new homes within a certain time period? Another big question to ask is, "Where do you get your funding to operate the rescue?" I don't know of any funding available to operate an animal hoarding operation and I've never met anyone that claims to be supporting one. Are we even speaking with an animal lover, or is it someone with a backyard filled with highly aggressive dogs tethered with heavy chains? If so he probably does not keep them that way because he loves dogs. If you encounter this situation, back out the door and contact your local authorities—you didn't meet a legitimate animal rescuer at that address. Distinguishing an animal hoarder/collector from someone operating a legitimate animal rescue or shelter is all in the eyes and nose . . . your surroundings will tell you pretty quickly what you have in front of you.

We have thus far been talking about the differences between animal hoarder/collectors and people who operate legitimate rescues to try and make a better world for animals. My coauthor will discuss some further points on how to distinguish animal hoarders from legitimate rescuers, as well as strategies for resolving animal hoarding cases, in Chapter Seven. For the remainder of the chapter, then, I will turn to some actual situations involving hoarding cases that I have encountered over the last ten years. . .

You are now entering the real world of a State Humane Officer, or as we are more affectionately called in some of the more difficult neighborhoods, "State Dog." We get all the calls. If it is animal-related in the least little way, sooner or later it ends up with us. The Animal Rescue League of Boston likes to say that "Rescue is our Middle Name" and some people take that pretty literally in their interpretation.

Please keep in mind that the popular perception of an animal hoarder/collector is a middle-aged, white female who lives alone in a somewhat less than immaculate domicile, heavily populated by an overabundant number of cats. Okay, now that I have made that statement just hold on because in a little while we are going to tear it apart!

The least favorite call any humane officer, animal control officer, or health worker wants to receive is the one telling them about where they can find a house or apartment full of animals. It never comes in early in the morning and without fail, it always happens on one of the hottest days of the summer. First thoughts through the lucky recipient's head probably are, "Damn, I knew I should have taken this week for vacation!" But like the good person you are, off you go to the address, and the start of another adventure.

For the first twenty-plus years I didn't have these feelings too often because as a police officer I only had to verify the complaint and then I called animal control and handed it off to them. All of that changed about ten years ago when I started to devote my efforts more toward finding a solution to these and other animal-related calls the police received. Two years ago I became fully involved when I started working as an investigator for the Animal Rescue League of Boston. Now I would have my own personal animal hoarding complaints to work on . . . boy was I in for an education.

The first summer I was with the League my nickname became "Cat Man Do" as it seemed every other call I went on dealt with an animal hoarding issue. By July I was pleading with anyone to give me a plain old "lack of shelter" complaint to do, anything to provide some change of routine. If you ever want to learn something new and learn it fast, try repetition—it does wonders. As it turned out, it was far from a wasted effort as I learned an awful lot in a very short span of time. The most interesting fact was that my whole idea of what made up a hoarder's profile was wrong, very wrong. . .

It was a nice day in late May and my boss said to me, "I just received a call from the Board of Health about a problem they are having and we need to meet with them." Since it was a nice day for a ride we both got into his truck and drove out to this picture-perfect New England town hall about three hours west of Boston. Once there we met with the local Health Department Official, Building Inspector, and Fire Chief who presented us with the following situation:

"We have a guy that lives on the family land with his wife and an unknown number of cats. He may be dangerous, and the neighbors want us to do something about it," the Chief says.

Right away I start to wonder about this picture. Why are we here? And why is the local animal control officer missing? We come from three hours away, where does the ACO live? How did you get our number and why not call someone else that must be a little closer? Well, we were here now and they seemed like nice people so what the heck, I think, let's take a look at the place.

Being the cop for so long my next question was: are there any guns in the house? The Fire Chief responded with a comforting answer of, "Maybe, could be, I think so, but I went to high school with him and he wasn't violent." Okay Chief, but when did you get out of high school, and what's he been doing since then? I now notice for the first time that someone else is missing from our little group. Where are the police? They were tied up, was the answer, but they said to call if we needed them. Okay I think, must remember this fact also.

Off to the house in question we go, three four-wheel-drive trucks and a Suburban. Nothing like having numbers on your side for the first visit. Up a dirt road we go, bushes overgrown so badly that the road is almost invisible, up a small incline we go, watching out for the wash outs. Then suddenly . . . oh, oh, what's that in front of us! I thought for a minute that the ground was moving. There are cats everywhere, going in all different directions! There must be over one hundred of them out here. . .

A gray, weathered, shingle-covered 2½-story house is on the left of a small knoll with a big blue tarp covering the front third of the roof and hanging over the doorway area. The garage ahead of us has an abandoned station wagon outside the door. There's a small out-building to the right of the garage and another abandoned car to the right side of the driveway opposite the house. The place looks like a big yard sale was held here a few years back and the stuff is still here waiting for pick-up. We stop our vehicle and step out on to a pine needle covered driveway that is now visible as by now the cats have run into the woods that surround the house. There is an instant attack by mosquitoes from every possible direction. I feel like I've got to move or they'll fly away with me.

I start toward what I believe is the front door and as I walk I look up to the second floor windows. All I can see is cats looking at us. There must be at least ten in every window, and I see about five windows. I reach the front door and knock on a nice new steel door, newly installed, quite a contrast to the rest of the property. No answer so I knock again, a little harder, and wait for a response from within. As I am waiting the mosquitoes back away for a moment and now I get hit with a new problem. Oh man, the smell, it is incredible. I am standing in front of a window fan exhaust sending the air out full-force from the first floor. Suddenly I hear my boss say something to someone and I quickly move around to his side of the house and away from the fan.

I see my boss standing at a side porch door with a white male approximately in his forties. The male is wearing a pair of pants and nothing else. I approach and he turns towards me and I notice he has tubes sticking out of his upper left chest area and he is covered with what looks like recent scars on his upper torso. I stick out my hand and introduce myself and he says his name is Dana.

I quickly start the conversation going by stating that his neighbors were worried about him and we came along with them in case we could be of assistance. He says that he appreciates us coming by. Then he turns and starts talking with my boss about some health issues he has been enduring. I look for the people from the town agencies. Where are they? Oh, there they are— all nicely lined up on the far side of the vehicles we came in. Guess they didn't know what Dana had been up to since high school graduation after all.

To make a long story short, we spent about half an hour talking with Dana about his cats, both feral and house versions, and how we could help him get the numbers under control. Dana was open to our offer and we set up a schedule to do some spay/neuter visits with our mobile clinic as well as to bring some food and supplies to him for the cats. As we were finishing our initial visit I got the idea I just had to make sure everyone from the town got to come forward and shake Dana's hand before we left.

Returning to Boston we set up a schedule to start providing services to Dana and his family of cats as well as learn more about how it all got so out of control. It was going to be an interesting case, I could just tell. On my next visit a week later, I delivered cat food, litter boxes, liners, and kitty litter. I also went to town hall and made arrangements with the Board of Selectmen to have a large dumpster dropped off at the house to start cleaning up the area. By now I have learned that Dana and his wife Beth live in the old family home with approximately sixty indoor cats and maybe another hundred that live outside as a feral colony. Beth works a full time job and Dana is unemployed. (He was employed until he got sick with serious kidney problems the previous year.) They have so many cats inside the house that they use plastic pick-up truck bed liners as litter boxes inside the house. Definitely the source of the odor I had caught wind of coming from the house interior.

Next visit we bring the mobile clinic and we spay/neuter twenty-plus cats, as well as start trapping and removing additional cats from the outside population. The numbers are so large we decide to start trapping and removing on a weekly basis.

Around my fourth visit Dana invites me to watch something I thought could only happen in a movie. Dana feeds the outdoor cats on a pretty much daily basis at 3:00 p.m. On this day he says to me, "Sit over there and watch them come to eat." I sit to the side of the driveway and stare in amazement. Just before 3:00 p.m. cats start coming from everywhere, in all directions, walking slowly toward the side porch door. I have never seen so many cats in my life! They are every size, shape, and color you can imagine. I lose count at over one hundred and fifty cats and they are *still* coming out of the bushes. After this sight I realize we have a major problem and still have a long way to go before we cure it.

Another visit is scheduled for the mobile clinic and we now double our trap-and-remove efforts to twice a week and now use two ambulance crews. My weekly trips are now routine: bring supplies out and return with trapped feral cats. After about ten visits Dana, Beth and I are now good friends and getting along well. One hot afternoon Dana comes out of the side porch door and presents me with a plastic bag of significant weight and says, "I guess I won't need these. You're my friend!" I open the bag and see that it contains bullets, lots of bullets. Without any further comment I say, "Thank you" and quickly lock them in my vehicle. The following day we inventory the ammunition and find that Dana had presented me with over three hundred rounds of ammunition.

Work progresses, slowly at times, but changes are being noticed. The dumpster is filling with rubbish, the odor is diminishing from inside the house, and the biggest improvement for all of us working outside is that the mosquitoes' numbers are finally dwindling because birds have returned to the trees around the house now that the number of cats has been reduced.

Spay/neuter efforts combined with our trap-and-remove trips have made significant changes in the entire situation. Dana and Beth are now hoping to sell the property and move to Florida taking less than ten cats, all spayed or neutered, with them.

In December we make our final trip to pick up the last few stragglers living out in the woods. The dumpster is filled and waiting to be removed, and there is no more need for a truck liner to serve as a litter box indoors. The overall count of cats removed from the property or spay/neutered and released was over 300. A routine situation involving a little old lady with a house full of cats? Not quite!

Our law enforcement secretary contacted me one day to say she had just been called by one of the shelter staff reporting a situation and would I please contact the shelter. When I contacted the staff member she relayed a strange incident that had happened to her the night before. She had been in a Dunkin Donuts and a woman had approached her and started to cry and tell her about a friend who needed help. It seemed that the friend lived alone with a house full of cats and they were taking over her life. The staff member was given an address and then the woman begged her not to tell anyone where the information came from.

I drive to the shelter and pick up the information she had been given the night before. The address is in a town close by so I take a ride over to check out the address. The house in question is a large, older 2½-story single-family dwelling located at the dead end of a short little alleyway. An abandoned automobile engine is laying in the very small yard to the right of the house and a large bag containing recycling cans and bottles is on the very weathered front porch with some old newspapers and rubbish in paper bags. The house is in need of some serious repairs to its exterior and gutters.

I walk up the alleyway and while still in front of the house next door to the house in question, I get my first whiff of that unmistakable odor . . . cats, and lots of them. Well I know I have the right house. Let's see if anyone's home. Up to the front door I go and knock on the door, no response, so I knock again, still no response. Time to look into the house and see what I can see. Cats, lots and lots of cats, that's what I see. Looks like an abandoned building except for the cats, lots of cats. Guess I'll leave a courtesy notice saying that we came by to see if there was something we could do to help out and hope for a response. Notice is posted, now its time to visit Town Hall and see if they can tell me anything. The Board of Health seems like a good place to start my inquiries. The people who work there are very helpful but have no complaints about the property. I do manage to get the occupant's name; it's a start if they call back.

Next morning I check my voicemail and hear the sound of a woman's voice speaking very softly about the address I looked at the day before. I can just barely hear her message, but I think she said she would call back later and left the name I was looking for. Its noontime when the phone rings, the lady on the other end gives her name—the same name I'm looking for regarding the house full of cats. As she starts to speak she breaks into sobbing and starts apologizing for what she has done. Time to calm her down; I sure hope she hasn't done something that bad, I think to myself. She regains her composure and says, "I'm sorry but the numbers just got away from me. I'm not home enough to watch them." Sounds like she is reaching out for help now that it has been offered, good sign. We make arrangements to meet at her house, outside, and she says, "Please don't wear any uniforms or come in a marked vehicle." OK, I think, if that's what it takes, can do.

The next morning, bright and early, I have my first meeting with the occupant and get the needed information to start helping her. It turns out this is her mother and father's house and she grew up here. She never married. She's now in her forties, works three jobs, and has brothers and sisters in the area. She started with three cats that were the only things left from her mother and father. Sadly they were not spayed or neutered and have grown by leaps and bounds. All the cats are indoor cats and have never been outside nor seen a veterinarian.

She tells me she had no heat in the house last winter and no water on the second floor. She had a small fire on the first floor last year that started as a result of one of the cats pulling on an electrical cord at the wall socket. She has no idea how many cats are in the house, but she knows it is close to seventy-five and she needs to do something about it. She also stated that some of the cats have very nasty dispositions, "Tom Cats" in the mix it appears.

I make plans to start removal of the cats the following day before she leaves for work. She is only willing to let a few go at a time, but some is better than none, I think to myself, and we can work on the numbers later. Let's get started first.

The next morning we arrive with an unmarked van and she takes the cages to the house. We only get as far as the front porch, still half a loaf is better than none, I think. We remove about ten cats the first day—all black cats. There are no white, no gray, and no other color. Just black. The veterinarian gives them an examination and discovers multiple health problems. Not exactly a big surprise considering the circumstances, but we will try and downplay the problems for now in the spirit of keeping the removal efforts going.

The weekly pickups continue. Luckily the next-door neighbor is more than willing to help her stay focused on her efforts. We are up to about week five on the visits and now speaking freely, she is starting to see the damage that has been done to the house by the cats and is feeling pretty bad about it. There is lots of reinforcing needed to keep her from giving up; her neighbor is being a huge help.

Nine weeks and still no end in sight to the number of all the black cats we are removing. What happened to that original number of about seventy-five, I ask? She states that she has since discovered there are also cats living in the crawl spaces and the eaves of the house and so she no longer has a firm estimate anymore of how many cats there actually are.

By the end of week eleven there is finally good news. There are only three or four more cats in the house; one more trip should do it. We arrive the next week and find the last three cats already on the front porch in crates ready to go. The total number removed from the house was 127 cats, all jet black. Never saw anything like that before. Stereotypical little old lady who lived alone, with no interaction with others and compulsively collected strays? Not quite. This was a forty-six-year old woman who worked three jobs to help feed cats, interacted with her neighbors and had close family living in the area. She lost control of the situation and then was too embarrassed to ask for help.

This last case is also my most recent "large numbers" of animals case, but this one has a slight twist to it. Two weeks prior to sitting down at this keyboard I had the pleasure of taking an early morning ride to a town in Massachusetts known for its great beaches and wonderful restaurants. Not a bad place to spend a nice, sunny workday. The call concerned a local resident who reportedly had at least fifty dogs supposedly hidden in her house and barn. She was reportedly out of control and her neighbors were up in arms. The local animal control officer had no place to put fifty dogs so he called the Animal Rescue League for help in investigating the complaint. We had our resources available if the fifty dogs needed transport and our local rescue groups were more than willing to pitch in if needed.

I arrived at the local police station to meet the animal control officer and assess the situation before we moved in on the location (yes, just like they do on those T.V. shows). I guess the police chief watches a lot of television because the A.C.O. said he was big on staging and assessing before he makes any moves. I can live with it, I think to myself, it's his town, not mine.

The first thing we do is check to make sure everyone has all the license plates numbers, names and descriptions of all parties associated with the address in question. I'm starting to get a little nervous. I thought we were here for a dog-related complaint.

Once everyone is briefed, all three of us, it's time to send someone to "scout the location." I'm getting very nervous now! I stay at the police station with the A.C.O. while the scout does whatever he is supposed to do. Twenty minutes later the scout returns (a positive sign, I think), and says, "Are you sure of the address? I can't find anything at that location." The scout now has to complete another assignment but says he will be back. I suggest to the A.C.O. that we take my unmarked vehicle and check out the area ourselves. He agrees and we drive off.

We get to the neighborhood and find the house with no problem. We also see two barns to the rear of property. The entry to the barns is off a side road adjacent to the property and from the main road it looks like they are actually on a different property. We drive into the parking area for the barns to have a look around and listen for any barking. No barking is heard, but looking through the open doors and windows of the barn there is evidence noticeable on the floor of the horse stalls that a number of dogs have been living there. Nothing else to see here, so we decide to have a talk with some of the neighbors.

The next house up the road has a doghouse. This looks like as good a place as any to stop. We introduce ourselves to the female occupant and explain our reason for being in the area. We have made the right move; she fills us in on everything we need to know. It turns out she sold the house in question to the current occupant who has a large number of dogs, but isn't living in the house herself at this time. The former owner visited the house on Sunday past and was very disappointed with its condition. It was reported that the first floor was dirty, dogs were running all around, and the basement was a mess with even more dogs running around. The house looked terrible and the previous owner was quite distraught over something she wouldn't talk about.

We thank the neighbor for all her assistance and head back down the road. I suggest we stop at the house this time and see for ourselves what is going on. We enter the yard to knock on the door and can hear the barking. Yep. There are definitely dogs in the house. We wonder what house our scout has been at? Looking through the glass panes of the door we observe a number of dogs of many different breeds running around the interior of the house. This has to be the place, all right. Stepping down off the porch we are near the cellar bulkhead and we can hear more dogs barking from that location. It confirms that we have at least ten dogs in the house, but I am not sure about the report of fifty. No one is at home but the A.C.O. feels the owner can be reached through another means, and I am willing to give it a try.

Upon our return to the police station the scout is nowhere in sight. Things are looking better. The A.C.O. makes a few phone calls and finds a friend of the woman who can contact her and have her call us within the next half-hour. Coffee time. Sure enough the phone rings within the stated time frame and it is the owner of the house. "Am I going to jail?" is her leadoff statement to the

A.C.O. "Not if you let us help you straighten this situation out," he responds. "We need to meet you at the house."

"I'll be there in twenty minutes," she replies. Fair enough, see you then. Twenty minutes later and we have our potential animal hoarder right where we want her, on the front steps of her secret lair. Now this is where you have to pay attention because the story turns into something of an English Mystery Movie from here on.

"Are these all your dogs ma'am?"

"No, not really."

"Well, would you mind telling us to whom they belong?"

"Well, I'm not really sure, someone gave them to me."

"How many do you have?"

"I only have eleven now."

"Do you usually have more?"

"Well, sometimes I have close to fifty."

"What do you do with them?"

"I put some of them in the barn, some in the house, and some in the cellar."

"Do you sell them to people?"

"No, I just keep them until someone takes them."

"I think it's time we sit down and go over this again. I'm having trouble following all of this. Let's start once again, but at the beginning when you got the first dogs, where did they come from?"

"My friend got them for me."

"Does your friend have a name?"

"Yes, but I don't want to get her in trouble."

"Where does your friend get them?"

"From her friend down South somewhere."

Suddenly a light went on, I think we may have entered the right road.

"Your friend gets them from down South somewhere and gives them to you, am I correct?" "Yeah that's right, how did you know?"

"Do you get them delivered to your house for awhile and them someone else comes and picks them up?"

"Oh, do you know those people, too?"

"No ma'am but is it possible it is some kind of a dog rescue group?"

"Yes, I believe that's what my friend said they were, they are trying to keep the dogs from being put down."

Okay, we have answered our hoarding/collecting question and have something else for later, but now to close the hoarding issue once and for all.

"Ma'am your intentions are honorable but not allowed under the law so it is time to stop helping your friend. Secondly, you cannot handle that large of a number of animals properly and it is only going to lead to additional problems down the road. Just take a good look at your house and barn and their present condition, sanitation is already becoming an issue for you. The A.C.O. is going to help you get back on track and we are available to assist him if needed. Do we have an agreement?"

"Yes, you do, and thank you for your help."

Did we have an animal-hoarding situation here? It certainly was on the verge of that classification. Fluctuating numbers of dogs arriving and leaving almost weekly, being stored indoors, in a basement and in the horse stalls of a barn. Different from the typical animal hoarding case, to be sure, but it still meets the criteria—especially the part where the caretaker was completely overwhelmed by the number of animals under her care.

In following up it was learned that the woman in question was, to an extent, coerced into providing a place for the dogs to stay by her so-called friend who was actually working with dog transporters from down south. It turns out that the so-called dog rescue was less than reputable and had been bringing dogs north to be sold, not saved from being euthanized, but that is another issue we are working to resolve with various agencies.

The major points in this case are that the original call was for an animal hoarding situation. From the looks of the first visit to the house it certainly met the criteria: multiple animals, sanitation issues, and so on. The homeowner was certainly becoming overwhelmed with the numbers of animals and she couldn't keep up. But the bottom line was that no intentional hoarding had been occurring. There was only someone trying to do the right thing for animals.

Once again not the stereotypical little old lady with a house full of cats, but this situation certainly puts a little different twist on how we need to look—and respond—to animal hoarding complaints in the future.

Chapter Seven

It Takes a Village: Obstacles and Solutions to Stopping Animal Hoarding in Your Neighborhood

Now that you have a solid understanding of the factors associated with animal hoarding, this chapter will highlight some of the obstacles and offer some strategies and techniques for dealing with animal hoarding cases. Also included will be tips for preparing for large-scale seizures, a review of the importance of building collaborative partnerships to prepare for and handle hoarding cases in your community, a review of what to expect when dealing with hoarders and the best methods for success, a recap of how to recognize potential hoarders, and an at-a-glance summary of how to distinguish between suspected hoarding cases and legitimate animal rescues and shelters. Following this, my coauthor offers a reality check about the obstacles encountered in real world animal hoarding cases and examples of a community partnership approach to resolving animal hoarding cases in your community.

OBSTACLES TO DEALING WITH ANIMAL HOARDING CASES

Animal Hoarders Always Have Excuses for What They Have Done

It is difficult to get hoarders to recognize that what they are doing to animals is wrong (Allen, 2004). In fact, according to Patronek (2003) one of the most frustrating parts of dealing with hoarders is the wide range of excuses they offer to justify their behavior and the conditions of the animals under their care. Hoarders rarely, if ever, admit to intentionally harming animals or purposefully failing to provide proper care for animals. Additionally, hoarders rarely acknowledge their own intentional actions or choices that have led to cruelty to animals. In fact, those who have worked with them know that animal hoarders usually deny that they have done *anything* wrong or inappropriate to animals. Instead, they offer excuses or justifications such as 'no one else would help' or they needed to do what they did in order to 'save the animals from being euthanized'. Hoarders frequently talk about how difficult and challenging it has been to care for so many animals with so little help or resources. They may claim that humane shelters, law enforcement, animal control, or even neighbors or family are out to get them. Common excuses offered by hoarders for the poor environmental conditions and poor health of the animals in their homes include low income, no one to help, poor health, or unanticipated personal problems. Hoarders will usually try to steer the conversation to focusing on the number of animals they have helped (Patronek, 2003).

Animal Hoarders are Difficult to Question, Treat and Study

Randy Frost, Ph.D. (2004), a member of the Hoarding Animals Research Consortium (HARC) has been studying the link between hoarders who collect inanimate possessions and animal hoarders. Animal hoarders are very difficult to garner information from; all people in positions of authority are looked at with distrust. The bottom line for law enforcement, humane investigators, ACOs, therapists, researchers and others is that getting animal hoarders to open up and talk is very difficult.

Animal Hoarders Tend to Be Socially Isolated

It is common for hoarders to be so isolated that they may have no human contact—sometimes for months or longer (Allen, 2004). When the ACO or humane investigator arrives on the scene it may be the first human interaction the hoarder has had in a very long time. Therefore that first interaction is critical, as it will set the tone for the entire process of rescuing and helping both the animals and the human victim(s). A gentle approach has been shown to be the most effective.

Animal Hoarders Tend to Be Highly Suspicious

According to Dave Pauli, HSUS Regional Director, animal hoarders tend to be a highly suspicious lot. They may tend to view the professionals dispatched to the scene in one of three categories: an authoritarian, a neutral person, or a resource. The key, Pauli says, is to make yourself the hoarder's 'resource' person. This can be done by offering the animal hoarder recommendations for problem solving with important issues such as food, transportation, medical attention, counseling, housing issues, and so on (Allen, 2004).

Animal Hoarders Require a Lot of Patience

It is very important to work with the person hoarding animals to improve the conditions the animals are living in and to reduce the numbers of animals. This is a long-term project and requires assigning those professionals who can exercise a good deal of patience (Allen, 2004).

Animal Hoarders Need Long-Term Supervision

Hoarders are usually isolated from a social support network. Even if they are successful in their professional lives, their personal lives are frequently isolated. Randy Frost says that in order to lower the likelihood of the hoarder becoming a repeat offender, a multidisciplinary team of people should be involved with the primary goal of bringing the hoarder back into contact with other people. Given hoarders' basic love for animals, experts have even had success getting them to come around by permitting recovering hoarders to have contact with animals under a highly controlled environment such as limited, supervised volunteer opportunities at animal shelters where professionals oversee the hoarder's activities (Allen, 2004).

SOLUTIONS FOR DEALING WITH ANIMAL HOARDING

Humane investigators, shelter directors, animal control officers, social workers and psychologists have all dealt with animal hoarders at some point—according to HSUS (Allen, 2004) most have developed operational strategies to address the problem. . .

Be a Good Listener

According to experts a significant amount of the interaction between the animal control officer, law enforcement officer or cruelty investigator and the hoarder should involve gentle, compassionate and persuasive conversation (Allen, 2004). Hoarders are oftentimes lonely people. Investigators and animal welfare professionals need to do a good job of listening to the hoarder before s/he will be at the point of being receptive to the investigator's message.

Use Empathy

Compulsive animal hoarding is a psychological disorder. Because of the hoarder's mental illness and lack of intent, prosecution under existing cruelty laws is not always the preferred method of problem solving. In order to resolve the current crisis and to prevent future episodes by the animal hoarder it is recommended that investigators and other professionals resolving animal hoarding cases develop understanding and empathy for the perpetrator. This is not to say that animal hoarders should be completely absolved of all liability for what they have done—only that the most effective approach used by professionals is one of more compassion and less strong-arming (Allen, 2004).

Animal Hoarders and The Law

Shelters can use existing laws to receive help in handling expenses associated with large seizures of hoarded animals—bonding laws compel the perpetrator to help with costs of care. Other laws allow animal owners to be declared "unfit" to care properly for animals. Civil unfit laws work like this: Once the hoarder has been declared unfit, the seized animals become the legal property of the seizing agency. The animals can then be adopted or euthanized rather than remaining long-term in a kennel throughout lengthy court proceedings. Remember that seizure of all animals and prosecution of the animal hoarder are not always the answer (Allen, 2004).

Document All Interactions with the Animal Hoarder

According to HSUS, all interactions that investigators and other professionals have with the animal hoarder need to be documented. Records should include all advice offered, all observations, and all the things that have changed over the course of the visits (Allen, 2004). Be sure to also note carefully the condition of the animals (and whether and how the condition changes over time) as well as the competency and willingness of the hoarder to make the recommended changes. This allows for clear communications between agencies and if the need arises, such documentation will facilitate possible prosecution. If the situation continues to deteriorate, legal action may become necessary. In the meantime, the goal should be to offer resources and information in the hopes that legal action is never needed.

Remember the Psychology of Animal Hoarders

According to experts in this area, the more shelters understand the psychological issues associated with animal hoarders and the most effective strategies for dealing with it, the more success they will have (Allen, 2004). Psychological treatments for hoarding are still in their infancy as researchers and clinicians are still trying to learn about and understand the disorder. Because animal hoarding remains a mystery, solutions to the problem have often involved treating the symptoms rather than the underlying illness. Working to change that is the Hoarding of Animals Research Consortium (HARC). The partnership was formed in 1997 and utilizes an interdisciplinary approach to understand and develop treatment strategies for animal hoarding. HARC searches for underlying causes and treatment for animal hoarding. HARC includes professionals from animal welfare fields, psychology, sociology, human and social services and veterinary medicine. To educate members of your organization or agency about the psychological factors associated with animal hoarding behaviors, visit the HARC web site. Contact information is available in Chapter Ten of this book.

Develop Collaborative Partnerships to Solve Animal Hoarding Problems

Animal hoarding often calls for a less punitive and more people-friendly approach requiring more informational and practical resources than a single organization or agency can provide (Allen, 2004). To help end the recidivism rate of hoarders many animal protection groups have now begun to develop and utilize partnerships and connections with non-animal professionals.

Animal welfare and humane organizations need to form multidisciplinary partnerships with other animal welfare organizations to pool resources and space for animal victims of hoarding. But they also need to form partnerships with professionals from non-animal agencies to address multiple concerns regarding the human victims. Partnerships should include professionals from elderly services, housing agencies, mental health services, child and family services, and so on.

Experts say that establishing a multidisciplinary task force *in advance* of hoarding situations in your community is really the only way to address a hoarding crisis adequately. It is important for the various individuals and agencies to already know one another and have had at least initial contact so that when the emergency situation occurs (as it does in so many communities these days) people and organizations can be pulled together quickly and efficiently (Allen, 2004). Collaborative partnerships established before a hoarding situation is uncovered allow for developing a task force, a plan for who will do what, and the organization of multiple resources so that early intervention is possible before the hoarding situation gets terribly out of control. And, if the situation is already out of control by the time it is discovered, having your collaborative partnership already established will greatly reduce the level of suffering of both animals and humans and reduce the burden of the agencies and organizations who intervene (Allen, 2004).

Additionally, a multi-agency partnership is necessary to address the problem, not just the symptoms of hoarding. In this way the needs of the hoarder are met as well, greatly reducing the chances of a situation spiraling out of control or repeating the cycle in "frequent flyer" style. Typically adult protective services, animal care and control, code enforcement and the health department are necessary components of task forces for animal hoarding cases. In order to be fully effective, all aspects of an animal hoarding case must be treated in a holistic fashion. This includes having professionals on your team to handle psychological issues, sanitation issues, animal care and human health problems (Allen, 2004).

Chapter Nine will outline the specifics of establishing a multidisciplinary partnership to deal with all types of animal-related issues in your community. The Humane Society of the United States (Allen, 2004) recommends that the multidisciplinary partnership you develop for a hoarding task force should include:

- Public and private animal welfare/animal care organizations
- Animal Control
- Adult protective services/elderly care
- Psychologist/therapist
- Veterinarian
- Code enforcement official
- Fire department official (If you are unable to get a hoarder to cooperate, consider asking fire officials on your team to investigate as the hoarders can frequently be cited for fire code violations.)
- Board of Health official
- Other professionals to educate/alert about hoarders:
- Prosecutors
- Judges
- Media
- Meter readers, utility employees, mail carriers, and cable television company employees (These people have access to the home and may be the first to notice a potential hoarding problem. They need to be educated as to what to look for and what sort of things are worthy of reporting to your task force.)

Preparing for Animal Hoarding Seizures

Experts advise that if possible, arrange to make several interventions before seizing animals in a hoarding situation. The point is to avoid large-scale seizures of animals if possible. They are costly, tiring, strain resources and frequently cause many animals to have to be euthanized. Avoiding large-scale seizures can be done if the hoarder agrees (1) to release the rest of the animals to your custody; (2) to not acquire anymore animals; (3) to permit unannounced visits to the home to examine the animals and the conditions; (4) to permit your agency to spay-neuter the animals and provide veterinary care to the animals who will remain in the home with the hoarder (Crosetti, 1999).

Remember That Animal Hoarders Can be Manipulative and Dangerous

Seasoned professionals warn that caution is advised for investigators and others entering the animal hoarder's home. Animal hoarders frequently put on a good show of crying and pleading in an effort to garner sympathy. They can also be filled with rage, screaming obscenities and can be a genuine physical threat when angered (Crosetti, 1999).

Preparing for Entry

Based on information from interviews and an article written about handling hoarders by the executive director of an animal shelter that has made many seizures of animal victims of hoarders (Crosetti, 1999) the following steps should be taken when preparing to enter the animal hoarder's home. . .

Preparing for Entering the Hoarder's Home:

- Create a plan of action
- Transfer animals at receiving shelter to partnering shelters with available space
- Notify law enforcement and other agencies and individuals in your multi-disciplinary partnership/emergency team
- Gather video camera, equipment (including masks), insecticide, safety gear, drugs and carriers
- Assign staff to specific duties
- Upon arrival put on masks, safety gear and insecticide
- Secure all doors and windows of house
- Send in scouts to assess the situation
- Briefly review the game plan with all involved
- Enter the house all together
- Begin video taping as animals are gathered working as quietly as possible (both for the animals' sake and for the fact that an evidentiary videotape is going)

- Call ahead to shelter when in route with animals
- When animals arrive at shelter assign each a number, weigh, photograph and give a complete veterinary examination
- Carefully log all information about each animal
- Bathe and groom each animal

Prepare Against a Public and Media Relations Nightmare

Animal hoarders can be a public relations nightmare because they may elicit sympathy from an uninformed, uneducated public and media (Crosetti, 1999). Additionally, lawsuits brought about by hoarders against humane agencies have become common in recent years. The buzz may become that the hoarder is simply a caring rescuer of animals who works to save animals from being euthanized and that law enforcement, animal control and animal shelters have an agenda to "kill these animals." It is critical therefore that the key agencies and organizations involved in the animal hoarding case carefully manage a media and public relations campaign before the animals are seized from the hoarder. Crosetti recommends calling the media promptly upon responding to cruelty cases such as animal hoarding. The media will then get the entire, accurate story as an early "scoop" and the proceeding public outrage about the cruelty that has happened to the animals under the hoarder's care can motivate the district attorney to move forward with the case with vigor.

Long-term Solutions for Animal Hoarding

The best solution for dealing with animal hoarders is still up for debate. Due to the horrible suffering of animals, criminal charges are becoming more common. However, given the proclivity of animal hoarders to repeat their collect-and-neglect cycle with animals, this is not always the best long-term approach to the problem. Additionally, hoarders have not typically received jail time for their actions. To date it appears that the optimal approach may be a combination of psychological counseling by therapists specializing in animal hoarding and long-term monitoring of the offender (HSUS/Simmons).

What Happens to Animal Hoarders?

In a survey of animal cruelty investigators from 10 agencies across the U.S. Patronek (1999) found that. . .

- 10% were ordered to cooperate with long-term monitoring of their actions
- 17% were prohibited from owning animals for a specified length of time
- 13% were ordered to have a psychological examination

Additionally, the results showed that animal hoarders were eventually institutionalized or had a court-ordered guardian in 26% of the reported cases.

Identifying Animal Hoarding in Your Community

Chances are professionals will become aware of animal hoarding because of a concerned citizen's call to an animal control officer or animal cruelty investigator. Or perhaps the hoarder will do something to catch the attention of the housing code enforcement department, or maybe the local fire department. It is also possible that law enforcement will be called by neighbors or a human/social services professional who has visited the hoarder's home. As you can see there are multiple agencies that have the potential for identifying animal hoarding. There are also multiple agencies and individuals needed to problem-solve once an animal hoarder has been identified.

Veterinarians as Frontline Professionals for Recognizing Animal Hoarders

Of course, one of the frontline professions to interact with animal hoarders is a veterinarian. According to the Hoarding Animals Research Consortium (HARC) veterinarians may encounter animal hoarders in the following ways:

- as clients
- as staff members or volunteers
- as colleagues (HARC reports they are aware of several veterinarians in active clinical practice who are themselves animal hoarders)
- through their professional relationships with animal rescue groups and shelters
- through law enforcement when asked to evaluate the animals of an alleged hoarding case
- when asked to participate in the rescue and rehabilitation of animal victims of hoarding

HARC cautions veterinarians that they must become aware of the warning signs of animal hoarding and to actively avoid becoming an enabler for the animal hoarder. For more information on the veterinarian's role in helping or hindering animal-hoarding cases please see Chapter Ten for contact information for HARC and other organizations.

Distinguishing Animal Hoarding from Legitimate Animal Rescue

According to the Hoarding Animals Research Consortium (HARC) there are some general characteristics that professionals from outside the animal welfare arena can use as red flags to differentiate an animal hoarder from a genuine animal rescuer or animal shelter. Probe further if the person under investigation:

- is unwilling to let visitors see the facilities where animals are kept
- is unwilling to say how many animals are actually present on-site
- lacks evidence that demonstrates due diligence to adopt animals in his/her care
- appears more focused on acquiring animals than adopting them
- has continued to acquire more animals even when existing animals have declining care
- claims to provide excellent lifetime care for special needs animals (paralyzed animals, blind animals, animals with diseases such as feline leukemia or extreme aggression) yet has no verifiable resources for providing such care
- the number of staff/volunteers seem inconsistently low with the number of animals on-site
- insists on receiving animals at a remote location rather than on-site

Public Education about Animal Hoarding

If you do not have the ability to establish a multidisciplinary partnership or cross-training a task force, then the Humane Society of the United States (HSUS) recommends that early education should be done. The public, courts and local media should all receive information about the important facts about animal hoarding so that they understand its seriousness, what to look for, and who to contact should they suspect a hoarding case in the community (Allen, 2004).

Chapter Nine will offer you guidelines for establishing a multidisciplinary partnership and Chapter Ten has important resources to help you learn how to successfully deal with animal hoarding cases in your community. For now, though, let's take a look at my coauthor's real-world experiences solving animal hoarding cases. . .

IT TAKES A VILLAGE: A REALITY CHECK ON THE OBSTACLES AND SOLUTIONS TO DEALING WITH ANIMAL HOARDING CASES

"It takes a village", a very popular statement, possibly used somewhat to excess during the last few years, but nonetheless quite fitting in so many situations. In the previous chapter we discussed the phenomenon of what is most often referred to as animal collecting or hoarding. If there is a place, time, and reason to get the "village" involved, this is surely near the top of the list if not, in fact, holding down the top position. If you want to test your available resources and the willpower of those individuals and agencies offering to pitch in and help, just invite them to your next large-volume animal hoarding case. You may be very surprised at how busy they can become in a very short time, or once at the scene how many of them are called away to emergency requests at other locations. I speak from experience as I have seen this happen many times. Some people have the best of intentions when they offer assistance, but if they don't know what they are getting into they are very quickly overwhelmed and looking for the nearest door. Don't get discouraged by this reality, there is a way to prevent most of this type of reaction.

It is now time to discuss the procedures for handling a successful animal hoarding intervention from start to finish. After that you will meet the residents of the "village" and learn what you need to do to have them properly prepared to take up residence.

Step number one, before we make any attempts in this area, is that *we* must go to the potential "villagers" and give them an opportunity to meet us. This very basic maneuver will give them a face to connect to the voice they will almost assuredly be hearing from at some point in the future. There is no more formidable task than asking for support from agencies or individuals that have absolutely no idea who you are. Get out into the "village", be seen, talk with the residents, offer to support their efforts, become known and established with them long before you seek their help. In short, become a "VILLAGER"!

In 1996, while working as the Community Service Supervisor for the Boston Police District that covered the Dorchester, Massachusetts's area, I started my first effort to make the Link-UP Program a reality. Link-UP was started originally to combat the use of vicious dogs as weapons of aggression and protection by gang members. During that summer we had become aware that the majority of the concerns facing the residents stemmed from these issues and were growing at a fast pace. The Boston Police knew how to handle gangs, but did not have extensive background handling animal issues such as these. Being the Community Liaison between the Department and the Dorchester Community at that time, it was up to me to do something about the problem, and to, as my ever-precise Captain said, "Do it quickly!"

As luck would have it I had met some members of the Animal Rescue League of Boston's Law Enforcement Department at a community meeting a couple of months prior to this. I placed a call to them and made arrangements to meet with two of their officers at the police station the next day. During my explanation for the meeting I observed the officers exchanging glances each time I mentioned specific troublesome locations within the district. When I had finished my combined story and plea for help they both stated in unison, "We go to those same addresses all the time." One of the officers then continued on by saying, "We do dogs, but we don't do gangs. I don't know if we can do much to help you out."

A very simple statement, extremely simple words, but oh-so-powerful in the impact that came about as a result of it. Quickly grasping what had just been placed in front of us I asked, "What about if we work *together* on these troubled areas?" My idea was discussed, some minor issues raised and resolved, and we all felt that it was a possibility. The common feeling was that we could pool our available resources and make a stronger effort to relieve the situation before it reached the critical level. It was now decided that we would bring in additional agencies such as the Boston Animal Control Unit as well as a new officer recently hired by the M.S.P.C.A. (In case any of you are wondering why the Boston Animal Control people were not involved from the start, at that point and time their function was mostly limited to barking, roaming, and unlicensed dog situations and their equipment was minimal.) At any rate, thus was born the "Task Force" of combined agencies, pooling their resources, to secure results of a positive nature.

The results were amazing and could be a story on it's own for a later time. Huge steps were made in a very short time and within four months the animal-related calls for service in Dorchester were reduced approximately 90%. We then went on to spread our focus area to include other parts of the city. And as we did this we also increased our scope of services provided. Our "village" was growing in numbers, our strengths and capabilities increased on a weekly basis, and before we knew it, people were calling and asking to become members of our "village." The Child Witness to Violence Project at Boston Medical Center became a resident of the "village," the local neighborhood health centers and senior service agencies arrived, and then the Juvenile Fire Setters Prevention Coalition became part of the "village."

Why did these people arrive at our gate? Because we had become a known member of the "village", we let people know that we were there to not only assist, but to also provide help when it was requested. We were helping to make the "village" grow stronger and the "villagers" believed in themselves more and more each day. This is how a strong "village" is built—slowly, carefully, and progressively. Be open-minded when someone approaches and asks to move to the "village." As a "village" grows it evolves in sophistication. It requires more and varied services. It needs new and different ideas to avoid becoming like so many old mill towns that suffered because they did not expand their horizons as time passed. The world changes constantly, and at an ever more rapidly increasing pace. What is new today is outdated in a week. The problem you encounter today is surpassed next month by something not even considered previously. People move in and out of the "village" all the time, jobs change, people age, lose interest, but the most important thing is to keep the basic premise of the "village" alive and well, as it will be needed as long as there are residents.

OK, we now know why we need the "village," but let's put that village together and understand why these people live in the "village." Each member has a specific function to perform so let's talk about how those functions are utilized in something like an animal hoarding situation. Even more important is to know what an actual animal-hoarding situation looks like. But before we get into the specific needs of a "village's" residents and how they are prepared let's fully understand what the "village" will be undertaking.

First off, someone has to become aware of the situation. The information may start with a call to 911 about a certain address and may simply say, "I think the police should check the house at the corner of, 'one way and do not enter'!" No more information may be supplied, but it will result in the police dispatching an officer to follow up on the call, nonetheless. The officer now arrives at the scene and observes a home with uncut grass in the front yard, overgrown shrubs, and a need for paint and some gutter repairs. The officer's first reaction is probably to hope the house is unoccupied and that the call was a prank. As he approaches the front door he now becomes aware of a strong odor coming from an undetermined location. Arriving at the front door he observes no mail in the mailbox, no flyers from local supermarkets lying on the porch. All the signs point to active occupants inhabiting the building. As he approaches the officer becomes well aware that the odor is getting much stronger, but maybe it is still unidentified to any of his past recollections of various odors.

A loud knock on the door produces the sound of some type of movement from within. Waiting an acceptable amount of time for a response and receiving none, he knocks again, and this time louder. After a few moments the door slowly starts to open and an overwhelming stench fills the officer's nostrils, causing him to step back quickly. A woman appears at the door, the officer's eyes are now watering and it is hard to focus on the occupant.

Stepping to the side the officer now regroups and asks, "Do you live here?"

"Yes I do, what do you want?"

"I was asked to come by and see if everything is alright."

By this point the officer can now see into the house and observes a large number of cats on the stairway leading to the second floor as well as in the first floor hallway area. The occupant states, "I am fine."

The officer says in return, "Okay, thanks," and quickly returns to the safety of the cruiser. Starting up and driving away quickly the officer calls head-quarters and says everything is fine at 'one-way and do not enter' and continues on patrol saying nothing about what was just witnessed at the house of odors. Case closed. Or is it?

We now have an opening in the "village" for a new resident, folks. That officer was just evicted. The proper thing for the first visitor from the "village" to do would be to establish some line of communication with the occupant. The door is open; you have just been presented with a golden opportunity. Police officers are supposed to be able to think quickly. It keeps them alive. This was a time to think here also. It was a time to ask about the cats, and to show interest in them and the occupant. That police officer is the first visitor to ever arrive from the "village" and their introduction is very important to everything that follows. Okay, so we learned from that scenario that we don't send that officer anymore because the situation won't help itself and another officer will just get the same call at some later date.

It is now a month later and you get a call to respond to. You guessed it, 'one-way and do not enter'. You arrive at the location and see *and smell* all the same things as the prior officer. But you live in the "village." Same procedure, same smells, same watering eyes when the door opens, and nothing has changed in a month, maybe just intensified. You start by saying, "Hi, I'm Officer Smith, how are you?" You know how to defuse potential bombs, and you like living in the "village." Quickly sizing up the situation you comment, "I see you like cats, too."

"Yes I do," says the occupant. The line of communication is starting to become established, but you are not out of the woods yet. Continuing what has been started you follow with, "Gee, what kind of cats do you have?" Show an interest, even if it is only temporary, even if you are really not into cats or even animals in general. A few more minutes of light conversation about the animals and anything else that may keep the conversation going and communication is getting stronger.

It is at this point that you can now start working on getting a name from the occupant. Make sure you provide your first name and let the occupant know they can call you by that name and that you don't need to be addressed as Officer Smith. As a police officer you have talked to enough people to develop a high level of skill in this area. Communication is quite possibly the most important tool a good police officer can have. You want to ask about possible family in the area, friends, how long they have lived there . . . casual conversation that will provide additional information, but not seem prying. Any information you come up with will go in your report about the situation.

Your report will most likely end your involvement with this situation unless you have encountered an emergency situation in which action must be taken immediately. The first visitor from the "village" has completed his visit and is now going to speak with the other "villagers."

Your supervisor now has your well-written report, which describes everything observed at the location completely and clearly. The supervisor asks you a few more questions about the call and then passes it on to Animal Control to do the follow up.

Animal Control receives the report the following day, and now the second resident of the "village" is about to become involved. A check is made of Animal Control's records regarding the address in question to see if they have made prior visits. No history appears for the address. The incident is now assigned to an Animal Control Officer. More residents of the "village" are becoming involved with each step. This member of the "village" plays a very crucial part in where this is going as the background work is very important before that actual visit to the house takes place.

A quick call or trip to Town Hall is next on the agenda to verify who owns the property, to find out if any back taxes are owed, whether there are any liens, and identify anyone who knows anything about either the location or the occupants. If you work in a small community you most likely hold the advantage here, as information is usually more readily available when there is a smaller number of residents. If the resident is a senior citizen it is time for a visit to the Senior Center and more background work. Don't forget to visit the local health center, if one is available. All of these people live in the "village" too and have a stake in the well-being of their fellow residents.

The local health center and senior center have now been visited, but only minimal information is available. It is time for Animal Control to take a ride by the address and check for vehicles possibly owned by the occupants that may be in the driveway, yard, or parked in front of the house. If so, the ACO will take down some license plate numbers and ask the police department to check for anyone registered to that address because this could be another good source of background information.

Additionally, when you drive by the house take notice of everything. Did you see any children's toys, or bicycles in the yard? Could there be children or grandchildren living there? If there are, the next stop is the local school district to talk to the school principal or guidance counselor and tell them what you are doing. After all, they are part of the "village" of residents. Don't be offended if they can't tell you much because of privacy rules, etc. It is more important for them to understand what is going on in the child/ children's home lives.

You have now exhausted just about all of your possible sources for background information and have very little to show for it. It is time to reach out to one last group before you knock on that front door. Head for the vicinity of 'one-way and do not enter', park your vehicle and hit the pavement. It is time to knock on some doors in the area and speak to the local residents. They probably know a lot about what is going on but may have chosen to not get involved. Many times these are the people who are your best sources of information when provided the opportunity to talk. A word to the wise though, be careful how you say things, you don't want to say the wrong thing to a friend or relative of the occupant and destroy all of your hard work. When this is completed it is safe to say that you probably have as much information as you are going to obtain.

Now comes decision time. Have you handled this type of situation before? Do you have the resources available to complete this without additional help from other agencies? Do you think that your assistance alone can actually help the resident of that house? I know of very few agencies that can do a proper job handling a situation of this magnitude alone.

Make sure you are ready for what is on the other side of that door. Line up all your "villagers," and have them ready when the time comes. When they are all ready and fully instructed as to just what the circumstances are, now you are ready. Remember, if you are not fully capable to handle the problem alone, don't knock on that door!

Is there someone else who lives in the "village" who has done these things before? Don't hesitate to reach out to the local humane society, S.P.C.A. Office, Animal Rescue League, or reputable cat rescue organization. Make sure all the organizations, including the animal rescue organizations, are capable of providing what they say. Most of them can, but like in all things, some of them have the best intentions but may be unable to handle large numbers of animals or crisis situations.

Okay, you have all your resources lined up, fully prepared and informed. Do you arrive at the house with a small army and attempt to speak with the occupant? Not quite! Only you and possibly one other person need to knock on that door. Remember, you are there to help, not frighten, the residents.

You have arrived, you have the occupant engaged in conversation, everything is going well but you are running out of things to say. Why didn't you bring some flyers with you? Props can be a big help when becoming tongue-tied. How about a flyer discussing rabies shots for cats, and why they are needed? How about FIV information for the occupant to look at? You have to keep the conversation going, you are there to inform as well as help. If the occupant doesn't know what you are talking about they certainly won't understand you are trying to assist them. This is a slow process; success will not be instantaneous. Remember, the person in the house is convinced they are already doing the right thing for the animals; you have to convince them they want to do an even better job.

The occupant and you are now engaged in meaningful conversation regarding the cats and how much they love them and don't want anything bad to happen to them. It is now your place to explain what happens to cats when they are too closely inbred, what FIV is, what Upper Respiratory Infection (URI) is. You have to know what you are saying here, so be able to back up your statements. You haven't even approached the spay/neuter question let alone the inevitable euthanasia inquiry from the collector. You are in a verbal minefield and one false step can set off a terrible series of explosions with you in the middle of it all. Right about now you are probably wishing that the "village" veterinarian was standing on that porch with you.

It seems like you have been standing on that porch for two weeks under a beating sun, but you have survived and the bomb never went off. Conversation is flowing well back and forth and you are each becoming more at ease with one another. It is time for the next big test, "How many cats do you have?" you ask. You hold your breath and wait for an answer or reaction.

"I think I have around forty" is the answer you receive, after a painfully long silence. Your answer hopefully is, "Not a bad number. They are lucky to have you to look out for them." I would say, by the way, that you are most likely dealing with between eighty and one hundred and twenty cats in the house. I have found, in the great majority of times, the number I get is usually one-half to one-third of the actual numbers at the location. Now do some quick math here, can you handle the numbers? I really doubt you can comfortably. Don't bite off more than you can chew.

How do you get at least some of the animals removed from the house with the permission of the hoarder? Make a good offer concerning the welfare of all the cats, "Gee how about if I take a few of the cats to the shelter so our veterinarian can check them out for any health problems?" If you are met with some resistance from the occupant who says, "I don't know. They are my babies." You counter with, "Don't you think it would be good to know if we need some medicine for them or if they may be exposed to possible health problems?" Remember this person is convinced that he or she is doing the right thing for these cats and you have to gently nudge them into believing they *want* to do these things and you are just helping them accomplish it. Animal hoarders have to feel empowered and believe that they want to do these things for the good of the animals or you will never be successful.

If after some serious thought you get permission to take five or so cats with you, this is a major step. Be happy, but conceal your joy until the appropriate time. The next major step is now to be attempted. Strive to get inside the house to catch the first five cats yourself rather than have the cats brought out to you. Anything else you can see inside may very well assist you in your next move toward actually solving this situation. An additional benefit to gaining entry to the house is that you can also ascertain what other members of the "village" will be needed to bring this to closure. If you and your assistant are allowed inside to remove a few of the cats, don't show any emotion to the living conditions once inside, no matter how bad they may be. Don't re-arm the bomb. When you get the few cats, take a quick visual count. It likely will be well over the original figure given of forty. Look for any photographs of possible family members, if you see any, comment on them. Try and find out who they are, and if they live in the area. Any awards, certificates of achievement . . . any personal information is evidence about the animal hoarder that may come in handy later. Look at the ceilings, walls, floors, water stains, ceiling cracks, and feces on floor. Try to see if the plumbing works. Try and get a look at other rooms when attempting to catch the cats. Be nosey but at the same time, not too obvious.

Once the cats are all safely loaded into cages and inside your vehicle, make arrangements for when you are coming back to see the occupant and ask if there is anything she needs. Does she need any cat food, litter box liners, kitty litter? All of these answers can provide more information. Remember, you are trying to get a complete picture of just what is going on in this person's life with regard to the animals and living conditions.

Okay that's enough; don't cause an overload on this person. You may be the first visitor in quite some time and you want to be welcomed back for return visits. Take your cats and head for the shelter. You now have a much better idea of just where you go from here and who needs to go with you as you make those future visits. Don't return too quickly. Give the animal lover some time to digest all that has transpired, but don't wait too long and risk losing all you have worked for. Re-contact within two to three days is usually adequate to maintain open communications.

You return to the address after three days and continue your efforts by having an honest discussion with the occupant about the physical ailments of her cat family. Emphasize that a veterinarian is making these determinations and not someone inexperienced. You have to keep building confidence in the occupant as to your overall intentions. In this case the veterinarian has determined that there is, at a minimum, major URI and FIV problems strongly developed within the cat population. It is now your function to convince the occupant that removal and veterinary treatment is in the best interest of all the cats. This is not an easy task and much care needs to be taken in how you say it. Remember to reinforce the fact that a veterinarian makes the determinations and no one else. At some point during this process, it may be worthwhile to mention that a replacement cat, spayed or neutered, would be available if none of the present cats can be saved. These cats may represent the only friendships the occupant has. You may very well be taking away the focus of their entire lives. So don't create a void for the hoarder, offer some form of replacement.

Perhaps your offer is met with approval after a long period of reflection on the part of the occupant. Once that is achieved make a schedule for removal of the cats in the most convenient manner possible for the animal hoarder. Don't stop the conversation. Reaffirm that the hoarder is making the right decisions for the welfare of their cat family. Try not to remove all the animals in one visit, unless you feel that is necessary. A gradual withdrawal seems to produce the best results. Let the hoarder place the cats in the cages if they request and the cats do not appear to present any safety issues.

All during this time you should still be learning more about the occupant and surveying the living conditions. Your job does not end with the removal of the last cat. By the time the last cat is removed you should know your client as well as possible and be ready to speak with the rest of the "village".

The Village as Partners to Resolve the Hoarding Problem

In addition to animal control and law enforcement, your animal hoarding situation may also involve a public health issue, senior neglect, domestic, child neglect, building code violations, truancy, fire safety issues, and any of a host of issues, all of which the police may respond to and then pass information on to the proper authorities for follow-up. In this case the follow-up goes to animal control, another member of the "village" has now come into the picture. Animal control does their background investigation by going to the town hall and checking with the Health Department, Building Department, Senior Services, Tax Assessor—four more members of the "village" have become involved and we haven't even set foot back on the front steps of the address. It seems like the "village" is larger than we thought at first, but every single "villager" has a stake in this entire process.

Once animal control has done their background work at town hall it is now time to get on the phone to the local humane society, cat rescue group, S.P.C.A., and Animal Rescue League asking if anyone has been to this address on prior issues. Four more members of the "village" are now involved and they will probably reach out to even more people looking for information. The "village" is growing by leaps and bounds at an incredible rate and has more growth in its future. Don't forget to check with the local health center staff. The nurses and doctors may have some insight for you—more "villagers" coming to the center of town.

We have now completed all our preliminary checks for the focus of our investigation. By now quite a few members of the "village" have already become involved, and we are just now ready to return to the animal hoarder's front door. The communications process has been established because we did our homework correctly and removal of the animals is starting. Removal to the shelter and examination by a veterinarian involves more "villagers" becoming involved in the process. After three weeks of scheduled visits to the house the removal of cat number 117 finishes the task, or does it?

While we were there we ascertained that the animal hoarder is a life-long resident of the town and has no surviving family members to fall back on. The house needs repairs to its roof and gutters and the heating system is balky. She lives on a fixed income and has been spending the great majority of her money on feeding the cats and has neglected her own basic needs. Are we finished at the location or do we need to visit more "villagers"?

My recommended first stop would be to the Common Council, Board of Selectmen or Mayor's Office to find out about any programs available to assist the elderly when they are in this type of situation. They are also public officials, often voted into office, meaning that they are also stakeholders in the welfare of one of their constituents. Times are tight and the assistance programs available provide only minimal help in monetary aid. It could be a good time to talk with some local firefighters, not just about what the possible fire safety issues are, but many of them are involved in various building trades on their time off and may know of a carpenter's union or group that might be able to help with some low-cost roof or gutter repairs. It might not be a bad idea to contact a local church, youth group, or Boy Scout Troop—cleaning up the yard and trimming the bushes would make a great Eagle Project or Community Service idea for them.

Well I'm glad I live in a large "village" because we have certainly needed the help of a lot of residents. From a simple call from a neighbor we have traveled through schools, churches, the town hall, police station, firehouse, animal shelter, and a health center. Along the way we have interacted with elected officials, doctors, veterinarians, police officers, firefighters, tax collectors, clerks, shelter staff, carpenters, laborers, social workers, and youth of the community. And before we are all done we probably have the media in our future as well. And just think . . . we could have needed a lot more "villagers" and a whole lot more resources if the door had been slammed shut on us the first day.

The Importance of Working Together as a Team

Before I end I would like to address the problem of making agencies more fully aware of what hoarding is and the proper procedures to follow when facing these situations. Over the last ten years I have spoken to anyone who will listen about the importance of coordinated efforts by multiple agencies. No agency I have ever dealt with has unlimited funds at their fingertips. We are all out there, we are all trained, and we are all functioning, but do we function efficiently? Not if we are not working together as a community team.

Put aside your turf battles and funding squabbles and don't hide behind so-called privacy rules and boundaries. Sit down and talk about your agency's capabilities and make sure everyone at the table knows what each other's agency can do. I tell people with privacy rules they must adhere to that I don't want their information but I do want them to listen to my information so they can do their jobs better. If you can't put these things aside and work for the betterment of your constituents it might be time to look for a new "village" to take up residency. I am looking for a strong "village" with educated residents willing to help less fortunate residents overcome animal, health, safety, personal problems, housing issues, and the like. I teach formalized training sessions conducted by employers, schools, and universities. I speak at P.T.A., fraternal, or community meetings. These training lectures are conducted to help people recognize and act at an early phase in hoarding problem cycles, long before the collecting reaches crisis levels. The earlier action is taken to make the correction, the better opportunity there is of a positive outcome, and the lower the chance of repeat problems.

The most important point to get out of this is to build a cooperative partnership to problem-solve with animal hoarding and neglect problems in your community. There are many great resources available to educate agencies and organizations about how to develop a multi-agency partnership to deal with animal-related problems before they become a crisis. Begin by using the guidelines presented in Chapter Nine and the resources listed in Chapter Ten of this book. And then go out and form your Village!

Chapter Eight

Recognizing Red Flags and Finding Those Who Need Help

Much of this book thus far has been devoted to helping professionals recognize the red flags for the specific types of animal abuse that have been covered. This chapter will focus specifically on how to identify red flags, understand what they mean, their importance as one of the key tools for helping to stop animal suffering, and what to do with them once you have spotted them.

HOW TO RECOGNIZE RED FLAGS FOR ANIMAL ABUSE

Red flags are the signs that something may be amiss. In essence, red flags are a result of your gut instinct—that "feeling" or sense you get that something is not quite right. There is no rulebook for how to learn to develop your gut instinct. Seasoned professionals will tell you that the ability just develops over time. But we can tell you that the important ingredient in developing your ability to recognize red flags is to be attentive. Carefully listen, observe, and remember. Do things look and seem reasonable? Is there consistency between the person's explanations? Do the facts add up in a way they should? Over time, carefully attending to a potential animal abuser's words, intonation, body language, surroundings, and so on will allow you to become highly perceptive and more apt to spot the red flags readily.

WHEN IS A FLAG ICE COLD RATHER THAN RED-HOT?

There are no hard-fast rules for immediately confirming the thing you encountered that set off bells and whistles that something may be wrong will actually amount to anything. So you have identified something that might be a tip-off that animal abuse is occurring. Now what? To help you understand the gravity of red flags for potential animal abuse you are likely to encounter throughout your professional career, let's examine the word "potential" in terms of the red flags you have identified. . .

For decades now—starting many, many years prior to today's high security to detect terrorists—I have been a "red flag" for every manner of security officials. For reasons that have always baffled me (but have amused my friends and colleagues), since adolescence I have been the object of scrutiny in any situation where security is an issue. I was being screened, searched, followed, interrogated, and placed under surveillance years before it was customary to be wary of the public at large. As a graduate student crossing the Canadian border in the 1980's after a day of sightseeing, the searching of my person, personal belongings, and entire car was so severe I swore I would never return. (I since have and to my relief only had to endure a lengthy verbal interrogation.)

In the days when I shopped at malls it was a regular event to have security with their "eye on me," speaking on walkie-talkies and following me around the racks of clothes. And, lest you think that maybe I am some closet shoplifter, the same has been true in places of public gatherings like music concerts, sporting events, comedy shows and ethnic festivals. In the days before intensive security at airports I was predictably pulled aside and patted down, asked questions, my bags gone through. Since increased airport security it has moved to the level of absurd. In one recent visit from New York to San Francisco I was pulled aside, patted down, had my purse and luggage searched and told to remove my blazer, my socks and my boots a total of six times—in one trip!

Over the years it has become clear that the level of suspicion sent my way surpasses the statistical odds. There must be something that is raising attention. So what are these "red flags" that security is seeing? I doubt it is my physical appearance. I am a small, white female. Always have been. So there's no claiming that minority status, a large, menacing size, or gender is sending them signals. I have no tattoos, no wild hairdo and my dress is usually restricted to blue jeans, nondescript shirt and a blazer. Pretty modest stuff. I learned years ago to always remove my sunglasses whenever security was around and I am conscious not to do anything overt that might raise the stakes even higher than they frequently are.

There seems to be no logical explanation. Unless, as it has been suggested, what security professionals are "reading" is my attitude. And herein lies my point: Professionals have to be careful to remember that red flags are just that—the *potential* for something more. As veterinarians can tell you there are any number of ailments and conditions that can cause animals to look as though they have been abused or neglected. Hormonal imbalances and skin conditions can cause cats and dogs to lose their fur, even to the point of baldness. Birds may develop nervous conditions where they literally pluck away all of their feathers. Arthritis may cause older dogs and cats to limp. Aging may cause poor vision and flinching to occur. Companion animals may be nervous, anxious souls (some are even placed on tranquilizers) and these behaviors may have little or nothing to do with their current family environment. In addition, there is any number of inheritable and age-related conditions that to the untrained observer may look like intentional harm or neglect has occurred to animals. In other words, sometimes a cigar is just a cigar. And moving forward with conviction before there is sufficient evidence can be very harmful to everyone involved—including the animals.

TAKE YOUR RED FLAGS TO A CONFERENCE

OK, you have learned how to listen to your inner voice, you have made your observations, asked all the right questions and recognized more than one red flag that says there is the potential for animal abuse or neglect going on. But now we have told you need to be careful. So what is a person to do with the red flags he or she has recognized? This is where the members of your multidisciplinary partnership come into play. If some activity has crossed your radar in enough ways to raise suspicion—even if it is a low-level of suspicion—now is the time to run it past your colleagues. This is precisely why it is important to have professionals from a wide variety of backgrounds on your team. Is the domestic violence shelter manager aware of any violence going on at the household in question? Has the ACO made any prior visits to that address? Law enforcement? What can the veterinarian on your team tell you about such-and-such symptoms? Has anyone from child and family services or elderly services visited the address before? If so, what can they tell you? In short, consider your red flags as indicators for the potential of animal abuse and then take that potential to a meeting. If there does not seem to be enough support among your colleagues that concern for animal abuse is merited, at the very least put the individual on a "watch." If there are any more red flags in the future, on behalf of the potential voiceless victims, move forward with your concerns. If over time nothing else surfaces, however, let it go. Sometimes the shoeless, sock-less girl being patted down in the airport has a smirk on her face for a reason.

WHEN THE FLAGS ARE RED HOT

Of course many of the indicator flags you will encounter are red-hot obvious. So obvious, in fact, you will wonder where everyone else was and why no one had taken any action yet. At FIREPAW we see a lot of these sorts of red flags. We host an international listserv that offers our members a daily online magazine of all the latest in the world of animals. We have been posting media reports of animal abuse—and the updated outcomes—for five years now. Every week there is at least one media report of some horrific act of animal cruelty somewhere in the U.S. and we too wonder, 'Where were the teachers? The parents? The neighbors? Didn't anyone see the warning signs? Or, did they see them and either not know what to do or choose not to get involved?'

Now of course one could argue that we see the reports of animal abuse after they have already ended in tragedy. Perhaps, one could argue, it may not be so easy to spot the potential for animal abuse before it actually happens. In some cases this may be true. As we have seen in the preceding chapters though, in most cases there are plenty of red flags a' waving well in advance of tragedy. A case of red flags missed happened just recently. . .

This winter I had the opportunity to meet with a group of children for a talk on animal abuse. About 30 minutes into my presentation about children witnessing and perpetrating acts of cruelty against animals a seven-year old boy raised his hand and asked, "Is *this* animal abuse?" He then proceeded to tell the story about his best friend who found an injured baby bird on the playground of his elementary school and began pummeling the bird with rocks repeatedly until it was dead. When the boy was asked whether he told anyone what he had witnessed his friend do he said that he had told his parents.

"What did they say about the story you told them?"

"Nothing."

"Did any adult see your friend stone the baby bird to death?"

"Yes. My teacher who was watching us on the playground."

"And what did your teacher do or say about what happened?"

"She didn't say anything."

This story probably plays out with a fair degree of frequency all over the country. To the professional who has received education about animal abuse the red flags are obvious. After having read the previous chapters you now know what to look for and what is likely to happen if you do not take action. But to those people who have not been educated about the antecedents and consequences of animal abuse or about the red flags and what they should do when they see them, the ability to help by using early warning signs is lost on them.

This is why it is crucial to educate the general public and other profession-als about the information you have learned in this book. It should be one of the primary goals of the community partnership you create to stop animal abuse. As my coauthor will reiterate later in this chapter, public education is as easy as creating an informational brochure. Nowadays with computers, brochures can be created easily at a very affordable price. Your brochure should include some of the key red flags people are likely to encounter and contact information for the various agencies and organizations they can call to report what they have witnessed or heard. These brochures should be dis-seminated to places where the general public and other professionals can be sure to see them. Send some to school administrators, asking them to be sure their teachers see them. Place them inside veterinarian offices and animal clinics, public libraries, town hall, and other places the public visits. Once you begin to educate your community you actually make your own job far easier and more effective. Now there are not only the members of your part-nership of professionals working to identify and stop animal abuse but the eyes and ears of many others who will now know what to look for and who to contact.

TALES FROM THE STREET: REAL LIFE STORIES FOR RECOGNIZING RED FLAGS AND FINDING THOSE WHO NEED HELP

How do we find those people and animals who are in need of our assistance? They don't advertise in the daily newspapers or have paid television ads run-ning. They don't drive up and down streets calling out phone numbers and web addresses for people to contact them. So how can we reach those who need us most? We are born with the tools we need, they are part of our orig-inal package, included as standard equipment upon our delivery to this earth. What are they? They are our five senses: sight, smell, hearing, feeling, and tasting. I'll go over all of these as they relate to animal cruelty, and then I will tell you about the all-important sixth sense.

Now, just how do these great tools fit in to the overall scheme of helping an-imal victims? Let's take each one individually, starting with sight. If you see something that doesn't look right, and you give it closer inspection (very im-portant), then you are using one of your senses, sight. If you smell odors un-pleasant enough to raise your awareness you are using your sense of smell. If you are hearing stories, or rumors about a location or occupants, or when in close proximity, hear abnormal levels or styles of conversation coming from a certain address, you are using your sense of hearing. Your next sense may be activated almost unknowingly, your sense of feeling. You may pat a longhaired dog or cat and feel a rack of bones hidden under the fur; your sense of feeling has been activated. I talk about the last sense in a somewhat liberal form, your sense of taste. You may meet someone, stop somewhere, or see something that just leaves a sour taste in your mouth. And last, but by far not least is my favorite, "sixth sense"—your sense of intuition and thought. Without having a sense about what you have experienced and giving it all thought, none of the original five senses would accomplish a thing. If you encounter any of what we just mentioned above and gave them no thought it would be as though they never occurred and nothing would develop from the experiences. Now that we have used one or more of our senses where do we go next?

Two of the most effective means of successfully recognizing and stopping animal cruelty in your community are collaboration and communication. We have spoken about these two concepts many times prior. They are the cornerstones, the basic building blocks, of any successful program of this type. We need to talk to each other; we need to overcome the hesitation to exchange information. One of the biggest stumbling blocks always seems to be confidentiality and who is bound by it. Get over it folks, it does not control our lives, we don't need to know each other's last little bit of information. I know there are a lot of agencies that have to work under confidentiality confines, it's fine with me, and I have no problem with that. I want to pass information to the correct agency for their follow-up or their needed contribution to the overall efforts of Link-UP; I don't have to know all their secrets. I need their help, and I need it in a timely manner. Period.

The second big factor is communication . . . talk to one other. If I run into a situation that needs a special agency's input I go to them. I seek them out, I don't wait for them to call me, no one has a crystal ball, and those other agencies don't know what I have run into. If we all sat back and waited for someone else to do it, or show up, nothing in this field would ever be accomplished. If you are having trouble visualizing this take a minute and ask yourself, 'why do all the other agencies have phones'? Is it so they can call friends and relatives or is it so they can conduct proper business procedures, including talking to other professionals?

Some individuals I speak to look at me like I have two heads when I say these things. Why? We don't function in a vacuum. We are not secret agents. Our aim is to help an animal and human victim in need and we are certainly not so highly trained and capable that we don't need help from time to time. Stop for a moment and recall some of the cases I have described throughout this book. If there is anyone out there who can handle any one of those cases without someone else's help please contact me right away . . . I've been looking for you for a long time.

Communication can also prevent major blunders on the part of agencies that don't bother to check with someone else. There is nothing more embarrassing to professionals than to show up at a location all geared up and ready to go, and find out the situation was resolved two days prior. In addition it also exposes you to the very real threat of harassment on the part of the individual that was the focus of your investigation. To make it easy to understand, it would be like raiding a drug house two days after the D.E.A. had already served a search warrant and made the arrest and drug seizure. Talk to each other, it can avoid a lot of problems down the road.

Okay, so let's follow an actual case from start to finish. As you read along watch for things I just mentioned. . .

You are a social worker for a local children's social service agency in a major city. It's Monday morning and you have just sat down at your overcrowded desk with this week's new caseload. Not a good way to start your week, especially when you consider how much money you don't earn weekly. (By the way, I'm not picking on social workers, I just know what their work life consists of because I've dealt with so many of them.) As you are trying to place files on your desk in a spot not already filled, your supervisor appears with a file in hand. "I wanted to give you this report for the Child at Risk Hot Line. It's in your area," says the supervisor who then walks away. 'Thank you,' you mutter to yourself, 'like I need more to do.' You pick up the complaint folder and read: 'Children are living in a house with dogs!' Yeah, well, you think to yourself, so what? We don't *do* dogs. The complaint gets placed back on a heap of files and you continue working on your phone messages. Later something does not feel right and you return to the complaint about the children at risk with dogs. Opening the folder you start to read the report. It appears from the report that the police responded to the address for a barking dog problem late at night and observed children living in a house. A house, it seems, that has been the source of an exceptional amount of complaints to the police. Reading further it seems that the majority of the complaints have been animal-related but the children always seemed to be present no matter what the time of arrival by the officers.

You recheck the Child at Risk slip and see a callback number for the complainant and decide to give it a try. You dial the number and wait, five or six rings and finally a woman answers. You explain who you are and the woman says abruptly, "That house has too many dogs and the kids are never attended to correctly. I know. I have kids of my own." You ask for more specifics and she says, "Come look for yourself, you'll see what I mean." She now says that she has to go and she hangs up the phone. You re-read the paperwork in the folder in case you missed something but still don't see too much as far as the children go. You think to yourself, 'I have a complaint, I don't see much on the surface, but I feel something is going on.' It's decidedly time to talk with your supervisor.

A few minutes later you are standing in front of your supervisor who looks up and says, "Make it good. I'm buried this morning." You recite the information you have and finish by saying, "What do you think?" The answer is, "Hey, we have enough to do. It only says dogs and kids live in the same house, nothing more. We have more important things to take care of."

That answers your question. Or does it?

You walk back to your desk still having that funny feeling in the back of your mind, but for now it's filed. Later that afternoon at lunch you ask your co-worker for an opinion about the dogs and kids information. She thinks for a minute and then says, "Remember that conference we went to last year where they talked about the animal/domestic/child abuse Link?"

You wonder if you still have any of that paperwork from the conference and whether you held on to the phone numbers they had given to call for help.

Thoughts begin to flood back into your mind about what the speakers talked about at that conference . . . about the importance of seeing things that reveal other things, hooking up with other agencies, not letting things slide by, not ever trying to go it alone. I hope that stuff is still in my bottom drawer, you think as you head back to your desk.

Once back at your desk you discover the conference paperwork where you had filed it away last year. After ten minutes of review you uncover the best local number to call. It's an investigator at the local humane society who also spoke at the conference. You dial the number and while it is ringing you are hoping he still works there. A male voice answers the phone and identifies himself as the person you wanted. You tell him about attending the conference and remembered what was explained about the importance of reaching out to other agencies when in doubt. You tell him you hope he didn't mind the call. He assures you that he is more than happy to help.

Just as you begin to speak and tell him the reason you called you suddenly think, 'OH NO! Red lights are flashing, sirens are going off, confidentiality rules control the day, and I can't say anything, DAMN! Now what do I do?' You start to stutter and stammer and feel like a real dope.

"Uh . . . I can't tell you anything."

"Relax," says the man's voice. "You can't tell me anything, but I don't need anything more than a call about an animal situation and an address. Remember what we talked about at the conference? Confidentiality rules don't have to be violated. I don't need any more than an address. I'm concerned with helping the animals and from the sound of what you've told me that seems to be the major issue. We don't need to exchange any more than that."

You think back to what your supervisor said, "It only says dogs and kids live in the same house." You quickly look through all the paperwork you have again. All it says is kids and dogs live at the same location. No accusations of neglect, abuse, cruelty, or anything else other than the fact that kids and dogs live in the same house.

"We'll take it from here and I'll let you know if I come up with anything that needs your involvement," says the humane officer.

"Can I call you back and see what happened?" you ask.

"Sure no problem. We'll try and get by the location later this afternoon. Why don't you give me a call tomorrow morning around 9:30, here at the office number?"

"Okay, thanks," you respond and you hang up feeling better already. 'I hope this is what they meant at that conference when they said reach out to other agencies when you hear something that isn't in your realm of responsibility' you think to yourself. 'Well, at least I didn't disregard it or bury it in my pile of paperwork.'

You can't wait for the clock to reach 9:30 the next morning. You are eager to know what happened but still a little uneasy about whether you did the right thing by making the phone call. The clock finally drags it's way around to 9:30 and you are quickly on the phone. It seems like the ringing goes on forever before someone finally picks up the phone.

"Hello," says the voice from the day before. You identify yourself and he says, "Glad you called back. I wanted to thank you for yesterday. You did the right thing and helped us a lot."

You breathe a sigh of relief and ask, "What happened?"

"That address you gave us ended up as the house of someone we've been looking for. We had a previous tip about dog fighting in that area but could not find it. It seems this is one of the main players, but it ended for him yesterday afternoon. He's been arrested, his dogs are confiscated and they are being treated for bite wounds. And you may want to watch your incoming reports. We filed a report out on the three little kids living there along with their mother who is a domestic violence victim. All three kids and the mom have now been relocated to a safe shelter. The police took them there yesterday because the house was deemed unfit for habitation by the health department inspectors. I would like to personally thank you for your initial phone call. You made a big difference in the lives of both the animals and the humans by making it."

As you hang up the phone you don't know whether to yell from anger or cry with happiness. Your emotions are understandably mixed. What if I just said, 'Its only kids and dogs living in a house' and had let it go? What would I have allowed to continue? You think to yourself. What if I had said I cannot call because of confidentiality rules and never picked up the phone? What if I had come back to my desk and stuck the paperwork on the bottom of the pile because we had more important things to handle?

The 'what ifs' could go on for a long time, but they needn't. The red flag of warning had been recognized and action had been taken. The social worker didn't try and do it alone. She reached out to others . . . the person that made the original call to the Hot Line, her supervisor, her co-worker, and finally, to an outside agency—the humane society. She kept trying once she felt that something wasn't right, she didn't give up or say to herself, 'Someone else will do it.'

The social worker did not violate her confidentiality rules, but at the same time did her job by helping out someone in need. Let's do a little review of the entire incident: How many of our senses were used? Sight, someone in the neighborhood saw something that didn't seem right. And the social worker seeing the report had the same reaction. Smell, the complaining neighbor stated the property had bad odors (you will recall the house was condemned as uninhabitable).

Hearing, the social worker listened to the complainant's remarks during her telephone call. Taste, the overall condition of the incident certainly left a bad taste in someone's mouth. And last but not least, the sixth sense . . . someone used her intuition and gave it some thought, they didn't say, 'That's a shame,' and keep on going. The social worker and the complainant both thought about what their senses were relaying to them and acted on the conclusion that something was wrong at the address in question.

Next we get into the communication part of the scenario. Plenty of communication here, from the Hot Line, to the supervisor, to the co-worker, to the humane group—plenty of people talking with one another, keeping the communication pipeline open until it reached the proper point. The communication could have been cut off at many points along the way, but luckily it wasn't. It kept momentum, moving from person to person, until it reached its goal.

Collaboration now kicks into gear as a result of that ongoing communication. How many agencies and people were involved along the way? There was the original phone caller, and how about the report the social worker received in the folder? It came from someone, too. The social worker spoke with her supervisor, she spoke with her co-worker, and she called the humane agency and spoke with the officer. The humane agency responded to the address about a dog complaint. The police department responded at the request of the humane agency. The building department responded at the request of the police department. Animal control officers may very well have responded to assist with removal of the animals. Emergency medical services may have responded to examine the mother and children before they went to the battered woman's shelter. Domestic violence advocates would have interviewed the woman at the shelter. Counselors may have worked with the children. There could have been any number of individual professionals and agencies involved in this incident before it was completely over and done with. So here we have a social worker on a Monday morning conducting a complete mobilization of multiple agencies. All of which came about by being able to see the "red flag" of warning and knowing what to do about it.

This is a good point to talk about another powerful tool. I am speaking about, "gut instinct." The number one scenario in which I would never make a move without consulting someone with a seasoned gut instinct or "sixth sense" is anything involving a domestic violence case. I can go to a scene and see abused, mistreated animals, neglected children, and a female victim, but to maximize my fact-finding I have to look at the same scenario using my sixth sense before any decisions are made. My belief in the importance of using my gut instinct was fortified when I went through the training for the Child Witness to Violence Project back in the early 90's. The instructors were all extremely talented social workers and they taught me a new way to view what I had been looking at for years . . . crime scenes, call locations, anywhere people required assistance from the police. I was instructed to REALLY see what were there . . . the children, the victims, the surroundings, and the entire scene. Of course there is no harder group to teach than police officers because we know all the answers, but I finished that training with an entirely new understanding of *really* seeing people and places. The Child Witness to Violence Project was quite possibly the most important training I ever received in my law enforcement career. I never saw things in the same light after that and I now fully see everything there is to observe.

When the time came for me to put the first outreach efforts of the Link-UP Program to the test I was accompanied by a very special type of professional, Aimee Thompson. She was working for the Child Witness to Violence Project at the time and previously had spent time in Palestine working with children. Knowing that she was no stranger to violence and dangerous situations I felt she would be the person to talk to about my plans. I had in the back of my mind a thought to develop a flyer that could be utilized as a handout when doing follow-up visits to prior animal cruelty investigation locations. Aimee and I put together a flyer that was entitled, "Do You Know a Child Who Cries at Night?" The flyer contained some information about child abuse and domestic violence issues on the inside. On the back cover was a listing of agencies, churches, and assistance groups that were available to contact for additional information or help. With the flyers in hand and a list of the top one hundred "hot spots" compiled, it was time to hit the streets. I won't get into the actual cases here, but I will say that the flyers were accepted in a much more positive way than either of us had ever imagined. I will tell you that the program was a success and the services offered in the flyer were utilized by some of the people we visited.   What is all of this meant to convey? The importance of collaboration in resolving violence situations involving animals and humans . . . we worked for two different agencies. And the importance of communication . . . we talked over our thoughts and ideas before anything was formalized and we were able to reach far more people because of it. And finally, the importance of using your sixth sense to help animals and people suffering from abuse. I could see what the suffering of animals looked like. I had learned to look beyond the obvious signs I had initially been trained to see and observed so much more. The bottom line is to really find that "red flag" indicator of a problem, and to do that you need to learn to hone your secret weapon, the power of the sixth sense!

How do you start to develop your sixth sense? Start by listening closely. For instance, calls will also provide you a little head start as what to expect or look for when arriving at locations with suspected animal abuse. You certainly don't want to arrive at the location of an alleged serious violation and make opening statements that will result in the door being slammed in your face or putting an innocent victim in harm's way when you leave. Try and visualize what you are being told before you even leave your office. It is often much easier to form images in your mind while still in a neutral location with no elevated stress levels to overcome. This doesn't mean to let your mind run wild either. Don't overthink a situation; use only the information that was provided.

Now bring in the communication and collaboration aspects. Once that call has been made, do your homework; find out if the location has a past history with any local public safety or humane agencies. If children are mentioned, check with local school authorities to see if they attend area schools. Give some thought as to what additional agencies may need to be utilized before this incident is brought to a close. Don't be afraid to talk it over with co-workers and supervisors, get their input, what do they think? Fully understand to the best of your ability just who and what you are going to be dealing with. Don't be in a hurry to jump into a situation with both feet if you don't know where they will land. Someone has given you information—it is incumbent upon you to develop it as well as possible. You may be investigating a bona fide incident or you could be dealing with someone making a spite call as a way to seek revenge for some unknown reason.

Finally, when you do knock on that door, don't arrive with an attitude; offer some help before you make a decision that dramatic measures are needed. That complaint about poor living conditions for animals and children at the location could stem from cultural differences. The first step you make should be from an educational angle as opposed to one of strictly enforcing criminal codes. An immigrant family may only be doing what was natural in their native country and have no criminal intent at all. You may also be dealing with someone who has multiple pressing issues in their daily life and as a result things look much worse than they actually are. Perhaps with just a little help they can get back on track. Don't make a hasty decision about an individual or a situation without thoroughly investigating. Some fences are much harder to mend than others after the damage has been done.

Recap of the Essentials

Now let's go through one of the scenarios I use in actual training sessions to determine whether a "red flag" is being waved and whether the professional is recognizing it and making all the right moves. The case is real and it came to a happy conclusion thanks to someone who used his or her five senses along with that wonderful gift of gut instinct. . .

It is Tuesday morning and you are at the veterinary clinic where you work. There are four veterinarians and seven veterinary technicians who staff the practice. A tall, well-dressed woman in her mid-30's enters the waiting room accompanied by a girl of about 12 years of age and a boy approximately 10 years old. You observe that the woman is carrying a cat. You ask if you can help her and she replies that the cat is injured and she would like the doctor to look at it. You ask her if she has been to the clinic before and she replies, "Yes." You ask for her last name and when you bring it up on the screen of your computer you observe from the address that she lives in an affluent area of an adjoining town. You proceed to fill in the blanks on the computer screen to facilitate proper treatment of the animal.

The woman tells you that the cat, which is the family pet, appeared at the door this morning crying and limping. One of the veterinarians is available so you bring the woman and the cat into the examining room and ask the children to wait in the reception area. Once in the examining room you ask the woman to hand you the cat. As she extends her arms you observe what appears to be bruises or rope burns on both of the woman's wrists as well as what appears to be small burn marks on her left forearm. The woman sees you looking and quickly pulls her arms down to her sides, almost dropping the cat. Another one of the vet-techs comes into the room to help and you return to the reception area. You observe the children sitting in the waiting area and you approach them to reassure them of the cat's condition. As you start talking to them they become very stiff in their actions, avoid making eye contact, and their verbal responses are limited to one or two words. The most you find out is that they moved to town two years ago.

You continue about your work and about forty-five minutes later the mother comes out of the examining room with the cat, which now has a cast on its leg due to a fracture. The woman pays cash for her bill and as she turns to leave the little girl asks, "Are you going to yell at daddy about Mittens?" The woman gives the girl a stern look, and says curtly, "Shut your mouth and get out that door!" After they leave the clinic you discretely bring up their record on the computer and find that they have been to the clinic eight times over the past eighteen months with injured animals—all of who were suffering from apparent traumas. Is something going on here? Who do you talk to? What do you tell them? Is it your job to get involved? Are you crying wolf? Is it all just a coincidence? What do you know about anything like this?

So here you are, "red flags" waving all around you. You know that you would never be able to live with yourself if you didn't do something. But where do you go? What do you do first? Should you call the police? What can you tell them? You have no concrete evidence, just a lot of suspicions. They would most likely tell you to stop watching Animal Planet and leave police work to the trained professionals, and anyway, they may add, it's only a cat.

It's time for our five senses to kick in, what did you see? The apparent injuries to the woman's arms and possible burn marks. Additionally, this is during very warm weather and the woman had on a long sleeve blouse of heavy material pulled all the way down and buttoned at the collar and both cuffs. So your sense of sight has provided some good preliminary information regarding the woman's possible physical injuries. Did your sense of feel get involved? Did you carry the cat into the examining room? How did the cat feel to you? He was a little on the thin side, very nervous when held and he acted like he was uncomfortable from more than just a leg injury. On to the next sense, your sense of hearing. Did the woman's answers to questions asked make sense or seem out of sync with the information presented? What about her reaction to the girl's comment about telling daddy? How about the answers the children provided and the manner in which they were made when you talked with them in the reception area? It certainly didn't seem like the normal reaction one would expect from children of this age group. Now let's return to your sense of sight. How did the children physically react when spoken to? Most children that age like to be included in conversation and have outgrown the avoidance of eye contact. How many ten- and twelve-year-olds sit stiffly when not in the presence of a parent, strict or otherwise, especially when in a relaxed setting such as the reception area? Remember they are not strangers to the clinic; they have made many prior trips. You're really starting to use that sixth sense for this, aren't you? So many things seem out of place or not fitting into a pattern of normal living for a family, especially one from a fairly affluent neighborhood.

You're doing your background work now. You already looked at the history and saw some major problems glaring back from that screen. You have enough doubt to justify more searching into this entire incident. What's the next step? Some discrete inquiries with your co-workers could provide some more light on the subject. Has anyone dealt with them before? Do they remember anything unusual about the woman or the children? Do they remember any unusual statements? Did anyone seem injured other than the animal? Do you have any close relationships with employees of neighboring clinics or humane groups who you may be able to make inquiries to about the family? Yours may not be the only clinic they visit. Do you know anyone who works at a local domestic violence program who you can talk with about mom who can give you suggestions on how to possibly approach her in the future? Any friends or confidants who may work in the local school system that the children possibly attend? Do you have a close friend or relative who works in law enforcement in the town they reside?

The entire list of possible people to communicate with has been established. Now, what do you do with it? Some of the people on the list are bound under confidentiality rules, but that is okay because you just want to relay information, not receive it.

You do ascertain that yours is not the only clinic visited by the family. You also find out that accidents have been happening to animals for longer than the last eighteen months. Another fact discovered is that the family has moved a number of times over the last six years. The injured animals have consisted of smaller breeds of dogs, cats, gerbils, hamsters, and on one occasion, a bird. The first incident uncovered in your search was five years prior and was for an injured puppy recently adopted from a shelter. Now new potential contacts suddenly come into view—local animal shelters and possible adoption records. Two days later you have a list of six animal shelters, all involved in prior adoptions to this same family over a four-year period. You now have all of your ducks in a row. It's time to talk with the right people and present your findings.

Your local humane law enforcement agency is contacted by phone. The scenario has been explained to them in full and you have further substantiated your suspicions with the veterinary technician's report.

So now let's go through everything that follows. . . The officer from the law enforcement division of the local humane agency responded to the clinic that afternoon and met with the veterinary technician who placed the call. She presented all of the facts gathered and was informed that it certainly was enough evidence to conduct an investigation. In fact, the law enforcement officer was rarely presented with so much information at the start of a case. The veterinary technician was asked if she would be willing to speak to other investigators as the case progressed, which she agreed to.

The law enforcement officer proceeded to conduct an investigation. After collaborating with local police agencies and the state attorney's office, he compiled enough evidence to request a court complaint to be issued for the owner of the animals in question. A court hearing was held and following that an actual trial for animal neglect/cruelty was conducted. As a result of the trial it was revealed that the father in the case was, in fact, injuring the animals and the woman as part of an ongoing domestic violence situation. It was also revealed that the father was addicted to cocaine causing frequent job terminations, multiple changes of housing locations due to the employment situation, and violent acts of cruelty directed toward his family members. The father was sentenced to a term in jail and mandatory drug counseling upon his release. The woman was to receive treatment through a battered woman's program and the children were also placed in a program to help get their lives back in order. The veterinary technician, though required to talk with people from other agencies as part of the follow-up investigation and prosecution, never had to appear in court. The initial amount of information she provided the humane law enforcement officer was enough to give a good strong basis for her feelings.

Now let's stop a minute and look back at what we have covered. During the past two real-life stories we saw two people from different backgrounds seeing the "red flags" of warning and making the proper moves to affect differences in the lives of both animals and humans. We also touched briefly on the importance of approaching problems in the correct manner so that progress can be made.

Tools to Assist You to Recognize and Act on Red Flags of Animal Abuse

A key tool to help you in your effort to stop animal cruelty is an educational/informational flyer or brochure. Flyers and brochures can provide the facts you forget to mention while talking with the people you are trying to reach. I carry flyers from a number of different agencies that offer various types of information about juvenile fire-setting, animal abuse, domestic violence, rabies prevention, licensing requirements, even proper feeding of animals. These items are packaged together to prevent people from thinking I am focusing on just a single issue. More than one type of information can also allow the conversation to continue for a longer period of time on first visits.

The first visit is when you want to try and use as many of your five senses as possible, and the longer time you have to do it the more success you will have. If you're there about a dog issue, it doesn't mean you can't look at the kids. If you're there about a housing code issue it doesn't mean you can't take a good look at the people and animals who live there. You don't even have to be at an address for any official reason, it can be as simple as walking by a location. You may be out walking for some exercise and pass a yard that has a dog tied on a short leash, with no visible shelter or water available. The dog may look fine or it could look like a rack of bones, it makes no difference. You've seen enough to justify a call to the local humane agency. A dog needs shelter and water and, while it is preferable that dogs are never tethered long-term, at the very least, dogs must have a long enough leash to move around. You've just been handed that "red flag" and the next move is yours.

Now what about dogs who live in apartments? Is it possible that one of the dogs living in an apartment never gets taken outside for exercise or relief? I have seen a number of these situations and some of them have involved fairly large animals. I had one case where the occupant of an apartment was using a spare bedroom basically as a kennel for five fairly large dogs. He was breeding and selling the pups. Neighbors on both sides knew he had the dogs because they could hear and smell them but they never bothered to call authorities. Needless to say, the apartment was condemned for habitation after we removed the dogs and the occupant. And how did we get the necessary information? A worker for the local utility company called after he refused to enter the apartment for a service call. In addition to the suffering of those particular animals, what effect do you think that situation had on the next dog owner who tried to rent an apartment in the building?

It is important to mention again that the situation will not always involve some kind of criminal intent. It could be a matter of cultural differences. I worked for ten years in an area of the city in which people from many different cultures resided. It was a very enjoyable experience for me, as I never had to travel far for an educational opportunity to see firsthand how other cultures lived. I could pass from one country to another simply by walking through the streets of the district I was assigned. I learned a tremendous amount of wonderful things. I also saw things that I needed to help people to correct. Just because something is done one way in the United States does not mean that new residents will automatically adapt immediately. Old customs die hard and I personally would not want to see many of them disappear. There are, however, a few that definitely need modification and some that need to stop all together. My main involvement was animal-related issues concerning the proper care of domestic pets. There are a number of ways people may treat their pets that is just unacceptable in our country. Sometimes, especially if the people have recently arrived from a different country with different customs, they will need to be educated about the appropriate way to treat companion animals. Needing to be educated does not equate with criminal intent.

Not all cases require a response of multiple agencies to affect change. Remember that while red flags may appear on the horizon the storm may be much less than first anticipated. Encountering situations such as these do allow you to breath a little easier, but there is still work to be done before you consider the case closed. I'll let you in on a local secret: Education, Direction, and Discipline or EDD. It's our secret weapon for approaching a problem while still maintaining a good relationship with the suspect and the community. EDD is a great way to reach your objectives while continuing to maintain good communication with the neighborhood. Any time we respond to a location we always approach with the intention of offering assistance. I can't repeat often enough how important it is to open your conversation with an offer of assistance if it is needed. An unsubstantiated accusation thrown at someone when they open the door is definitely not the way to start the day. Believe me, I have worked with certain agencies that feel they need to introduce themselves by informing people how long they can go to jail for as their initial opening statement. I always thought it was a good idea to introduce myself and provide a business card if available, but this group certainly didn't agree. Needless to say I limit my interaction with them to the bare minimum, as I don't like doors slammed in my face and I don't see how it helps to stop animal suffering. There is a time to be forceful but it isn't when you knock on the door for the very first time at what could be much less than a life-threatening situation.

Now let's get back to EDD, step one Education . . . not everyone knows how to care for an animal properly, not everyone is a good parent from the beginning, not everyone has the same mental capacities, not everyone is from the same cultural background. Take the time to find out what the situation is. The best way to do that is to establish open communication. An offer of help does wonders in this area. Have those flyers or brochures with you that we spoke about earlier. Make sure the person understands what you are saying; communication won't be too effective if you both speak different languages. Once you have this sorted out, discuss the reason you are there in general conversation. Once we have the door open and conversation started it is time to steer the individual slowly towards your appointed target. "Do you have any animals? You do? Oh that's good, what kind are they? Can I see them?" You're on the right track. If their animals include a dog ask, "How old is he? Does he have his rabies shots? No! Oh, you have to be careful, rabies can be a serious health threat to humans and animals." We can get into the fact that it is the law later, but right now we are still strengthening our communication. The conversation can go on to include licensing requirements, fees, when it needs completion, and so on. And remember, during all of this conversation you have also been using your other senses to make a better determination as to what it is you are really seeing.

When all of this is over and done with, you should have a feel for the actual circumstances at the location. Hopefully you have seen the animal, child, and the woman who were the focus of your visit. You have presented your message and information in a manner that is understood by the occupants. I also make a date for a return visit to just check and see how everyone is doing. At this point you have completed the Education phase of the EDD program.

During the ten years we have used this system, eighty-five percent of our complaints have been completed at this level. Then again, what if we go back for the follow-up visit and things are no better than they were on the first visit? It is time for step two: "Direction." This is where your partnerships start to become very important. You certainly don't need to run off to the local courthouse and start filing applications for complaints. The court does not need to build its statistics; they have enough cases already without your help. So where do you get some "Direction"? How about an animal control hearing or a local mediation board? Time to find out what your jurisdiction offers in the form of hearings. I encounter people all the time who are not even aware of what they have available in this area to assist them. Remember, you have to know what tools are available for your use to be effective, but please find out what they are before you start something. There is nothing worse than to think you can do something, start the ball rolling and find out later that you can't finish what you started.

We are very lucky in Boston because we have a dedicated Hearing Officer, Sergeant Charles Rudack, of Boston Animal Control to conduct the hearings. I have seen him render some very unique decisions after listening to cases that would easily have tripped up the "Wisdom of Solomon." The hearings are comparable to a mediation session, as both sides get to be heard, and the use of an attorney is not needed. The majority of the time both parties reach a mutual agreement and don't require a written decision handed down by the Hearing Officer. The Hearing Officer's decisions can be appealed to a local Clerk Magistrate of the Court within ten days if it is not acceptable to all the parties involved. We have now solved ninety-five percent of our problems by utilizing the first two levels of the EDD Program. Your local jurisdiction may have similar types of hearings available or some other form of legal recourse available. But you should look into it before there is a problem.

Now, what about the rest of the problems, you ask? An arrest made at the scene is a rare occurrence. A much more standard outcome is a little help offered, some educational guidance, a follow-up visit and things are corrected. Some of the time you are going to see things that need immediate action far above an offer of assistance. This is where we end the Mr. Nice Guy conversation and take control. It does not happen often, but when it does you need to make the right move, and make it right away.

Of course an alternative scenario to those discussed here is that the "red flag" is ignored by the professionals involved, things get worse not better, no one becomes aware, and sooner or later a tragedy of some type results. "Red Flags" do not always indicate a hurricane; they also mean small craft advisories and storm warnings. They are just what they are meant to be: indicators of *potential* problems brewing on the horizon. A prudent individual takes notice of the warnings and reacts correctly. The environment you live in depends on you and those around you. When you see or become aware of something that does not seem right it is your responsibility as a professional to make the right move.

I hope this 'tales from the street' segment has increased everyone's understanding of "red flags" as real world indicators of potential suffering to animals and humans in your community, the proper way to react when you become aware of them, and the importance of maintaining proper perspective when setting out to investigate the legitimacy of those red flags.

A Final Note: Sometimes the Best Tool for Stopping Animal Abuse is One That is Outside of the Box

The final lesson when it comes to stopping animal cruelty is that the obvious solution may not always be the best one. Sometimes you have to dig around in your bag of tricks to find the best solution. Think on your feet and look around at all the resources you have available. Remember, no matter what your profession, when it comes to helping animal victims of abuse, collaboration, communication and your own gut-instinct or sixth sense are the best items you have in your toolbox.

Chapter Nine

Partnering and Seeking Solutions for Abused Animals

So far we have learned about the magnitude of animal abuse, the key antecedents and consequences, the profiles of the primary perpetrators, and why it is critical we all begin to recognize and speak up for these silent victims. It is now time for some practical, pragmatic, real-world tools and strategies for seeking solutions to stop the abuse directed at animals in your community. Based on the knowledge gathered from decades of clinical, research, consulting and fieldwork experience this chapter will begin by discussing traditional obstacles to resolving animal abuse problems (such as problems with lack of agency and community support, inappropriate priorities, resistance, ignorance, lack of adequate training, miscommunication between agencies, etc.) Next, the chapter discusses supporting arguments for creating a multidisciplinary partnership as the most effective solution to stopping animal abuse. Following this, the chapter will offer profession-specific techniques for recognizing the warning signs of animal abuse and taking action. Included will be a discussion of successful programs already in place to stop violence to companion animals. The chapter then presents a Tales from the Streets segment offering anecdotal examples and no-nonsense strategies for solving animal abuse cases. The problem-solving strategies offered throughout this chapter are designed so that all agencies and individuals involved—law enforcement, animal control, humane investigators, fire officials, veterinarians, therapists, human services (including elderly services/child/family services), municipal leaders and the community at large—can work together to stop the abuse of companion animals in their community.

COMMON OBSTACLES TO HELPING VICTIMS
OF ANIMAL ABUSE

It would be great to report that helping animal victims of abuse is a relatively easy venture and that all that is necessary is to educate people about the problem and they will offer their assistance. But such a perspective is Pollyanna at best. The truth is that helping victims of animal abuse can be an uphill battle—at least initially. Even at FIREPAW where we have the ability to devote our primary focus to projects that help stop animal suffering, we face roadblocks. When professionals can only devote a small amount of time to this effort these roadblocks can be devastating to their goals. Before going on to the strategies that can and do work, therefore, it is important to first examine these potential obstacles. This will not only help to prepare you for issues that may run interference to your efforts but will also allow you to develop a Plan B to overcome potential roadblocks.

Lack of Agency and/or Community Support

A decade and a half ago while doing consulting at a domestic violence shelter I got a firsthand look at how stretched the caseworkers and shelter managers were. Back then there was never enough staff, too many fires to put out, and always more need than funding to pay for it. And now? After all these years of public education campaigns and social enlightenment about violence, interviews with caseworkers and shelter managers reveal that things have not changed all that much. The caseloads and stress levels are still frequently high, the resources limited and the burnout always just around the corner. And that is for helping people. Ask most professionals helping domestic violence victims to add more to their list of responsibilities by also helping animal victims and you are likely to hear a laundry list of reasons why this is not possible. The reason is because those domestic violence shelters and helping agencies that are not part of a partnership to assist animal victims simply do not have the resources to stretch themselves any thinner than they already are. When there are no alliances with other agencies in the community there is also frequently a lack of support from within one's own agency. In these scenarios helping animal victims of abuse requires caseworkers to use their own time, energy and resources to take that animal to safety. Caseworkers must establish a network of potential fosters on their own, call around on their own time trying to place the animal, and drive the animal (frequently long distances) to a safe house, usually without any hope of being reimbursed for their gasoline and certainly little hope of being paid for their efforts. Without the support of one's agency and the community at large there is little time, energy or opportunity and therefore little incentive, to take on yet more responsibility to help animal victims.

A lack of agency and/or community support will be an obstacle for other professionals as well. Whether you are in law enforcement, animal control, social services, a veterinarian in a multi-partner practice, or some other profession entirely, if there is not support at the systemic level of your organization or agency and there is no support within the community it will be an uphill battle to assist victims of animal cruelty. That is not to say that it cannot be done. All across this country there are lone advocates working to help animal victims on their own time. Frequently these folks become known as "the animal victim person" in their field and before long their reputations allow them to establish a sizeable network and add many potential problem-solving strategies to their bag of tricks. Unfortunately, such reputations also present these lone advocates with more work than they can easily handle on their own. As we will see later, there are detours around a lack of agency or community support but it is a potential roadblock that needs to be anticipated.

Skewed Priorities

Students and neophytes might find this hard to believe, but not all agencies or organizations have their priorities in order. This is said tongue-in-cheek of course, but the truth of the matter is agencies frequently function on the strength of their weakest link. If those in power lack strong management and organizational skills, organizations—even those whose primary objective is to serve, protect and assist those in need—can be functioning far below what is normative for the field. Professionals who work at such agencies spend their energy treading water far more often than swimming laps. Still other organizations and agencies may place more of a priority on gathering forces and power or getting good publicity than following the mission statement or pursuing the stated objectives of the agency. If you are trying to establish a working relationship with such an agency to help animal abuse victims you may discover it takes more energy to make it work than it is worth. Again, there are solutions for working around such scenarios but anticipating and recognizing organizations that are operating with skewed priorities is important to keep your own plans on track.

Ignorance and Resistance

If you are a professional and reading this book, chances are you already "get it." You see the bigger picture and can appreciate the impact that violence has on the entire community whether that violence is directed at people or companion animals. But not everyone you approach is going to understand the importance of stopping animal cruelty. In fact, you can pretty much expect that when you start the initial steps of bringing professionals together in your community to problem-solve, not everyone is going to get on board. Some people may be completely uninformed and others may be mindful of the general problem but resistant to devoting energy and resources to resolve it. Again, this potential obstacle does not have to curtail your efforts. Rather than use up precious time and energy trying to convince an organization that is not ready to be convinced, it is far more effective to put your energy in to locating *individuals*. If your community social service agency or law enforcement department seems uninterested in becoming officially involved in partnering to stop animal abuse, start asking around about individual professionals who work within these agencies. All you really need is one committed person who is sympathetic to your goals. Inviting them to attend your meetings could mean you will have a valuable ally interested in becoming part of your efforts. These folks may end up being more helpful than if their agency as a whole was involved.

Lack of Adequate Training

Another potential obstacle that can run interference with the goal of stopping animal cruelty in your community is the lack of adequate training for all participants. While you and/or professionals from your organization may be well trained in recognizing the red flags of animal cruelty and in taking the appropriate action, that does not mean that professionals from other organizations will be as well-trained. Success in curtailing animal abuse in your community depends on all participating agencies receiving adequate training to identify and take action to bring animals to safety and to take the appropriate steps with the alleged perpetrator. One of the important first steps therefore is to identify whether partner agencies have the training they need and if they do not, to make sure they get it. There are multiple resources offered in Chapter Ten that can guide you as to where and how such training can be obtained.

Miscommunication Between Agencies

Nearly everyone can identify with the troubles that can occur when there are miscommunications or a lack of communication between departments, divisions or agencies. If there is any surefire way that animal victims of violence will fall between the cracks, it is poor communications between agencies responsible for ensuring their safety. In order to keep this obstacle from blocking the success of your efforts there must be a clear plan and a backup plan in place to assure that everyone involved is notified in a clear and timely manner. Establishing a phone tree with a designated, capable and willing central contact person can help ensure that animal victims are rescued and taken to safety and that all the appropriate agencies are notified about the suspected perpetrators and human victims. This central contact person should also be in charge of follow-up telephone calls where participants are apprised of the current status and given an opportunity to pass along any important messages about the case to the central contact person. While this obstacle has the potential to prevent animal victims from being rescued in a timely manner, it is such a common problem that other organizations have already found ways to work out the bugs. Contacting the organizations listed in Chapter Ten will allow you and your fellow professionals to set in place a system that prevents this obstacle from running interference with your efforts.

Difficulty Finding Fosters or Safe Houses

Locating temporary safe havens for victims of animal cruelty can be a major obstacle. Ideally your community has an animal shelter or veterinarian practice willing to participate in offering temporary housing and care for these animals. If this is not possible, it will require building a reliable network of foster families that can take animals into their homes at a moment's notice.

Unfortunately, many communities do not have a safe haven system in place for animal victims. Another relatively common scenario is when a particular agency such as a domestic violence shelter creates an agreement with a specific animal shelter to offer a safe haven for the animal victims coming through that particular domestic violence agency. This works out perfectly for the two organizations involved in the agreement but leaves other domestic violence shelters and other agencies in the community trying to find safe havens for animals out twisting in the wind.

Because of our interest in stopping animal abuse, FIREPAW regularly gets calls from domestic violence shelters needing emergency foster homes for their clients' pets. They have nowhere else to turn. Frequently these animals have already been threatened and/or harmed by the batterers so there is always a sense of urgency requiring that everything be dropped immediately to try and secure safe housing for these creatures. We put out the call to a network of people who have previously done emergency fostering of animals, say a prayer, and hope for the best. But the best does not always happen. Foster families may already have foster animals in their homes. They may be unavailable. The animal victim may not get along with the foster family's own animals. The animal victim may lack evidence of proper vaccinations or have a medical condition that prohibits their stay in a home with other animals. And then there is the common occurrence that the only fosters available to help live too far away for the caseworker to drive the animal. Due to these obstacles, animal victims are frequently left at risk living in the home of the batterer. Sometimes domestic violence caseworkers and other professionals risk problems with their landlords or their own animals in order to take an animal victim into their home for safety.

This seat-of-the-pants approach to problem solving can be a significant obstacle to achieving the goal of helping animal victims of abuse. For those professionals who offer to get involved this method is stressful, time and energy consuming, expensive and has a low likelihood of a successful outcome making the volunteer less likely to want to get involved the next time an animal is in need. In order to keep this obstacle from running interference with your goal to stop animal abuse in your community, you will need a structured plan of action for getting animal victims to safety. Your action plan for bringing animal victims to safety should be highly detailed. Who will pay for the animal's housing, food and veterinary care if the guardian has no money? How long will the foster or safe haven be expected to house the animal? What will happen to animals whose guardians cannot get back on their feet for a prolonged period of time or cannot secure housing that permits pets? Should the human victim/guardian know where the pet is being housed? Should the guardian and the children be permitted to visit the pet? These are all critical questions that need answered prior to establishing a program to help animal victims. Again we return to the concept of creating a multidisciplinary partnership of agencies and organizations in your community. Ideally, this partnership will include a veterinarian, an animal shelter and animal welfare organization that organizes and trains fosters. To find strategies around this potential obstacle you should also consider contacting the resources listed throughout this chapter and Chapter Ten. Of particular value is talking with professionals from communities that have already established successful pet safe havens and reading the book, *Safe Havens for Pets: Guidelines for Programs Sheltering Pets for Women Who are Battered* by Frank R. Ascione, Ph.D.

Lack of Commitment

Another potential obstacle is people who pay lip service but lack commitment when they are called on to get involved. This can happen at any stage but professionals have reported it more frequently in the early stages of developing and working with community partnerships. Obviously if you are depending on people to follow through and they drop the ball, the animals can be at increased risk and perpetrators may slip between the cracks.

Strategies that can help reduce the risk of bringing people who lack commitment on board is to be clear and up front with the level of responsibility involved and offer a detailed outline of each person's or agency's responsibilities when a call of possible animal cruelty comes in. All involved should have a clear understanding of the importance of each person/agency as a link in a chain and the potential problems involved if someone drops the ball. Ask each person who has made a verbal commitment to be a part of the effort to stop animal cruelty if they have any reservations. All reservations should be put on the table for discussion and if necessary either establish a backup plan or appoint an alternate person to take on the responsibility. There is no way to completely prevent those who lack commitment from signing up, but with clear statements of the needs and expectations of participants, problems can be kept to a minimum.

Political Infighting

Even with the most admirable of intentions and goals, participants whose top priority is their own political aspirations can make efforts to help animal victims of abuse dicey at best. If your partnership begins to experience an individual or agency that insists on taking control, starts requiring that all communications are first filtered through them, starts dictating changes not supported by the other participants, leaves others out of the loop, becomes competitive, manipulative, or engages in other behaviors that undermine the primary goal of helping animal victims it is time for a change. People who bring their own political agendas into such partnerships can cause resentment and make the air thick enough to cut with a knife—not exactly the type of atmosphere that fosters a spirit of cooperation. To prevent this potential obstacle from sabotaging your efforts it is important to lay clear ground rules up front about participants' roles and the importance of maintaining mutual respect, open communications and cooperation.

Unclear Which Agency Has What Responsibility

Confusion about who is supposed to call whom and who is suppose to do what can cause chaos and become a real obstacle to your efforts. As with overcoming potential problems of miscommunication, avoiding this obstacle requires clear boundaries and guidelines being communicated to all participants, preferably in writing. If a participant is unable to attend critical meetings in which changes in who will be responsible for various duties are laid out, be certain that person receives notification of those changes—again, preferably followed up in writing.

Institutional Limitations

Systemic and institutional limitations inherent in participating agencies and organizations can cause roadblocks in your efforts to stop animal cruelty. As Aimee Thompson, founder of the Close to Home Domestic Violence Prevention Initiative has pointed out, a number of institutional limitations can act as obstacles to achieving the overall goal of stopping violence in your community (Herbst, 2003). In terms of stopping violence directed toward companion animals these limitations include: (1) institutions responding to violence have an inherent lack of capacity to address the magnitude of the problem. Institutions can only reach a fraction of those who need help; (2) institutions provide after-the-fact crisis interventions but do nothing to modify the social norms that could prevent violence from occurring in the first place; (3) those institutional interventions that fail to draw on the leadership of a community can fall short in making long-term changes, especially in communities with ethnic groups who have specific cultural attitudes and traditions that are harmful to animals.

The first obstacle will take time, but you can begin to address the second and third limitations by implementing a public education component to your program. It can start with something as simple as creating an informational brochure about animal cruelty and progress to professionals offering educational materials at local shopping or meeting places and holding town-hall-meeting-style educational forums during community and school events. Be certain you consult members who live and work in the community as you design and develop educational materials and programs.

THE MULTIDISCIPLINARY PARTNERSHIP SOLUTION

As the previous sections suggest, the magnitude of the problem and the challenges involved in stopping it make a compelling a case for professionals from multiple fields to come together, link up and pool their resources to stop animal cruelty. The most effective method for stopping animal abuse in any community is to have an active, open line of communication between all individuals and agencies who are on the frontline and are most likely to interact with the victims and/or perpetrators of animal cruelty. Municipalities, officers of the court, veterinarians, animal control officers, animal welfare shelters, law enforcement, fire officials, social service agencies—especially domestic violence case workers and family and elderly services professionals —as well as therapists should all be active players in stopping animal cruelty in their communities. A number of professionals and organizations have called for a multidisciplinary approach to stopping animal abuse in their communities. According to the National Center for Victims of Crime (2001) it is critical to include animal control officers and veterinarians in any cooperative community partnership to stop animal abuse. Let's take a look at what some others have had to say:

A Specialist in Animal Law

The overwhelming majority of states in the U.S. do not have state laws mandating reporting of animal abuse cases. Until that day comes individuals and agencies can make dramatic differences in reducing animal cruelty in their communities simply by linking up, forming alliances and creating their own system of cross-reporting (LaCroix, 1998). Such a multidisciplinary approach would ideally involve social service workers, family service workers, and domestic violence caseworkers trained to recognize and report animal abuse to other agencies when investigating child, spousal and elderly abuse cases. Likewise, law enforcement, animal control and humane investigators investigating animal abuse cases should contact social service agencies in cases where children are involved. Such an alliance should also encourage veterinarians encountering suspected animal abuse cases to notify humane officers who would in turn notify social service professionals if children are residing in the home where the animal abuse has taken place.

Linking all the key agencies, a cross-reporting system allows for a network of professionals who are on the front lines as the most likely to recognize animal abuse to create a far more effective solution than when such professionals are isolated from one another. A multidisciplinary cross-reporting system holds the potential for expanding the current pool of trained professionals who are the most likely to encounter victims and/or perpetrators of animal abuse. Additionally, such a system enhances early detection of all forms of family violence and other problems, thus improving the success of both intervention and therapy. As LaCroix has pointed out, although there are no laws requiring social service agencies to report animal cruelty, several jurisdictions have established a network of professionals in social service agencies, animal care, law enforcement, humane investigators and animal protection agencies who volunteer to participate in such a partnership.

Animal Welfare Organizations Specializing in Education and Training Programs to End Animal Cruelty

The Humane Society of the United States (HSUS) has developed the innovative First Strike, an educational training program for professionals on the frontline for identifying and taking action in cases of animal abuse and other types of violence. Reviewing successful multidisciplinary partnerships already in existence HSUS representatives have stated, "Critical to the success of the program [is] training on the link between animal abuse and domestic violence provided to all professionals who encounter abused adults, children or animals," (Ponder and Lockwood, 2000).

The American Humane Association (AHA) has fostered inter-agency co-operation by training humane agents to recognize signs of possible child abuse and training social and family service workers to recognize signs of possible animal abuse. Several communities across the U.S. have implemented cross-reporting and cross-training cooperative partnership programs. Existing programs such as those in California and Michigan share inter-agency information, offer training seminars and partner with child welfare workers, animal control, humane officers, social service workers, veterinarians, therapists and police officers in their communities (Kowalski, 1995).

HSUS offers First Strike seminars across the country to educate professionals and community leaders about the link between animal cruelty and violence directed toward humans and the importance of utilizing a multidisciplinary approach to stopping animal abuse. AHA holds training workshops, seminars and community forums nationwide on issues involved in the link between domestic violence, child abuse, juvenile delinquency and animal cruelty. See the resources listed in Chapter Ten for contact information.

A Psychologist Specializing in Training Therapists to Treat Child and Adult Perpetrators of Animal Abuse

Ken Shapiro, Ph.D., executive director of Society and Animal Forum (a.k.a. Animals and Society Institute; previously Psychologists for the Ethical Treatment of Animals—PsyETA) has argued that only by sensitizing both social service professionals and the general public about violence directed at both humans and animals can we reframe animal abuse as a highly charged social issue deserving of considerable resources. Cross-reporting of violence directed at humans and animals is the only solution to what he refers to as the "current culture of violence," (Shapiro, 1996).

A Researcher Who Studies the Factors Associated with Animal Abuse

In a forum addressing family relations professionals, researcher Clifton Flynn argued that cross-training and cross-referrals between animal control officers and human service professionals is important in recognizing and dealing with the link between animal abuse and family violence. According to Flynn, policies that enable the sharing of information between both groups of professionals could result in a more effective response to both human and animal victims of violence (Flynn, 2000a).

COMMUNITY PARTNERSHIP MODELS

The next section offers some basic tips for specific professions on how to get started developing a multidisciplinary partnership. Included in the section are examples of some successful community partnership programs already working to stop animal cruelty. Before moving on however, we will take a brief look at two unique partnership programs. While these programs have a slightly different focus and goal than those of applied fieldwork/cross-reporting partnerships, their key ingredients make them models for successful partnerships worthy of consideration.

A Multidisciplinary Educational Network

The Human/Animal Violence Education Network or HAVEN as it is commonly known is the brainchild of veterinarian Lorna Grande, DVM. Together with educator and author Christopher Nye, Ph.D., Grande formed a network of professionals from a variety of disciplines to provide an educational resource for professionals and the public about the link between animal and human violence. What makes this partnership work are some key elements that can make other programs successful as well.

Atmosphere fosters respect and cooperation. The atmosphere fosters network partners to have a genuine mutual respect for one another and for newcomers. Every person's input is respected and valued. This means that participants regularly offer their thoughts so that a free exchange of ideas is the norm at regular meetings. Along with this mutual respect comes the fact that members actually enjoy one another's company such that meetings are actually an enjoyable experience—this, despite the fact that the subject matter is oftentimes difficult.

Highly diverse group. The partnership is comprised of professionals from a wide variety of backgrounds: social service and family and child services professionals, animal shelter management, domestic violence services professionals, law enforcement, fire department officials, researchers and educators, authors, animal control professionals, and a film/media professional, to name a few. This leads to a rich mixture of input from a variety of perspectives.

Efficient use of members' time. Additionally, there is never any drag time during meetings. Grande, who leads the meetings, always has critical discussion items and updates ready so that the time is used effectively. By the time the network's meeting time is over members have a clear sense of where projects stand and what needs to be done next.

Growth is nurtured rather than feared. The network is always growing. Grande actively seeks out professionals who may be interested in participating in the network, calling them personally, explaining the history and goals of the network, and inviting them to attend a meeting. When they attend they are greeted warmly, introduced and asked to share their interests in helping to stop animal cruelty in the community. Newcomers are always made to feel welcome and that their ideas and experiences are valued.

In summary, this community partnership has clear goals, is always moving forward to meet those goals, and does so in a manner that is receptive and respectful of members and visitors so that the partnership itself encourages its own growth and success.

A Bridge with the Community Initiative

The Close to Home Domestic Violence Initiative is the brainchild of social services professional Aimee Thompson. What makes this program unique is that it works to build bridges between community members and institutions in order to educate the community about services that are available to them. In turn this helps law enforcement, and criminal justice, health and social service agencies make their services more responsive to community needs. The program has invited counselors and advocates from a group of local community centers to attend kitchen-table conversations so they can share information and receive feedback about what community members want from them. To this end the program seeks to find the balance between being an action-oriented group that wants to do something, and allowing people to come together to process their own experience and what this issue has meant in their community (Herbst, 2003). While this program focuses on human victims, the features driving it can be incorporated in to partnership programs focusing on animal victims as well.

GETTING STARTED:
PROFESSION-SPECIFIC FINDINGS AND TIPS

Domestic Violence Caseworkers, Shelter Professionals and Social Service Professionals (Family/Child/Elderly Services)

Researchers and other experts recommend that (1) Databases currently being established for tracking reported domestic violence cases should include family pets who have also been abused, and (2) Shelters should expand their services to include the needs of pet-owning clientele. Safe houses need to be established for animal victims of domestic violence. For example, domestic violence shelters should establish referral programs with animal shelters to provide emergency short-term housing or foster care for human victims' pets (Arkow, 1996). The majority of shelters do not provide temporary shelter or emergency services for the pets of clients. Pets may still be at risk if left behind to live with the batterer when human victims flee the violent home (Ascione, Weber, and Wood, 1997a; Ascione, 1998a); (3) Shelters for battered women must incorporate questions about pets and pet abuse during the intake interview. While shelter staff are frequently aware of the link between animal abuse and domestic violence, few ask about pet abuse at intake or offer safe haven arrangements for their clients' pets (Ascione, Weber, and Wood, 1997b).

Getting Started: Domestic Violence Caseworkers and
Social Service Professionals . . .

- collect data to determine the level and type of need in your community. How many animals on average need temporary shelter or fostering? Are they mostly dogs? Cats? Birds? Other small mammals?
- contact your local animal shelter and arrange a meeting.
- come prepared with a detailed outline of what is needed and how you propose to accomplish it.
- explain to the animal shelter professionals what their level of involvement would be and why it is critical that they participate.
- find out the shelter's conditions: how long can temporary shelter be provided? Do animals need proof of vaccinations to be boarded? Would owners need to help pay for their animal's housing and care? If owners have no available funding, who will pay?
- consult the resources listed in Chapter Ten to learn the steps involved in establishing a pet safe haven. Talk to your peers who have already set up a safe haven for pets to learn both the shortcuts as well as the pitfalls to avoid.
- explain to the animal shelter why it is beneficial for them to participate, both in terms of helping animals and in terms of good public relations from being involved in an innovative program.
- arrange a follow-up meeting with your local animal shelter to arrange preliminary logistics of how to coordinate getting the animals to the shelter when victims flee the abusive home.

Child and Family Service Professionals

Child and family service professionals who work with victims of child and partner abuse need to ask questions about abuse that has occurred to the family pet. Counselors should be aware that children who are cruel to animals might have the propensity for other types of interpersonal violence. Both perpetrating and witnessing animal cruelty can have potentially harmful, long-term psychological consequences. Possible reactions to experiencing animal abuse (including witnessing animal abuse) include: sense of loss, guilt over not preventing the abuse, grief, or even no emotional response at all (Flynn, 2000a).

Law Enforcement Professionals

Animal cruelty and the link with violence to humans have been given increasing attention by law enforcement. Articles about the link have appeared in material provided to all chiefs of police across the country. Experts recommend that databases currently being established by law enforcement for tracking reported domestic violence cases should also include family pets who have been abused.

Getting Started . . .

- Begin by setting up a preliminary meeting with leaders of community social services, domestic violence shelters and animal shelters/animal welfare organizations in your area to begin a dialog about assessing the level of need in your community and potential problem-solving strategies.
- Use the resources in Chapter Ten . . . contact other multidisciplinary partnerships that have already established programs to stop animal cruelty in their communities. Several of the videos, educational materials, programs and training manuals are profession-specific and can help guide you and your colleagues to lay the groundwork for starting your own community partnership.

Law Enforcement Collaborative Partnerships to Stop Animal Abuse: Model Programs

Police chiefs from several cooperative multi-agency partnership programs say that since joining forces with other agencies there has been a significant increase in successful convictions of animal abuse perpetrators. In fact, when multiple counts of violence are on the table sometimes the animal abuse charge is the only thing that sticks.

The following highlights model programs for law enforcement agencies partnering with anti-violence organizations to develop inter-agency collaborations for reducing family violence and animal cruelty. The programs are in both rural communities and large metropolitan areas and offer methods that police chiefs can apply to decrease violence directed at both pets and people in their communities (Ponder and Lockwood, 2000).

The Baltimore County Program

In Baltimore, Maryland after learning of the connection between animal abuse and domestic violence in 1997 the police chief felt it was critical to work with animal protection and the veterinary community. (They were already part of an established network to curtail domestic violence and had developed an outreach campaign educating school officials, hospitals, child protective services, adult protective services and other community agencies.) The police chief decided to implement a cross-training and cross-reporting system to stop human and animal violence in their community of Baltimore County.

The police chief began with an educational campaign to educate the public, police officers, domestic violence advocates, child protective services, animal control officers, and veterinarians about the link between animal abuse and family violence. The department started by including information about pet abuse in its domestic violence brochures and posters. They also worked with several local domestic violence shelters and animal shelters to establish an informational network of emergency shelters or "safe havens" for animal victims of domestic violence.

In 1999 Baltimore County Police Department became one of the first agencies in the country to address the connection between animal abuse and family violence. The department then started providing training on the connection to officers at the police academy, animal control officers, child protective services and veterinary professionals. Their next step is to refine a data base system for the collection of both animal abuse and domestic violence incidences (Ponder and Lockwood, 2000).

The DVERT Program

DVERT is a nationally renowned program launched by the Colorado Springs, Colorado police department in 1996. DVERT or Domestic Violence Enhanced Response Team, was developed to reduce the high number of lethal domestic violence incidents each year. DVERT's primary objective is to identify individuals who pose a significant risk to their intimate partners. It entails an intake team that reviews every domestic violence case that comes in to their jurisdiction's police department. After the case is assessed the team classifies it as either a DVERT case or not and then refers it on to either a primary or secondary response team. The primary response team is on-call 24 hours a day and includes a detective from the police department, a district attorney, and a victims advocate from the domestic violence prevention services. The purpose? To assist the initial patrol officers in the investigation and to provide support services for the victims. When animal abuse is involved a secondary response team is created with professionals with specialized expertise. Approximately 40% of DVERT cases involve animal cruelty and 50% involve child abuse. A coordinator of the DVERT team has stated that DVERT has played a part in reducing the number of perpetrators who re-offend (Ponder and Lockwood, 2000).

DVERT serves as a national model for law enforcement agencies across the country. The program offers onsite visits and opportunities from other law enforcement agencies, animal control and social service agencies around the country. Interested in learning more about this or other programs? See Chapter Ten for contact information.

The Link-UP Program

Link-UP is a proactive approach to child abuse, domestic violence and senior abuse through the investigation of animal cruelty incidents. The strengths are drawn from the linking up of multiple agencies to prevent abuse to animals and humans. The program focuses on the generation of potential abusers that are now in the early development stages of life. It includes an educational and enforcement program offered by the Animal Rescue League of Boston Law Enforcement Department, in which the Child Witness to Violence Project, Link-UP Educational Network, and The Northeast Animal Control/Humane Task Force are major components. The program has been in existence more than seven years. Link-UP was formulated as a result of ten years of research and over five years of field development.

The Link-UP Program can be used by such varied agencies as law enforcement, animal control, veterinary sciences, medical, child welfare, educational, parents' groups, courts, and youth groups aimed at both young children and teens. The educational portion teaches professionals how to recognize the three major early indicators of violent behavioral development: animal abuse, arson, and "battering reaction syndrome." Additionally, follow-up steps are taught to increase one's confidence when approaching someone displaying the indicators. Factors such as where to turn for additional assistance, how to validate assumptions of a potential problem and the caution needed to prevent overreaction are stressed.

A component of the Link-UP program is the Education, Direction, and Discipline (EDD) system. The EDD is utilized by the Task Force and is taught to law enforcement officers, social service agencies, and animal control officers in a combined classroom and field exercise setting. The EDD is a three-step system of investigation that enhances the chances of success by coordinating the resources of multiple agencies in one direction. The Task Force has utilized EDD with great success since it's inception.

Another component of Link-UP is Animal Protection Training (APT). APT is a program that is taught to various community groups and focuses on common every day incidents concerning the treatment of animals. The APT system covers the many aspects of animal ownership, including proper handling, legal responsibilities and acceptable training standards. The goal is to make better animal owners, especially within the adolescent age groups. This program has been well-received by educational, youth, and parents' groups.

The Link-UP Program is being utilized by multiple agencies throughout the Northeast and continues to expand and refine its major components on an ongoing basis.

Tips for Getting Started: Law Enforcement

For those professionals considering starting up a program in their community, Ponder and Lockwood (2000) of the Humane Society of the United States (HSUS) have some tips:

- Much can be gained from implementing multidisciplinary programs to prevent family violence and animal cruelty.
- Existing programs have become highly diverse and are designed to meet the conditions of individual communities.
- Law enforcement officials considering implementing a program on the connection between animal abuse and family violence should start by contacting their counterparts in social services and animal protection agencies and joining their local anti-violence coalition. These contacts can be used to develop cross-training, cross-reporting and multidisciplinary response teams.
- Law enforcement should include questions about animal abuse in their domestic violence intake forms. Data collection of this type can be very important when applying for funding or demonstrating the need for such a program in your community.
- It is important that police chiefs and other wishing to launch an animal abuse/violence education program talk with members of existing programs.
- Law enforcement officials can receive technical assistance, training and educational materials from the Humane Society of the United States (HSUS) First Strike Campaign. The program works to raise public and professional awareness about the connection between animal abuse and family violence. See the resources listed in Chapter Ten for contact information.

For a list of nonviolence offenses correlated with animal abuse (Arluke, Levin, Luke and Ascione, 1999) see Chapter Ten resources.

Animal Control Officers, Humane Investigators and Fire Officials

Getting Started: Humane Investigators, Animal Control Officers . . .

- Begin by setting up a preliminary meeting with leaders of community law enforcement, social services, domestic violence shelters and animal shelters/animal welfare organizations in your area to begin a dialog about assessing the level of need in your community and potential problem-solving strategies.
- Use the resources in Chapter Ten . . . contact other multidisciplinary partnerships that have already established programs to stop animal cruelty in their communities. Several of the videos, educational materials, programs and training manuals are profession-specific and can help guide you and your colleagues to lay the groundwork for starting your own community partnership.

American Humane Association (AHA) has published a training manual for animal control officers and humane investigators on the strategies for recognizing and reporting child abuse. See Chapter Ten for contact information.

Getting started: Fire department officials.   Firefighters are frequently on the frontline to recognize hoarding and intentional juvenile fire-setting (the latter a symptom that may accompany animal cruelty in cases of childhood Conduct Disorder). Fire department officials should learn the factors associated with childhood animal cruelty outlined in Chapter Four, and hoarding which is covered in Chapter Six and Chapter Seven. Utilizing the resources outlined in these chapters and those in Chapter Ten is a good place to start. The next step is to contact law enforcement officials, social service professionals and animal welfare officials in your community to begin the process of communicating and developing a solution-oriented plan for putting an end to animal abuse in your community.

Veterinarians

It is imperative that veterinary professionals begin to play an active role in helping to stop animal cruelty. Veterinarians are on the frontline of professionals who can identify animal abuse and neglect. It seems only natural that they would report such findings, right? Unfortunately, this is not always the case. One of the primary reasons veterinarians hesitate to become actively involved in reporting animal cruelty cases is that they are often not a part of the humane investigation-animal control network in their community. On the issue of barriers for veterinarians making charges of animal abuse and neglect, Patronek (1997) has the following: ". . . veterinarians may be unaware of the appropriate agency responsible for investigating animal cruelty in their community. When humane societies are the agencies responsible for investigation of these cases, some veterinarians may be reluctant to become involved. This could be due to general mistrust, historical adversarial relationships, or simply a lack of confidence and unfamiliarity with the personnel who would conduct an investigation. However, these reservations could be addressed through improved communication and mutual effort to develop effective working relationships."

Getting Started . . .

- Begin by setting up a preliminary meeting with leaders of community social services, domestic violence shelters and animal shelters/animal welfare organizations in your area to begin a dialog about assessing the level of need in your community and potential problem-solving strategies.
- Use the resources in Chapter Ten . . . contact other multidisciplinary partnerships that have already established programs to stop animal cruelty in their communities. Several of the videos, educational materials, programs and training manuals are profession-specific (including several resources specifically designed for veterinarians) and can help guide you and your colleagues to lay the groundwork for starting your own community partnership.

Animal Shelters/Animal Welfare Organizations/Animal Protectionists

Getting Started: Animal Welfare Organizations/Animal Shelters . . .

- Determine how much space you have available for temporary shelter of animal victims of violence and how long you can offer shelter for any one case.
- Determine payment options for care of the animals you will offer temporary shelter for. . . Will there be a special fund established for animal victims? Who will do the fundraising? Is there grant funding available?
- Contact your local domestic violence shelter and arrange for a meeting to discuss their level of need and request that the shelter begin tracking the number and types of animals needing temporary housing each month.
- Consult the resources listed in Chapter Ten to learn the steps involved in establishing a pet safe haven. Talk with other animal shelters that have already established a safe haven program in their community.
- Work with the domestic violence shelter to create a plan for bringing animals to the safe house, including arranging for a foster network that can

take the animals in at a moment's notice and bring them to the animal shelter when it opens.

- Write up the conditions for housing of animals including who is responsible for payment of care, what documentation such as proof of rabies vaccines are required and what will happen if the victims are unable to obtain such documents, whether and under what conditions animal owners can visit their companion animals, etc. Create a release form for animal owners to allow their animals to receive veterinary care in the case of an emergency.

Getting Started: Animal Protectionists . . .

- Establish a network of volunteers for emergency fostering of animal victims of domestic violence.
- Create an action plan detailing the logistics . . . who is part of your network calling tree? Who is responsible for being the first responder when animals need shelter? What is your back-up plan if key people are unavailable? Who will be responsible for the costs involved with animal feeding and care? Do you have a veterinarian willing to offer care to animals who may have an emergency?
- Consult the resources listed in Chapter Ten to learn the steps involved in establishing a pet safe haven through fostering. Talk with other animal protectionists who have already established a safe haven foster program in their community.
- Contact local domestic violence shelters and social service agencies to arrange a preliminary meeting to discuss how your foster network can work in partnership with human service professionals to help animal victims of domestic violence.

American Humane Association (AHA) conducts a training program for animal welfare professionals to recognize and report child abuse. See the resources in Chapter Ten for contact information.

Therapists and Counselors

Getting Started . . .

There are now several assessment tools for therapists to identify animal abusers as well as approaches for treating animal abusers—both adults and juveniles. Therapists and others involved in assessment and treatment are encouraged to seek out the available resources listed in Chapter Ten.

Therapists and counselors who help battered women will encounter the need to deal with the range of emotions likely to accompany the loss of a separation from a pet. Children may need attention in this area as well, either because of trauma from witnessing abuse of their pet or because they have learned to begin abusing animals themselves (Ascione, Weber, and Wood, 1997a; Ascione, 1998a).

Policy Makers/Legislators/District Attorneys/Prosecutors and Judges

Animal cruelty is now included in the training programs of all newly-appointed juvenile prosecutors as early warning signs of potential criminal or antisocial behavior (APRI, 1999). This is an important beginning, but there is still much to be done. Experts in the field of animal abuse argue that policy makers and legislators should strengthen laws and penalties for perpetrators of animal abuse (Flynn, 2000a). Prosecutors trying domestic violence cases may actually improve chances of securing orders of protection, custody of children and arrest of the batterer by using evidence of animal cruelty to support their case. Given the limited success of the criminal justice system in dealing with male batterers (Barnett, Miller-Perrin, and Perrin, 1997) stricter enforcement of animal cruelty laws may be an effective way to hold perpetrators responsible who have previously avoided penalties in the past for these violent acts.

As a footnote, according to Susan Urban (2002) of the American Society for the Prevention of Cruelty to Animals (ASPCA), some states embody their animal cruelty statutes under Agriculture and Markets laws. This means that police officers and court officials may be unfamiliar with the animal anti-cruelty laws, leaving it to those advocating for abused animals to educate them. It is critical that policy makers, legislators, district attorneys, prosecutors and judges become active players in creating, staying informed, and vigorously upholding animal anti-cruelty laws. An important variable in this process is to become a member of the multidisciplinary team to stop violence in your community. Being a part of the team—even if you can only attend an occasional meeting—allows you to see firsthand how the link between animal and human violence plays out at the ground level.

TALES FROM THE STREET: "WORKS WELL WITH OTHERS" . . . MULTIDISCIPLINARY PARTNERSHIPS

"Works well with others," a category often seen on my report card while attending grammar school, but never understood until much later in life. As I prepared to write this final section I recalled the timeframe from when very

few agencies even spoke with each other to today's rapidly developing practice of efficient collaboration between various agencies when investigating
and resolving cases of abuse.

From the start of my career as a street cop back in the days just after the
assassination of Dr. Martin Luther King, Jr., every shift produced a new experience. When I began in law enforcement, police work was still a basic
function and many of the changes seen today had not started to be implemented. There was no animal control unit and the Department of Social Services wasn't to come until years later. Back then the police made the arrests
and the court provided the conclusions, pretty cut-and-dried but also seriously
lacking in efficiency. There were not many opportunities to link with other
agencies or pass on information to someone who might be able to do some
follow-up work. Certainly not a very positive experience for human or animal
victims and definitely lacking when considering the long-term effect on witnesses to some of these horrific incidents.

As the years went by incidents such as these kept happening and arrests
continued to be made but I always felt that there had to be a better way to
approach this entire process. I was getting very tired of going to the same
address over and over for the same problems each and every week without
fail. There had to be a way of stopping the repeat offender short of long-term
incarceration or execution, but what was it? Police Departments throughout
the country had tried many new and innovative approaches to fighting crime
but it all ended with the same answer: the public wanted quicker response and
more officers responding to calls.

We went to the 911 system to provide quicker responses to calls for assistance, and when that didn't stop crime we invested in a program called "rapid
response," a total disaster for the officers on the street due to a breakdown of
communications between units responding to calls.

Eventually we were introduced to a "new" concept in policing. It was
called, "Community Policing," the police and the community working together to get results. The police were going to walk beats and meet and talk
to people in their patrol areas. The ironic part of this entire premise was that
I had worked for one Police Commissioner years before who had forbidden
us to mingle with the community as he felt it bred corruption issues when the
local cop and the neighborhood became friendly. Oh well, he was gone so it
was time to change the music.

But was this really a "new" concept in policing? It resembled an old song
I used to hear when I was young. My dad was a police officer before World
War II and he walked a beat and knew all the people who lived and worked
in his area. They had a friendship and open communication between police
and the community was ongoing. That was the way police work was done in

those days and had been done that way for years. Police officers walked beats and knew who belonged and who didn't and who to talk with and who not to talk with. Community policing was the latest thing in police work, and it introduced a very important word that would really make the difference, "PROACTIVE." Here was a word that would make an entire concept perish or bloom, one simple little nine-letter word that would be the backbone of an entire new phase of policing that would be embraced throughout the entire country: "PROACTIVE"!

Here was my panacea, my "holy grail" in the search to put an end to repeat-offenders. My entire future world would focus on this one word. Proactive, a total change for policing practices that had based itself on reacting to calls since the birth of law enforcement. We were going to be interested in looking at how to prevent an incident from happening *before* it took place, not waiting to get calls from victims after the crime had occurred. We were also going to involve other agencies from outside law enforcement in our latest efforts, we were going to exchange information, we were going to meet and talk with people from other disciplines. Our doors would be open; we would contact and work with people from health centers, schools, social service agencies, humane groups, churches, and any number of people trying to make a difference.

It sounded wonderful at the strategic planning sessions we attended; everyone was going to be proactive in his or her efforts to reduce incidents of crime. Well it was a hit for a while and everyone was on board to an extent, but as time passed old habits returned and some of the luster wore off the magic bullet of being Proactive. New and bigger problems arose and pretty soon the bill came in for community policing and the price was steep and the Federal Government had other things to pay for. Funding dried up and programs started to disappear. Proactive initiatives dwindled to few and far between causing most to sink into the sunset.

I was still a firm believer however, and had developed my own form of a proactive program, the Link-UP Program. I had assembled a number of people from multiple agencies to work on problems surrounding issues of animal/child/domestic/senior abuse issues. Link-UP had no budget or funding. We utilized people already trained in their own field of expertise and already funded and working day to day. It worked when it first started and it functions today in an even more efficient manner while covering a much larger area. We are still proactive in our efforts to find problems before they happen by looking for indicators when involved in other activities. In my present position we are now able to utilize proactive efforts in a much larger geographical setting than ever before and some of the results have been amazing!

So let us leave the old ways of policing to history and enter the modern age of "working well with others." I will leave you with a story that involves the efforts of multiple agencies, so read closely and see how many you can identify. . .

It was Halloween night and I was in the office helping with our annual Halloween Party for neighborhood children when a call came in from a supervisor on the street. It seemed that the officers had received a call to a local address for "dogs barking continually in a backyard." Upon arrival the officers had observed three large dogs in a fenced backyard barking and fighting with each other. Closer examination of the yard revealed what appeared to be the body of a dead dog also within the enclosed area. The supervisor contacted me once he arrived and made an assessment of the overall scene, and asked if assistance from any of our Task Force members was available. I made a couple of phone calls and was able to locate a nearby animal control officer to respond, as well as a veterinarian and a member of law enforcement from the Animal Rescue League of Boston who also happened to be in close proximity. I would not be responding due to my prior commitment but would be coordinating communications from the station. Within a matter of ten to fifteen minutes four agencies were on the scene and in the process of controlling and removing the animals before any more injuries were incurred. The deceased animal was removed from the yard and preliminary inspection revealed that the possible cause of death resulted from multiple tearing wounds and major blood loss.

Once order was returned to the scene determination of ownership of the animals was needed and officers turned their attention to the house itself. The building appeared uninhabited upon first observation but closer inspection revealed the presence of a small child standing on the back porch. It was Halloween Night, as I said, and as is usual this time of year in New England the temperature was in the low forty-degree range yet the child was observed to be wearing only a t-shirt and diaper. Officers now proceeded down the driveway and approached the front door of the house seeking identity of the occupants. After knocking and waiting a fairly long time considering the present circumstances, a female appeared at the front door and asked, "What do you want?" A somewhat surprising response to all those present when you look at what had happened over the last twenty to thirty minutes in the immediate backyard.

Not to be placed at a loss for words the police supervisor on the scene quickly asked, "Do you live here?"

"Yes I do," was the slowly worded response.

"Do you own those dogs in the backyard?" was the next question posed to female.

"No I don't," was the next slowly and somewhat slurred response.

"Do you know who owns them?" "

"My boyfriend, he's not home."

The slurring of the words seemed to be more pronounced the longer this went on. Clearly present at the outset of this entire incident was the neglect of the animals on the part of the owner/caretaker. This had clearly deteriorated to the status of animal cruelty. There was obvious prolonged failure to provide proper living conditions for the dogs in the yard. The fatal dog attack and injury situation had drawn us to the location and it was now incumbent upon us to observe any other potential problems and provide the necessary follow-up. Routine questioning continued in the search for more answers.

As open communication was slowly established between the female occupant and the responding officers, a level of trust was also developed. An offer to provide help as opposed to a threat of punishment for violations also removed barriers. The conversation was now flowing in both directions and answers were making much more sense.

As more questions continued to be asked of the occupant, multiple problems were revealed.

It turns out the location had ongoing animal cruelty, domestic violence, child neglect, heavy drug use, and multiple housing code violations. The focal point of these complaints was a dominant male occupant with a long criminal history, which included multiple restraining orders from various courts issued to multiple females.

Additional agencies were contacted as a result of these developments and immediate action began. Emergency medical services were provided to the female and her child. The Department of Social Services arranged to place the child in an overnight foster care home. All remaining animals were removed from the scene by animal control and taken to the animal shelter. Inspection Services responded to the house and after examination of the multiple code violations of a serious nature declared the residence unfit for habitation and removed all occupants. The local police district was made aware of outstanding arrest warrants for the male in question, who was not on the scene. His arrest was facilitated within twenty-four hours of the original incident after being stopped in a nearby town for a motor vehicle infraction.

The final result of the officers responding to a "barking dog" complaint was the arrest of a wanted felon and the prosecution of the perpetrator of animal cruelty. There was also the placement of a small child into a much better environment (who was also given counseling). There was also the removal of a drug-addicted female from a life of domestic violence and given appropriate rehabilitation and eventual return of her son. And last but not least, the rescue of three dogs that were eventually returned to physical health and later evaluated and retrained for possible adoption.

Did the police do all of this great work as a single agency? No, but they were the catalyst for all that followed. The original officers called for a supervisor. The supervisor was aware that assistance was available and made the call. The assistance was provided by the simple means of one more officer making a few phone calls. As a result of an already in-place network of agencies the phone calls brought Boston Animal Control, Animal Rescue League of Boston Law Enforcement staff, a veterinarian, and Code Enforcement Officers from the Inspection Services Department to the scene. But this was not the end of the collaboration. We also had Boston Emergency Medical Services, a local hospital, domestic violence counselors, a drug counseling program, the Child Witness to Violence Project at Boston Medical Center, local district court, District Attorneys Office, and the local police department that made that important traffic stop. There could be countless other individuals who were in someway involved that we may never know about, but it all comes down to one thing: We have to be able to "work well with others."

We've come a long way from the days when one or two agencies did the entire process, to a cooperative, team-oriented approach, capable of providing the specialized services needed to help both human and non-human victims. And the main message of this chapter? We cannot do it alone; we *need* those other agencies working closely along side us on a day-to-day basis for any of us to succeed. We certainly are not skilled enough to handle all facets of every situation we encounter. Open communication and a willingness to reach out to others for help are two of the most important tools needed to end the cruelty to animals and their human family members.

A Final Note

As we have demonstrated throughout this book, understanding what to look for and how to proceed is critical but it simply isn't enough to successfully end animal cruelty. Professional support and networking are critical. Community and municipal agency leaders hold the key to developing and maintaining a cooperative, team-oriented partnership approach. Only by supporting a *community effort* can we assure that companion animal victims no longer slip under the radar. Those professionals most likely to encounter perpetrators and victims of animal abuse must begin to be the voice for these most vulnerable and silent of victims. To save the animals is to save ourselves.

Chapter Ten

Getting Started: Resources for Speaking Out and Helping Silent Victims

Now that you have learned about the problems—and the solutions—of companion animals as silent victims, this chapter offers a myriad of resources to assist you in stopping animal abuse in your community. The chapter includes many action-oriented resources applicable to a myriad of professions. Included are profession-specific listings of resources for law enforcement, animal control officers, domestic violence advocates, veterinarians, humane officers, mental health professionals, child, family and elderly services professionals, and animal welfare organizations and agencies. Additional resources can help you locate agencies specializing in animal law, temporary safe houses, resources for helping animal victims of domestic violence, psychological services for human caretakers of victimized animals, therapeutic resources for identifying and treating adult and juvenile animal abusers, and much more. We hope you will become proactive in your use of the resources listed in this chapter. Like the rest of the book it is intended to give you the tools you need to begin building a multidisciplinary network and getting started in creating your own community program to recognize and help animal victims of abuse. And if you need to go it alone, or if you are a student setting out to learn more about the types of programs available, there's plenty of resources included to help you do that too. . .

ORGANIZATIONS

American Humane Association [AHA]
63 Inverness Drive, East
Englewood, Colorado 80112-5117

Tel: 1-800-227-4645
Web site: www.americanhumane.org
This is the oldest animal protection group devoted to national educational programs to stop animal cruelty.

American Society for the Prevention of Animal Cruelty [ASPCA]
424 East 92nd Street
New York, NY 10128
Tel: 212-876-7700
Web site: www.aspca.org
Their mission is to provide effective means for the prevention of cruelty to animals throughout the United States. They offer national programs in humane education, public awareness, government advocacy, shelter support, and animal medical services and placement.

Animal Legal Defense Fund [ALDF]
National Headquarters
127 Fourth Street
Petaluma, CA 94952-3005
Tel: (707) 769-7771
FAX: (707) 769-0785
E-mail: info@aldf.org
Web site: www.aldf.org

ALDF—Anti-Cruelty Division
919 SW Taylor Street, 4th Fl.
Portland, OR 97205-2542
Tel: 503-231-8480
Tel: (503) 231-1602
FAX: (503) 231-1578
Animal Cruelty Action Line: 1-800-555-6517
Email for the action line: action@aldf.org
The Animal Legal Defense Fund has been pushing the U.S. legal system to end the suffering of abused animals. Founded by attorneys active in shaping the emerging field of animal law, ALDF has blazed the trail for stronger enforcement of anti-cruelty laws and more humane treatment of animals in every corner of American life. ALDF's groundbreaking efforts are supported by hundreds of dedicated attorneys and more than 100,000 members. ALDF works to protect animals by:
Providing free legal assistance to prosecutors handling cruelty cases.
Maintaining a database of animal abuse crimes across the country.
Working to strengthen state anti-cruelty statutes.

Encouraging the federal government to enforce existing animal protection laws.

Nurturing the future of animal law through Student Animal Legal Defense Fund chapters.

Educating the public through seminars, workshops and other outreach efforts.

Supporting lawsuits that explore important issues and expand the boundaries of animal law.

ALDF—New ACT Program Targets Abusers

Now concerned citizens across the country will be able to join the fight against animal abuse. An outgrowth of ALDF's Animal Cruelty Actionline updates, ACT will keep animal advocates informed when new cruelty cases arise. After joining the team online, ACT members will receive e-mailed action alerts with contact information for prosecutors and judges handling cruelty cases. ACT will also be used to gather activists on a regional level, since a large turnout for a court date or sentencing hearing can reinforce that the community is watching and won't tolerate animal abuse — or lenient treatment of abusers.

Close to Home Domestic Violence Prevention Initiative
42 Charles St., Suite E
Dorchester, MA 02122
Tel: 617-929-5151
FAX: 617-822-3718
Email: aimeemt@earthlink.net
Facilitates coalition-building efforts among residents, civic groups, faith communities, health centers, elected officials, police, courts and other organizations to prevent domestic violence.

Dogs Deserve Better, Inc.
Tammy Sneath Grimes, Founder
P.O. Box 23
Tipton, PA 16684
Toll Free 1.877.636.1408
Tel: 814.941.7447
Web site: www.dogsdeservebetter.com
Email: info@dogsdeservebetter.org
Dogs Deserve Better (DDB) is a non-profit organization that works solely on the issue of chaining/tethering dogs. DDB has a pre-written, non-aggressive letter for the caretakers of dogs chained in your community. They will even sign and send the letter for you if you are nervous to do it yourself. They are working towards educating people and have even built fences and doghouses to make the lives of these animals better.

Doris Day Animal League [DDAL]
227 Massachusetts Avenue, NE, Suite 100
Washington, D.C. 20002
Tel: 202-546-1761
Email: info@ddal.org
Web site: www.ddal.org
The Doris Day Animal Foundation is dedicated to promoting increased protection for animals and accomplishes its mission primarily through educational programs that empower others to act on behalf of animals. They work with the U.S. Congress, government agencies, and state and local officials, to pass laws and enforce existing laws that reduce the suffering of animals anywhere they are mistreated.

FIREPAW, Inc.
The Foundation for Interdisciplinary Research and Education Promoting Animal Welfare
228 Main Street, #436
Williamstown, MA 01267
Tel: 518-462-5939
FAX: 518-658-0979
Email: info@firepaw.org
Web site: www.firepaw.org
FIREPAW is a charitable nonprofit research and education foundation dedicated to changing public consciousness about animal welfare and to reducing and eliminating the abuse, neglect, abandonment, overpopulation and unnecessary killing of animals.

Human/Animal Violence Education Network—HAVEN
Berkshire County, Massachusetts
Tel: 413-447-7878, ext 40
Web site: http://www.havennetwork.org/index.php
Focus is on the development and implementation of educational programming about the links between animal cruelty and human violence and the promotion of programs that encourage compassion and tolerance. Provides support for the creation and implementation of cross-reporting systems within human services agencies and animal welfare organizations.

The Humane Society of the United States [HSUS]-First Strike Campaign
2100 L. Street, NW
Washington, D.C. 20037
Tel: (301) 258-3076
Web site: www.hsus.org
A national nonprofit organization dedicated to animal welfare.

The Latham Foundation
Latham Plaza Bldg.
1826 Clement Avenue
Alameda, CA 95401
Tel: (510) 521-0920
Email: *info@latham.org*
Web site: *www.latham.org*
A national clearinghouse of information on the link between animal abuse and human violence.

Link-UP
Animal Rescue League [A.R.L] of Boston
Officer Tom Flanagan, State Humane Officer
Law Enforcement Department
or Jim Knight, DVM
10 Chandler Street
P.O. Box 265
Boston, MA 02117
Tel: 617-426-9170, ext.-115
FAX: 617-426-3028
A multidisciplinary partnership and educational program to stop animal cruelty.

PET-ABUSE.COM
P.O. Box 2995
Del Mar, California 92014-5995
Toll-Free: 866-240-1179
FAX: 858-225-0886
Email: info@pet-abuse.com
Web site: www.pet-abuse.com
Publicly accessible, interactive and searchable database on this website dedicated to cataloguing and archiving animal abuse cases throughout the United States. This extensive database is maintained in the hope of assisting law enforcement agencies to apprehend animal abusers.

Society and Animals Forum
(a.k.a. Animal and Society Institute; Previously Psychologists for the Ethical Treatment of Animals [PSYETA])
P.O. Box 1297
Washington Grove, MD 20880-1297

Tel: 301-963-4751
Email: kshapiro@societyandanimalsforum.org
Web site: www.societyandanimalsforum.org
Society and Animals Forum (formerly Psychologists for the Ethical Treatment of Animals) works with social scientists, mental health providers and other animal protection organizations to reduce the suffering and exploitation of both human and nonhuman animals.

Task Force for the Columbus Coalition Against Family Violence
Lesley Ashworth, Esq., Director/Project Coordinator
Karen Days, President
700 Children's Drive, 7th Floor
Columbus, Ohio 43205
Tel: 614-722-5985 (voice)
Tel: (614) 309-3905
FAX: 614-722-5995
Web site: www.theColumbusCoalition.org
Task force works with the Columbus Coalition Against Family Violence to create a pet foster-care program, train police officers and humane investigators about the link between animal and human abuse, provide public education about abuse prevention, and works to strengthen existing animal anti-cruelty laws.

The Vermont Animal Cruelty Task Force [VACTF]
General Information: Joanne Bourbeau
c/o The Humane Society of the United States
New England Regional Office
P.O. Box 619
Jacksonville, VT 05342
Tel: 802-368-2790
Email: info@vactf.org
Web site: www.vactf.org
The Vermont Animal Cruelty Task Force is a statewide coalition of private and governmental agencies and associations that have joined to coordinate Vermont's efforts to prevent and respond to animal cruelty through communication, education, training, legislation and enforcement. They are dedicated to providing the resources and networking opportunities that the state's law enforcement, social service, veterinary and animal welfare communities need to work together for the betterment of Vermont's animal and human populations alike.

BOOKS

Animal cruelty: Pathway to violence against people
(2004) Linda Merz Perez and Kathleen M. Heide
Walnut Creek, CA: Alta Mira Press

Animals and Women: Feminist Theoretical Explorations
(1995; 1999 *second printing*) Carol Adams and Josephine Donovan (eds.)
Durham, NC: Duke University Press

Brute Force: Animal Police and the Challenge of Cruelty
(2004). Arnold Arluke
West Lafayette, IN: Purdue University Press
With little legitimate authority to enforce the law, animal cops become humane educators who try to make people into responsible pet owners. With few victories in court, they look for other ways to feel effective in their fight against cruelty. And with different preferences for doing police or animal work, their department culture tolerates both styles.

Child abuse, domestic violence, and animal abuse:
Linking the circles of compassion for prevention and intervention
(1998) Frank R. Ascione and Phil Arkow (eds.)
West Lafayette, IN: Purdue University Press

Cruelty to animals and interpersonal violence: Readings in Research and Application
(1997) Randall Lockwood and Frank R. Ascione (eds.)
West Lafayette, IN: Purdue University Press

VIDEOS

Animal Hoarding: A Community Task Force Solution Video
Humane Society of the United States (HSUS)
The video is designed to educate agencies and organizations about hoarding.
The video is $6.00
(202) 452-1100

Beyond Violence: The Human-Animal Connection Video
Video was a joint project of Psychologists for the Ethical Treatment of Animals [PsyETA] and Doris Day Animal League [DDAL]
Psychologists for the Ethical Treatment of Animals
P.O. Box 1297
Washington Grove, MD 20880-1297

Tel: 301-963-4751
Web site: www.psyeta.org
Intended audience: humane educators, teachers, mental health professionals, professionals working to stop animal cruelty.
(*This video and accompanying workbook are also available at FIREPAW. Email:* info@firepaw.org)

Breaking the Cycles of Violence: A Guide to Multi-Disciplinary Interventions
Video and Training Manual
The Latham Foundation
Latham Plaza Blvd., 1826 Clement Avenue
Alameda, CA 95401
Tel (510) 521-0920
FAX: (510) 521-9861
For general questions please Email: Info@Latham.org
For order related questions please Email: Orders@Latham.org
A 22-minute video and 64-page training manual produced by The Latham Foundation to help human service and animal welfare professionals do their jobs more effectively by recognizing, reporting, investigating, and treating their interrelated forms of family violence. This practical "how-to" guide helps communities establish interdisciplinary coalitions against all forms of family violence. The manual and video are perfect for training personnel in a wide range of agencies, cross-training with other organizations, and sensitizing community groups to the problems and potential solutions.
Video + Training Manual: $29.75 (plus shipping and sales tax).

The Cruelty Connection—Documentary/Video (BBC and Arts and Entertainment Network, 1999)
British Broadcasting Corporation
BBC Worldwide Americas, Inc.
747 Third Avenue
New York, NY 10017-2803
Tel: (212) 705-9300
FAX: (212) 888-0576

First Strike Campaign Video
The Humane Society of the United States [HSUS]-First Strike Campaign
2100 L. Street, NW
Washington, D.C. 20037
Tel: (301) 258-3076
Web site: www.hsus.org

I am Unseen
Neglect Prevention Presentation/Education

Video/DVD
Dogs Deserve Better
Tel: 1.877.636.1408
If you prefer to order by mail, print out the order form at our web site: http://www.dogsdeservebetter.org/iamunseen.html, and send check or money order to P.O. Box 23, Tipton, PA 16684. If you are unable to print out the order form, you may also write your order on a sheet of paper and mail it to us. ($12.00 for video, $13.00 DVD, Includes $4.00 Shipping).
This video presentation is an overview of the services Dogs Deserve Better offers. It will help educate your audience, from school age to community adults and lawmakers, about the needs of chained dogs, penned dogs, and all dogs ostracized from the family. It will help people realize there is work to be done, and challenges them to help.

In the Line of Duty: Animal Abuse Video
Tel: 1-800-462-5232
Intended audience: Law enforcement, animal control officers, humane investigators.

Patterns of Abuse: Exploding the Cycle Video
Pyramid Media
P.O. Box 1048/WEB
Santa Monica, CA 90406
Tel: 800-421-2304
Tel (in Los Angeles, CA area): 310-828-7577
FAX: 310-453-9083
Email: info@pyramidmedia.com
Produced by Chicago Anti-Cruelty Society and Erik Friedl (1999)
Intended audiences: junior high- and high school-level students, college-level psychology classes, hospitals and current/potential pet owner-guardians.

MANUALS/EVALUATION TOOLS/TRAINING PROGRAMS

American Humane Association [AHA]
The Violence Link Training Program
63 Inverness Drive, East
Englewood, Colorado 80112-5117
P.O. Box 3597
Englewood, CO 80155-3597
Tel: 1-800-227-4645
Web site: www.americanhumane.org

AHA Link Training Program (Link Between Violence to People and Animals)
Tel: 1-800-227-4645 ext. 461
American Humane is the only national humane organization with divisions for protecting both children and animals from neglect, abuse, cruelty, and exploitation. The organization addresses the relationship between cruelty to animals and other forms of societal violence. American Humane is a leader in researching the problem, raising public awareness, and most importantly, providing tools for decision makers, social service providers, animal care and control professionals, veterinarians, parents, and concerned citizens to recognize problems and take appropriate steps to end abuse and protect its victims. AHA provides networking, training and a resource center.
Offers interagency cross-training programs to stop animal cruelty.
Offers a Cruelty Kit with specific instructions for taking animal abuse seriously by strengthening animal cruelty legislation in local communities. One of the kit's publications, "Growing up humane in a violent world," offers parent advice for teaching humane ethics to their children.

American Humane Association (1993). Protecting children and animals: An agenda for a nonviolent future. Englewood, CO: American Humane Association. Available from AHA; Original price listing: $6.00 ea.

American Humane Association (1995). The cycle of violence to children and animals. Englewood, CO: American Humane Association. Available from AHA; Original price listing: 100 for $20.00.

American Humane Association (1997). Growing up humane in a violent world: A parent's guide. Englewood, CO: American Humane Association. Available from AHA; Original price listing: $5.00 ea.

Animal Cruelty Training Sessions and Brochures for Mental Health Professionals
Society and Animals Forum provides free copies of its brochure:
"Workshops for Counseling Professions: Intervening in the Cycle of Abuse"

Society and Animals Forum (a.k.a. Animals and Society Institute; formerly PsyETA)
P.O. Box 1297
Washington Grove, MD 20880-1297
Email: *kshapiro@societyandanimalsforum.org*
Web site: *www.societyandanimalsforum.org*

Animal Cruelty Training Manuals for Mental Health Professionals *now on DVD*
AniCare Model of Treatment for Animal Abuse
AniCare Child

Society and Animals Forum (a.k.a. Animals and Society Institute; formerly PsyETA)
P.O. Box 1297
Washington Grove, MD 20880-1297
Email: *kshapiro@societyandanimalsforum.org*
Web site: *www.societyandanimalsforum.org*

Animal Hoarding sample bonding and "unfit" laws
Humane Society of the United States (HSUS)
Animal Sheltering Issues section
Call to request copies
Tel: 202-452-1100

American Society for the Prevention of Animal Cruelty [ASPCA]
424 East 92nd Street
New York, NY 10128
Tel: 212-876-7700
Web site: www.aspca.org
The ASPCA Animal Cruelty Prosecution Task Force:
An organization made up of prosecutors, attorneys and law enforcement officials, has been created to examine and track animal cruelty cases and promote effective prosecution. In addition, an intervention program has been launched by the ASPCA in which convicted abusers meet with our Director of Counseling Services.
Key goals of the program are:
Cross-training among human service and animal welfare agencies
Cross-reporting
Information-sharing among agencies and effective public education
Psycho-educational intervention for abusers
Foster care for animals at risk

Companion Animal Victims Educational Seminars [CAVES]
FIREPAW, Inc.
The Foundation for Interdisciplinary Research and Education Promoting Animal Welfare
228 Main Street, #436
Williamstown, MA 01267
Tel: 518-462-5939
FAX: 518-658-0979
Email: info@firepaw.org
Web site: www.firepaw.org
Companion Animal Victims Educational Seminars [CAVES] *Offers profession-specific educational seminars with a creative, user-friendly, prac-*

tical approach to training geared for specific professions. Seminars target the unique challenges and solutions for each profession. Seminars designed for specific professions include: animal control officers, humane investigators, law enforcement, prosecutors, judges, animal welfare protectionists, veterinarians, domestic violence caseworkers, social service professionals and mental health professionals/therapists.

Cruelty Statutes United States and Canada. Englewood, CO, 1994: American Humane Association. Web site: www.americanhumane.org

Cruelty to animals and other crimes: Program Manual
Massachusetts Society for the Prevention of Cruelty to Animals and North-eastern University (1997). Massachusetts Society for the Prevention of Cruelty to Animals [MSPCA] Boston, MA
350 South Huntington Avenue
Boston, MA 02130
Tel: (617) 522-7400

Doris Day Animal League [DDAL]
227 Massachusetts Avenue, NE, Suite 100
Washington, DC 20002
Tel: 202-546-1761
FAX: 202-546-2193
Email: info@ddal.org
Web Site: www.ddal.org
Doris Day Animal Foundation:
Beyond Violence: The Human-Animal Connection: *This program provides resources to professionals that work with perpetrators and victims of animal abuse, such as police officers, child psychologists, animal control officers and teachers.*
Training Workshops: *Beyond Violence staff conduct training workshops on the violence connection and the AniCare prevention and intervention models. Workshops can be tailored to the concerns of a particular group or community agency.*
Intervention Tools: *The* AniCare Model of Treatment for Animal Abuse, *for use with adults, is an original approach to therapeutic intervention in animal abuse.* AniCare Child *is the only published treatment approach to focus exclusively on juvenile cruelty to animals.*

Understanding the Violence Connection: The Violence Connection *publication examines the link between animal abuse and other violent crimes. This 12-page booklet describes a range of efforts underway to implement legislative, program, and policy responses to animal abuse with a view toward prevention and treatment.*

50 Strategies To Prevent Violent Domestic Crime Program Manual
National Crime Prevention Council
Web site: http://www.ncpc.org/
ISBN 1-929888-18-X. 144 pp. $19.95
M81: $13.95
From the United States, you can order our publications by calling
800-627-2911. From countries outside the USA, call 518-843-8161.
*This manual takes readers behind the scenes of some of the best programs in
36 states with a discussion of the partnerships and components necessary to
successfully apply the strategy in any setting. With tips from the field provided
by program organizers, and lessons learned from the obstacles they faced,
readers will be equipped to take these exciting strategies back to their own
community. This collection of promising programs was designed to inspire
readers to seek out new and alternative methods to aid under served victims
of violent domestic crime including teens in dating relationships, elderly victims of late-life abuse, child witnesses to violence, battered immigrants, male
victims, and survivors in the gay and lesbian community.*

Forensic Investigation of Animal Cruelty: A Guide for Veterinary and Law
Enforcement Professionals to be published in 2005.
Randall Lockwood, Ph.D., Leslie Sinclair, DVM and Melinda Merck, DVM

Guidebook for the Visual Assessment of Physical Child Abuse. (Englewood,
CO, 1996). Englewood, CO, 1995: American Humane Association. Web site:
www.americanhumane.org

The Humane Society of the United States [HSUS]
First Strike Program
2100 L. Street, NW
Washington, D.C. 20037
Tel: (301) 258-3076
Web site: www.hsus.org/firststrike
HSUS-First Strike Campaign
Tel: 1-888-213-0956
Email: firststrike@hsus.org
First Strike music video: http://www.hsus.org/video_clips/page
.jsp?itemID=27259993
On-line Directory of Safe Havens for Animals Programs
*Humane Society of the United States (HSUS) First Strike Campaign: to edu-
cate the public on the connection between animal abuse and human violence.
The campaign is designed to addressed interaction, education and prevention
of animal abuse at the local level. One of the goals of the campaign is to train
law enforcement officers about the connection between animal abuse and violence in the home (Turner, 2000).*

First Strike Workshops:
First Strike workshops are designed to train professionals such as educators, humane investigators, veterinarians, law enforcement officers, prosecutors, judges, domestic violence and child welfare advocates, adult protective service professionals, and other anti-violence advocates to recognize the connection between animal cruelty and human violence, and to intervene effectively before violence occurs.
Through these workshops they provide the support and foundation necessary for the development of human violence. Specifically, the workshops fulfill the following goals:

- *Provide an opportunity to introduce local professionals involved in animal care and control to their counterparts in human services who deal with abused children, women, and other victims of family and community violence.*
- *Educate representatives of the law enforcement and legislative communities about the seriousness of animal cruelty cases in the larger context of family and community violence. This is particularly helpful if there have been recent cases that have attracted attention due to insufficient enforcement.*
- *Provide a foundation for the establishment of a local antiviolence coalition. Such coalitions might then meet on a regular basis to discuss issues such as cross-training, research, legislation, intervention strategies, and community education.*
- *Bring these issues to the attention of the local media. This is particularly helpful if there are local media people clearly identified as advocates for animal protection, domestic violence, or child welfare issues.*

First Strike Directory of Violence Prevention and Intervention Programs:
Special attention is paid to animal-related programs that focus on victims and perpetrators of violence and on those who are considered to be at risk of becoming entangled in the web of abuse. Also included are programs that reach out to the professionals—teachers, social service workers, and law enforcement authorities—who work with these populations.
Updated directory (2004) in order to provide current information on the original programs highlighted in 2000. The HSUS is pleased to make this revised edition available online as a PDF file.

Mental health professional manual to evaluate child/adolescent perpetrators of animal cruelty
Lewchanin, S., and Zimmerman, E. 2000. *Clinical assessment of juvenile animal cruelty.*
Brunswick, ME: Biddle Publishing

Recognizing and Reporting Animal Abuse: A Veterinarian's Guide.
Englewood, CO: American Humane Association.

American Humane Association (AHA)
63 Inverness Drive, East
Englewood, Colorado 80112-5117
Web site: www.americanhumane.org

Safe Havens for Pets: Guidelines for Programs Sheltering Pets for Women
Who are Battered
Frank R. Ascione, Ph.D.,
Department of Psychology, Utah State University
2810 Old Main Hill
Logan, Utah 84322-2810
Tel: 435-797-1464
FAX: 435-797-1448
Email: FrankA@coe.usu.edu,
Sponsored by the Geraldine R. Dodge Foundation.

Society and Animals Forum (a.k.a. Animals and Society Institute; formerly
PSYETA)
Kenneth Shapiro, Executive Director
Tel: 301-963-4751
Web site: www.societyandanimalsforum.org
*Society and Animals Forum offers Powerpoint presentations on the relation-
ship between human violence and animal abuse and workshops on the as-
sessment and treatment of animal abusers.*

Society and Animals Forum Workshops—For mental health, education, and
criminal justice professionals
Assessing and Treating Juvenile Animal Abuse
Assessing and Treating Adult Animal Abuse
Animal Abuse: Understanding, Identification and Action Planning

The Connection Between Animal Abuse and Violence Against Human Beings.

A Training Guide for Recognizing and Reporting Child Abuse for Animal
Control Officers and Humane Investigators. Englewood, CO, 1995: American Humane Association. Web site: www.americanhumane.org

The Vermont Animal Cruelty Task Force [VACTF] Manual
General Information: Joanne Bourbeau
c/o The Humane Society of the United States
New England Regional Office
PO Box 619
Jacksonville, VT 05342
Tel: 802-368-2790

E-mail: info@vactf.org
Web site: www.vactf.org
Provides a searchable online manual including an excellent chapter devoted to HOARDING.

LAW ENFORCEMENT MULTIDISCIPLINARY PROGRAMS: LINK BETWEEN ANIMAL ABUSE AND FAMILY VIOLENCE

Baltimore Police Department
Police Commissioner's Office
601 East Fayette Street
Baltimore, MD 21202
Tel: (410) 396-2600

Biddeford Police Department
Animal Control Officer
39 Alfred Street
Biddeford, ME 04005
Tel: (207) 282-5127
Email: aco@bpd.net

DVERT Program
Domestic Violence Coordinator
Colorado Springs Police Department
705 South Nevada Avenue
Colorado Springs, CO 80903
Tel: (719) 444-7813

Humane Society of Missouri
Rescue and Investigations Coordinator
1201 Macklind Avenue
St. Louis, MO 63110
Tel: (314) 951-1514

Link-UP
Animal Rescue League (ARL) of Boston
Tom Flanagan, State Humane Officer
Law Enforcement Department
10 Chandler Street
PO Box 265
Boston, MA 02117
Tel: 617-426-9170 X115

FAX: 617-426-3028
Email: tflanagan@arlboston.org
Part of the National Crime Prevention Council www.ncpc.org
An independent Link-UP style program has also been implemented in
Greenfield, MA. Contact Dee Clapp-Boyle, (dee@petz.org), Martha Cutt,
(humaneed@petz.org), or Jay Conway, (bluejaybluejean@yahoo.com).
*Link-UP educates law enforcement officers and first responders about the
connection between animal abuse and domestic violence.*

Link-UP Educational Network
Jim Knight, DVM
344 Old Greenwich Plains Road
Ware, MA   01082
Tel: 413-967-7325
*Link-UP officers partnered with a local veterinarian to create the Link-UP
Education Network. The Network is a group of 40 professionals from a variety of criminal justice and social service agencies convened to discuss the
Link and mobilize their peers to intervene. The group holds 10-week workshops with agencies to teach community leaders about screening for domestic violence when animal abuse is reported. The Link-UP Education Network
is currently exploring the creation of a program to provide temporary crisis
shelter for the companion animals of victims of violence.*

National Crime Prevention Council
Web site: *http://www.ncpc.org/*
*Offers numerous resources for establishing professional partnerships to stop
animal and human abuse.*

ANIMAL ABUSE ASSESSMENT TOOLS AND
TREATMENT APPROACHES

Ani-Care and Ani-Care Child Model of Treatment for Animal Abuse
Society and Animals Forum and Maryland Psychological Association, Co-
lumbia, Maryland
Jory, B. and Randour, M. (1999). The Ani-Care model of treatment for animal abuse. Washington Grove, MD: Psychologists for the Ethical treatment
of Animals

Society and Animals Forum (*a.k.a. Animals and Society Institute; Previously
Psychologists for the Ethical Treatment of Animals—PSYETA*)
P.O. Box 1297
Washington Grove, MD 20880-1297

Tel: 301-963-4751
Web site: www.societyandanimalsforum.org

Society and Animals Forum Workshops - For mental health, education, and criminal justice professionals
Assessing and Treating Juvenile Animal Abuse.
Assessing and Treating Adult Animal Abuse.
Animal Abuse: Understanding, Identification and Action Planning.
The Connection Between Animal Abuse and Violence Against Human Beings.

AniCare Child: An Assessment and Treatment Approach for Childhood Animal Abuse by Mary Lou Randour, PhD, Susan Krinsk, LMHC, and Joanne L. Wolf, MA, CAC.
Available through the Doris Day Animal Foundation http://www.ddaf.org/.

Boat Inventory on Animal-Related Experiences [BIARE] (formerly the Animal-Related Trauma Inventory)
Designed for screening and information-gathering to determine an individual's history of animal-related experiences including animal cruelty and trauma-related events involving animals. Covers the following: cruelty to animals, animals used to control another person, sexual interactions with animals, previous pet ownership, animal-related fears.

Boat, B. (1999). Abusive children and abuse of animals: Using the links to inform child assessment and protection. In P. Arkow and F. Ascione (Eds.) Child abuse, domestic violence and animal abuse: Linking the circles of compassion for prevention and intervention (pp. 83-100). West Lafayette, IN: Purdue University Press.

Community Intervention model for juvenile animal abuse
Zimmerman, E. and Lewchanin, S. (2000). Community intervention in juvenile cruelty to animals. Brunswick, ME: Biddle Publishing.

Cruelty to Animals Assessment Inventory [CAAI]—Children and Animals
Designed to uncover multiple aspects of animal cruelty and is intended for use with children five years old and up and their parents. The inventory explores ability for empathy/expression of remorse, settings for animal cruelty (doing it alone versus in a group setting with peers), the degree to which the child tries to cover up his or her animal abuse, and the ability to understand animal sentience. The inventory screens for duration, frequency and severity of acts of animal cruelty.

Ascione, F., Thompson, T., and Black, T. (1997). Childhood cruelty to animals: Assessing cruelty dimensions and motivations. *Anthrozoos*, 10, 170–179.

Battered Partner Shelter Survey/Pet Maltreatment Survey (BPSS)
Battered Partner Shelter Survey/Pet Maltreatment Survey—Mother/child version
Children's Observation and Experience with their Pets Survey (COEP)
Families and Pets Survey
Ascione, F. and Weber, C. (1995-1996) Logan, UT: Department of Psychology, Utah State University
Email: FrankA@coe.usu.edu

Miscellaneous Professional Resources

Arluke, A., Levin, J., Luke, C. and Ascione, F. (1999). The relationship of animal abuse to violence and other forms of antisocial behavior. Journal of Interpersonal Violence, Vol. 14(9), 963-975.
Listing of nonviolent offenses correlated with animal abuse.

Loar, L. (2000). Treatment for people who hurt animals: It's the law.
C.H.A.I.N. (Collective Humane Action and Information Network) Letter 13 (1): 10, 18.
Listing of professionals who conduct animal cruelty assessment and treatment for perpetrators involved in criminal cases.

Reisman, R. and Adams, C. A. (1996). Part of what veterinarians do is treat animal victims of violence. Should they also report abusers? Latham Letter, XVII (1), 8- 11.

ANIMAL SAFE HAVEN PROGRAM INFORMATION

A New Hope Center [ANHC]
20 Church Street
Owego, N.Y. 13827
Toll Free: 800-696-7600
Tel: 607-687-6887
Email: anhc@att.net
Web site: http:// anhc.home.att.net/

PetSafe
Janice Sojka, DVM
Department of Veterinary Medicine
Purdue University
Lafayette, Indiana

Tel: 765-494-8548
Email: sojkaje@purdue.edu

Task Force for the Columbus Coalition Against Family Violence
Lesley Ashworth, Esq., Director
Lori Barton, Task Force Director
700 Children's Drive, 7th Floor
Columbus Ohio 43205
Tel: 614-722-598
Tel: 614-722-6328
Web site: www.theColumbusCoalition.org

ADDITIONAL SOURCES

AARDVARC (An Abuse, Rape and Domestic Violence Aid and Resource Collection)
Catherine NeSmith
Executive Director
AARDVARC.org, Inc.
606 Calibre Crest Parkway, Suite 103
Altamonte Springs, FL 32714
Email: aardvarcinfo@aol.com
Web site: www.aardvarc.org
A Florida-based non-profit organization dedicated to combating family and relationship violence, sexual violence and child abuse.

AARDVARC :
Web site: http://www.aardvarc.org/dv/pets.shtml
Animal Abuse Resources . . . Entire section devoted to "pets as pawns in domestic violence" which includes extensive listing of resources.

Association of Veterinarians for Animal Rights [AVAR]
P.O. Box 208
Davis, CA 95617-0208
Tel: 530-759-8106
Email: Info@avar.org
Web site: www.avar.org
AVAR is actively seeking reformation of the way society treats all nonhumans.

Green Chimneys School
400 Doansburg Road, Box 719

Brewster, NY 10509
Tel: (845) 279-2995
Tel: (718) 892-6810
Tel: (203) 797-8320
FAX: (845) 279-3077
Web site: www.greenchimneys.org
Green Chimneys is located in the Town of Patterson, NY. The agency serves children and adults with special needs. To date the agency is considered the strongest and most diverse of its kind involving farm, animal, plant and wildlife assisted activities. They strive to develop a harmonious relationship between people, animals, plants, nature and the environment through an array of educational, recreational, vocational and mental health services. GC is a voluntary, non-sectarian, multi-service agency. Programs include a Farm and Wildlife Conservation Center, and the East Coast Assistance Dogs.

Hoarding of Animals Research Consortium [HARC]
Web site: www.tufts.edu/vet/cfa/hoarding
Offers information on the latest studies on anti-hoarding strategies. Topics available at this site include:

- *Animal hoarding and its relationship to elder neglect, child neglect and adult self-neglect*
- *Medical literature abstracts about animal hoarding*
- *Media reviews of animal hoarding cases*
- *Veterinarians' role in helping—and hindering—animal hoarding cases*
- *Veterinarian animal triage assessment scales (Tufts Animal Care and Condition Scales—TACC)*
- *Guardianship issues and animal hoarding*
- *Costs involved in resolving animal hoarding cases*
- *Benefits of multidisciplinary partnerships when dealing with animal hoarding cases*
- *Tools for therapists dealing with animal hoarders (including therapeutic techniques)*
- *Animal hoarding and the law*
- *Animal hoarding versus legitimate animal rescue/animal sheltering*

Hoarding and the Elderly Resources
Web site: http://www.wordbridges.net/elderabuse/AAR/Vol1Issue3/hoardinglitreview.html

National Center for Victims of Crime
2000 M Street, NW

Suite 480
Washington, DC 20036
Tel: (202) 467-8700
FAX: (202) 476-8701
Email: webmaster@ncvc.org
Web site: www.ncvc.org
NCVC: Forging New Collaborations: Victim Service and Animal Welfare Professionals
The nation's leading resource and advocacy organization for crime victims, providing direct services for victims, and technical training and assistance for professionals.

New York City Hoarding Taskforce, Cornell University
Web site: www.cornellaging.com/gem/hoa_nyc_hoa_tas.html
Offers information about frequently asked questions concerning hoarding
Offers a sample assessment form for professionals working with hoarders

Web site: http://www.helpinganimals.com/Factsheet/files/FactsheetDisplay.asp?ID=18
Animal Abuse Resources

Web site: *www.arkonline/violence.html*
A social sentinel: Acts of animal cruelty can point to an offender's potential for violence against humans

Web site: www.unchainyourdog.org
A site advocating on behalf of chained dogs.

Web site: *www.Pets911.com*
A site to locate humane agencies and animal control in your community

Web site: www.tufts.edu/vet/vet_common/pdf/petinfo/dvm/case_
Veterinarians help convict animal abuser: A groundbreaking study

Web site: http://www.animalsvoice.com/PAGES/invest/randour.html
The link between animal and human cruelty and the animal cruelty background of many serial killers. By psychologist and animal cruelty treatment expert Mary Lou Randour, Ph.D.

Web site: http://www.animaltherapy.net/

Web site: http://www.animaltherapy.net/Bibliography-Link.html
An updated listing of scientific publications on the topic of the link between animal abuse, domestic violence and child abuse by Phil Arkow

Web site: www.ncvc.org/newsltr/animalab.htm
National Center for Victims of Crime Newsletter (2001). Networks: Forging new collaborations—victim service and animal welfare professionals

Web site: http://www.pet-abuse.com/cruelty/risk.php
Factors in the Assessment of Dangerousness in Perpetrators of Animal Cruelty by Randall Lockwood, Ph.D.

Bibliography

Achenbach, T., C. Howell, H. Quay, and K. Conners. "National survey of problems and competencies among four to sixteen-year-olds." *Monographs of the Society for Research in Child Development*, 56, no. 225. (1991).

Adams, C. "Bringing peace home: A feminist philosophical perspective in the abuse of women, children and pet animals." *Hypatia*, 9 (1994):63–84.

—— "Woman-battering and harm to animals." Pp. 55–84 in *Animals and women: Feminist theoretical exploration,* edited by C. Adams and J. Donovan. Durham, North Carolina: Duke University Press, 1995.

Agnew, R. (1998). The causes of animal abuse: A social-psychological analysis. *Theoretical Criminology* 2: 177–209.

Albert, A. and K. Bulcroft. "Pets, families and the life course." *Journal of Marriage and the Family*, 50 (1988): 543–552.

Allen, C. "Opening the closed door: Strategies for coping with animal hoarders." *Animal Sheltering Magazine* (July-August 2004): 15–27.

American Humane Association, <http://www.americanhumane.org> (5 May, 2005).

American Psychiatric Association. *Diagnostic and statistical manual of mental disorders* (DSM-IV). 4th ed. Washington, D.C.: APA, 2000.

American Veterinary Medical Association (AVMA). "Veterinarians should report animal abuse." *Journal of the American Veterinary Medical Association (JAVMA)* 208 (1996): 175.

Animal Awareness.org: <http://www.animalawareness.org/pages/types_neglect .html> (4 May 2005).

Anon., "Cops, led by odor, find 145 cats at home," *Associated Press,* 19 August 2004a, 7(N).

Anon., "Authorities remove 160 rabbits from home," *Associated Press,* 10 August 10 2004b, 12 (N).

Anon., "165 Pets taken from California ex-mayor's home," *Associated Press,* (2005). 13 May 2005, 5 (N).

APRI. *Jumpstart: Resource manual for newly assigned juvenile prosecutors.* Alexandria, VA: American Prosecutors Research Institute, 1999.

Arkow, P. "Animal abuse and domestic violence: Intake statistics tell a sad story." *Latham Letter*, 15, no.2 (1994a): 17.

―――― "Child abuse, animal abuse and the veterinarian." *Journal of the American Veterinary Medical Association* 204, no.7 (1994b): 1004–1007.

―――― "The relationship between animal abuse and other forms of family violence." *Family Violence and Sexual Assault Bulletin*, 12 no.1–2 (1996): 29–34.

―――― "The evolution of animal welfare as a human welfare concern." Pp. 19–37 in Child Abuse, Domestic Violence and Animal Abuse: Linking the Circles of Compassion for Prevention and Intervention, edited by F. Ascione and Arkow, P. West Lafayette, Ind.: Purdue University Press, 1999.

―――― ed. Breaking the cycles of violence: A guide to multi-disciplinary interventions. A handbook for child protection, domestic violence and animal protection agencies. Alameda, Ca.: Latham Foundation, 2003.

___ "The veterinarian's role in preventing family violence." *Protecting Children* 19 no.1 (2004): 4–12.

Arkow, P. and H. Munro. "The Veterinarian's Role in the Prevention of Family Violence: The Experience of the Human Medical Profession Regarding the Recognition and Reporting of Non-Accidental Injury." In *International Handbook on Cruelty to Animals,* edited by F. Ascione. West Lafayette, Ind.: Purdue University Press. *In press.*

Arluke, A., F. Ascione, J. Levin, and C. Luke. "The relationship of animal abuse to violence and other forms of antisocial behavior." *Journal of Interpersonal Violence* 14, no.9 (1999): 963–975.

Arluke, A. and C. Luke. "Physical cruelty toward animals in Massachusetts, 1975–1990." *Society & Animals*, 5 (1997): (1997). 195–204.

Ascione, F. "Enhancing children's attitudes about humane treatment of animals: Generalizations to human-directed empathy." *Anthrozoos* 5 (1992): 176–191.

―――― "Children who are cruel to animals: A review of research and implications for developmental psychopathology." *Anthrozoos* 4 (1993): 226–247.

―――― "Domestic violence and cruelty to animals." *Latham Letter* 17, no.1 (1996): 1–16.

―――― "Battered women's reports of their partner and children's cruelty to animals." *Journal of Emotional Abuse* 1 (1998a): 119–133.

―――― "Children who are cruel to animals: A review of research and implications for developmental psychopathology." Pp. 83–104 in *Cruelty to animals and interpersonal violence: Readings in research and application*, edited by R. Lockwood and F. Ascione. West Lafayette, Ind.: Purdue University Press, 1998b.

―――― *Safe Havens for Pets: Guidelines for Programs Sheltering Pets for Women Who are Battered.* Morristown, New Jersey: Geraldine R. Dodge Foundation, 2000.

―――― "Animal abuse and youth violence." *Juvenile Justice Bulletin*, U.S. Department of Justice, Office of Juvenile Justice and Delinquency Prevention. (Sept. 2001):1–15.

Ascione, F. and P.Arkow, eds. *Child abuse, domestic violence and animal abuse: Linking the circles of compassion for prevention and intervention.* West Lafayette, Ind.: Purdue University Press,1999.

Ascione, F. and R. Lockwood, eds. *Cruelty to animals and interpersonal violence: Readings and research applications.* Lafayette, Ind: Purdue University Press, 1997.

—— "Cruelty to animals: Changing psychological, social and legislative perspectives." *The State of the Animals* (2001): 39–53.

Ascione, F., T. Thompson, and T. Black. "Childhood cruelty to animals: Assessing cruelty dimensions and motivations." *Anthrozoos* 10, no. 4 (1997): 170–177.

Ascione, F., C. Weber, and S. Wood. "Animal welfare and domestic violence: Final report." Morristown, New Jersey: Geraldine R. Dodge Foundation, 1997a.

—— "The abuse of animals and domestic violence: A national survey of shelters for women who are battered." *Society & Animals* 5, no.3 (1997b): 205–218.

AVMA /American Veterinary Medical Association. *U.S. pet ownership and demographic sourcebook.* Schaumburg, Ill: AVMA, 1997.

Baldry, A. "Animal abuse and exposure to inter-parental violence in Italian youth." *Journal of Interpersonal Violence* 18 (2003): 258–281.

Barnett, O., C. Miller-Perrin, and R. Perrin, R. *Family violence across the lifespan.* Thousand Oaks, Ca.: Sage Publishing, 1997.

Becker, F. and L. French. "Making the Links: Child Abuse, Animal Cruelty and Domestic Violence." *Child Abuse Review* 13, (2004): 399–414.

Beckett, V. "The silent victims of family violence." *AV Magazine*, The American Anti-Vivisection Society (Winter 2005): 16–18.

Beirne, P. "The use and abuse of animals in criminology: A brief history and review." *Social Justice,* 22, (1995): 5–31.

Boat, B. "The relationship between violence to children and violence to animals: An ignored link?" *Journal of Interpersonal Violence* 10, no.4 (1995): 229–235.

Boat, B. and J. Knight. "Experiences and risks of adult protective services case managers when assisting clients who have companion animals." *Journal of Elder Abuse & Neglect* 12, no.3/4 (2000): 145–155.

Bowd, A.D. and A.C. Bowd. "Attitudes toward the treatment of animals: A study of Christian groups in Australia." *Anthrozoos*, 3, no.1 (1989): 20–24.

Browne, A. *When battered women kill.* New York: Free Press, 1987.

—— "Violence against women by male partners: Prevalence, outcomes and policy implications." *American Psychologist* 48 (1993): 1077–1087.

Bryant, K. "The richness of the child-pet relationship: A consideration of both benefits and costs of pets to children." *Anthrozoos* 3 (1990): 253–261.

Cain, A. "A study of pets in the family system." Pp. 72–81 in *New perspectives on our lives with companion animals*, edited by A. Katcher and A. Beck. Philadelphia: University of Pennsylvania Press, 1983.

Canadian Veterinary Medical Association. "Animal welfare position statements: Animal abuse." <http://www.canadianveterinarians.net> (5 May 2005).

Carlisle-Frank, P. and J. Frank. "Owners, guardians, and owner-guardians: Differing relationships with pets." *Under review* (2005).

Carlisle-Frank, P., J. Frank, and L. Nielsen. "Selective battering of the family pet." *Anthrozoos* 17, 1 (2004a): 26–41.

—— "Companion Animals as Scapegoats, Property, and Victims of Abuse in Violent Homes." Paper published in Linking Violence: The Relationship Between

Violence Against Animals and Humans Conference Papers, University College of Cape Breton, Sydney, Nova Scotia, May 2004b.

Carmack, B. J. "The effects on family members and functioning after the death of a pet." Pp. 149–161 in *Pets and the family*, edited by M. B. Sussman. New York: Haworth Press, 1985.

Clarke, J.P. "New South Wales Police animal cruelty research project." Unpublished report, New South Wales Police Service, Sydney, Australia, 2002.

Clifton, M. "Animals in bondage: The hoarding mind." *Animal People*. Jan.–Feb.1999. <http://www.animalpeoplenews.org/99/1/hoarders.html> (20 May 2005).

Costin, L. "Unraveling the Mary Ellen legend: Origins of the "cruelty" movement." *Social Service Review* 65, no.2 (1991): 203–223.

Crary, D., "Animal cruelty as a warning," *Associated Press*, 20, Feb 2002, 18 (N).

Crosetti,V. "Handling hoarders." *Animal People*. Mar. 1999. <http://www.animalpeoplenews.or/99/2/handling_hoarders.html> (14 May 2005).

Dadds, M.R., C. Whiting, P. Bunn, J.A. Fraser, J.H. Charlson, and A. Pirola-Merlo. "Measurement of cruelty in children: The cruelty to animals inventory." *Journal of Abnormal Child Psychology* 32, no.3 (2004): 321–334.

Davidson, H. "What lawyers and judges should know about the link between child abuse and animal cruelty." *Child and Law Practice* 17, no.4 (1998): 60–61.

Department of Justice. "Bureau of Justice Statistics Crime Data Brief: Intimate Partner Violence, 1993–2001." Washington, D.C.: DOJ, 2003.

DeViney, E., J. Dickert, and R. Lockwood. "The care of pets within child abusing families." *International Journal for the Study of Animal Problems* 4, no. 4 (1983): 321–329.

Dogs Deserve Better (DDB). "The Facts About Chaining or Tethering Dogs." <http://www.dogsdeservebetter.com> (10 May 2005).

Douglas, J., A. Burgess, and R. Ressler. *Sexual homicide: Patterns and motives*. New York: Free Press, 1995.

Duel, D. *Violence Prevention & Intervention: A Directory of Animal-Related Programs*. Washington, DC: Humane Society of the U.S., 2004.

Dutton, M. *Empowering and healing the battered woman*. New York: Springer Press, 1992.

Edleson, J. and M. Brygger. "Gender differences in reporting battering incidents." *Family Relations* 35 (1986): 377–382.

Entin, A. D. "Pets, photos and family theory: triangles in the family." Paper presented at the 1983 Annual Convention of the American Psychological Association, Anaheim, Ca, 1983.

Felthous, A. "Aggression against cats, dogs and people." *Child Psychiatry and Human Development* 10 (1980): 169–177.

Felthous, A. and S. Kellert, S. "Violence against animals and people: Is aggression against living creatures generalized?" *Bulletin of the American Academy of Psychiatry Law* 14 (1986): 55–69.

Felthous, A. and S. Kellert. "Psychological aspects of selecting animal species for physical abuse." *Journal of Forensic Science* 32, no. 6 (1987a): 1713–1723.

——— "Childhood cruelty to animals and later aggression against people: A review." *American Journal of Psychiatry* 144 (1987b): 710–717.

Finkelhor, D., L. Williams, L., and N. Burns. *Nursery crimes: Sexual abuse in day-care*. Newbury Park, Ca.: Sage, 1988. Fish, J. "Life at the End of a Chain." <http://www.dogsdeservebetter.com/endofchain.html> (10 May 2005).

Flynn, C. "Animal abuse in childhood and later support for interpersonal violence in families." *Society and Animals* 7 (1999a): 161–172.

——— "Exploring the link between corporal punishment and children's cruelty to animals." *Journal of Marriage and the Family* 61 (1999b): 971–981.

——— "Why family professionals can no longer ignore violence toward animals." *Family Relations*, 49, no.1 (2000a): 87–95.

——— "Woman's best friend: Pet abuse and the role of companion animals in the lives of battered women." *Violence Against Women* 6 (2000b): 162–177.

——— "Battered women and their animal companions: Symbolic interaction between human and non-human animals." *Society & Animals* 8, no.2 (2000c): 99–127.

——— "Acknowledging the zoological connection: A sociological analysis of animal cruelty." *Society & Animals* 9 (2001) 71–87.

——— "Hunting and illegal violence against human and other animals: Exploring the relationship." *Society & Animals* 10 (2002): 137–154.

Frasch, P., S. Otto, K. Olsen, and P. Ernest. "State animal anti-cruelty statutes: An overview." *Animal Law* 5 (1999): 69–80.

Fucini, S. "The abuser: First a dog then a child?" *American Humane* 5 (1978): 14–15.

Ganley, A. "Court-mandated counseling for men who batter: A three-day workshop for mental health professionals." Washington, DC: Center for Women Policy Studies, 1985.

Galvin, S. and H. Herzog. "Ethical ideology, animal rights activism and attitudes toward treatment of animals." *Ethics and Behavior* 2 (1992): 141–149.

Gelles, R. *Intimate violence in families*. 3rd ed. Thousand Oaks, Ca.: Sage, 1997.

Gelles, R. and M. Strauss. *Intimate Violence*, New York: Simon & Schuster, 1988.

Gerbasi, K. "Gender and non-human animal cruelty convictions: Data from Pet-Abuse.com." *Society & Animals* 12, no.4(2004): 359–365.

Gershman, K., J. Sacks, and J. Wright. "Which Dogs Bite? A Case-Control Study of Risk Factors." *Pediatrics* 93, no. 6 (1994): 913–917.

Gottfredson, M. and T. Hirshi, eds. *A general theory of crime*. Stanford, Ca.: Stanford Press, 1990.

Herbst, K. "Close to Home: A Community Development Response to Domestic Violence." *Change Makers Journal*. September 2003. <http://www.changemakers.net/journal/03september/herbst.cfm> (18 Feb. 2005).

Hellman, D. and N. Blackman. "Enuresis, fire-setting, and cruelty to animals: A triad predictive of adult crime." *American Journal of Psychiatry* 122 (1966): 1431–1435.

Henry, B. "Exposure to animal abuse and group context: Two factors affecting participation in animal abuse." *Anthrozoos* 17, no.4 (2004a): 290–305.

——— "The relationship between animal cruelty, delinquency and attitudes toward the treatment of animals." *Society and Animals* 12, no. 3 (2004b): 185–207.

Herzog, H. and G. Borghardt. "Attitudes toward animals: Origins and diversity." Pp. 85–100 in *Animals and people sharing the world*, edited by A. Rowan. New Hampshire: University Press of New England, 1988.

Hirschauer, S.C., "Tethered dogs might be on short leash: The number of localities that prohibit keeping dogs tied outdoors increased nationwide," 16 March 2005, *Daily Press* 15 (N).

Hoarding of Animals Research Consortium (HARC) and Frost, R. "People who hoard animals." *Psychiatric Times* 17, no. 4 (Apr. 2000). <http://www.psychiatrictimes.com/p000425.html> (18 May 2005).

Humane Society of the United States (HSUS). "First Strike Campaign: Report of animal cruelty cases." Washington, D.C.: HSUS. 2001. <http://files.hsus.org/webfiles/PDF/2001AnimalCrueltyReport.pdf>

——— "What to Do About a Dog Who's Left Outside." <http://www.hsus.org/pets/issues_affecting_our_pets/animal_abuse_and_neglect/what_to_do_about_a_dog_whos_left_outside.html> (Apr 3, 2005).

Humane Society of the United States (HSUS) and Simmons, R. "Behind closed doors: The horrors of animal hoarding." <http://www.hsus.org/pets/issues_affecting_our_pets/behind_closed_doors_the_horros_of_animal_hoarding.html> (18 May 2005).

Hutton, J. S. "Animal abuse as a diagnostic approach." *Social Work: New perspectives on our lives with companion animals* (1983): 444.

Jacobson, N. and J. Gottman. *When men batter women: New insights into ending abusive relationships.* New York: Simon & Schuester, 1998.

Katcher, A. and A. Beck. *New perspectives on our lives with companion animals.* Philadelphia, Penn.: University of Pennsylvania Press, 1983.

Kellert, S. "American attitudes toward and knowledge of animals: An update." *International Journal for the Study of Animal Problems* 1 (1980): 87–119.

——— "Affective, cognitive and evaluative perceptions of animals." Pp. 241–267 in *Behavior and the Natural Environment*, edited by I. Attman and J. Wohlwill. New York: Plenum Press,1983.

——— "Attitudes toward animals: Age-related development among children." Pp. 43–60 in *Advances in animal welfare*, edited by M. Fox and L. Mickely. Boston: Martinus Nijhoff Publishers, 1985.

Kellert, S. and A. Felthous. "Childhood cruelty toward animals among criminals and non-criminals." *Human Relations* 38, no.12 (1985): 1113–1129.

Kidd, A. and R. Kidd. "Seeking a theory of the human-companion animal bond." *Anthrozoos* 1 (1987): 140–145.

Koop, C.E. and G.D. Lundberg. "Violence in America: A public health emergency: time to bite the bullet back." *Journal of the American Medical Association* 267, no.22 (1992): 3075–3076.

Kowalski, G. "Agencies team up to fight child, animal abuse." *The West Bloomfield-Lakes Eccentric* 9, (Feb.1995): 7–9.

Kuehn, B. "Animal hoarding: A public health problem veterinarians can take a lead role in solving." *Journal of American Veterinary Medical Association* 221, no.8 (2002): 1087–1089.

Lacroix, C. "Another weapon for combating family violence: Prevention of animal abuse." *Animal Law* 4 (1998): 1–32.

Lembke, L. "Bedwetting, fire setting and animal cruelty." *Latham Letter* 15, no.2 (1994):14–19.

Lockwood, R. and F. Ascione. *Cruelty to animals and interpersonal violence: Readings in research and applications.* West Lafayette, Ind.: Purdue University Press, 1998.

Lockwood, R. and A. Church. "Deadly serious: An FBI perspective on animal cruelty." *HSUS News* (Fall 1996): 27–30.

—— "Deadly serious: An FBI perspective on animal cruelty." Pp. 241–245 in *Cruelty to animals and interpersonal violence: Readings on research and applications,* edited by R. Lockwood and F. Ascione. West Lafayette, Ind.: Purdue University Press, 1998.

Lockwood, R. and G. Hodge. "The tangled web of animal abuse: The links between cruelty to animals and human violence." *HSUS News* 2, (Summer 1986): 77–82.

Merz-Perez, L. and K. Heide, eds. *Animal cruelty: Pathway to violence against people.* Walnut Creek, Ca.: Alta Mira Press, 2004.

Merz-Perez, L., K. Heide, and I. Silverman. "Childhood cruelty to animals and subsequent violence against humans." *International Journal of Offender Therapy and Comparative Criminology* 45 (2001): 556–572.

Miller, C. "Childhood animal cruelty and interpersonal violence." *Clinical Psychology Review* 21(2001): 735–749.

Miller, K. and J. Knutson. "Reports of severe physical punishment and exposure to animal cruelty by inmates convicted of felonies and by university students." *Child Abuse and Neglect* 21 (1997): 59–82.

Munro, H. "Battered pets." *Irish Veterinary Journal* 49 (1996): 712–713.

—— "The battered pet syndrome." Pp. 76–81 in *Recognizing and reporting animal abuse: A veterinarian's guide.* Englewood, Co: American Humane Association, 1998.

Munro, H. and M. Thrusfield. "Battered pets: features that raise suspicion of non-accidental injury." *Journal of Small Animal Practice* 42 (2001): 218–226.

Muraski, A. "Don't tell or I'll kill your pet." *California SPCA Monterey* (Spring 1992).

Myers, L. "The hoarding of animals: A rising problem in society." http://www.critter-haven.org/hoarding_animals.htm (18 May 2005).

National Center for Victims of Crime. "Networks: Forging new collaborations—victim service and animal welfare professionals." *NCVC.* 2001. <http://www.ncvc.org/newsltr/animalab.htm> (13 Apr 2005).

Nibert, D. "Animal rights and human social issues." *Society & Animals* 2 (1994): 115–124.

Novello, A.C., J. Shosky, and R. Froehlke. "From the Surgeon General, U.S. Public Health Service: A medical response to violence." *Journal of the American Medical Association* 267, no.22 (1992): 3007.

Offord, D., M. Boyle, and Y. Racine. "The epidemiology of antisocial behavior in childhood and adolescence." Pp. 31–54 in *The development and treatment of childhood aggression*, edited by D. Pepler and K. Rubin. Hillsdale, NJ: Lawrence Erlbaum Publishers, 1991.

Patronek, G. "Issues for Veterinarians in Recognizing and Reporting Animal Neglect and Abuse." *Society and Animals* 5 no.3, (1997). <http://www.psyeta.org/sa/sa5.3/Patronek.html> (15 May 2005).

—— "Hoarding of animals: An under-recognized public health problem in a difficult-to-study population." *Public Health Report* 14, no. 1 (1999): 81–87.

—— "The role of excuses in animal hoarding." *Report to Hoarding of Animals Consortium.* 2003. <http://www.tufts.edu/vet/cfa/hoarding> (4 May 2005).

Pet-Abuse.com, <http://www.Pet-Abuse.com> (15 May 2005).

Podger, P., "Cat hoarder freed on competency decision," *San Francisco Chronicle*, 17 Aug. 2004, 3 (N).

Ponder, C. and R. Lockwood. "Programs educate law enforcement on link between animal cruelty and domestic violence." *The Police Chief* (November 2000): 31–36.

Pope-Lance, D. and J. Engelsman. "A guide for clergy on the problems of domestic violence." Department of Community Affairs Division on Women, New Jersey, 1987.

Quinlisk, A. "Domestic Violence Intervention Project 1994–1995 Survey Results." LaCrosse, Wis, 1995.

Quinn, K. "Animal abuse at early age linked to interpersonal violence." *Brown University Child & Adolescent Behavior Letter* (March 2000).

Raupp, C. "Treasuring, trashing or terrorizing: Adult outcomes of childhood socialization about companion animals." *Society and Animals* 7, no. 2 (1999): 141–159.

Renzetti, C. *Violent betrayal: Partner abuse in lesbian relationships.* Thousand Oaks, Ca.: Sage Publications, 1992.

Risley-Curtiss, C., L.C. Holley, and S. Wolf. "The animal-human bond and ethnic diversity." Unpublished report, Arizona State University School of Social Work. Ariz., 2004.

Robin, M. "Minnesota Medicine Report Minnesota Medicine Report." *Minnesota Medical Association*, 82 (August, 1999).

Ruby, J. "Images of the family: the symbolic implications of animal photography." *Phototherapy* 3, no. 2 (1982): 2–7.

Sacks, J., L. Sinclair, J. Gilchrist, G. Golab, G., and R. Lockwood. "Breeds of dogs involved in fatal human attacks in the U.S. between 1979–1998." *Journal of the American Veterinary Medicine Association (JAVMA)* 217, no.6 (2000). http://www.cdc.gov/ncipc/duip/dogbreeds.pdf (4 Feb. 2005).

Sauder, J. "Enacting and enforcing felony animal cruelty laws to prevent violence against humans." *Animal Law* 6 no.1 (2000): 1–21.

Schenk, S., D. Templer, N. Peters, and M. Schmidt. "The genesis and correlates of attitudes toward pets." *Anthrozoos* 7, no.1 (1994): 60–68.

Serpell, J. *In the company of animals.* New York: Blackwell Publishing, 1986.

Shapiro, K. "Violence and animal abuse: All in the family." *The Animals' Agenda* (Jul.-Aug. 1996): 55–56.

Siegel, J. "Companion animals: In sickness and in health." *Journal of Social Issues* 49 (1993): 157–167.

Solot, D. "Untangling the animal abuse web." *Society & Animals* 5 (1997): 257–265.

Statman, J. *The battered woman's survival guide: Breaking the cycle*. Dallas: Taylor Publishing, 1990.

Tapia, F. "Children who are cruel to animals." *Child Psychiatry and Human Development*, 2 (1971): 70–77.

Tingle, D., G. Barnard, G. Robbins, G. Newman, and D. Hutchinson, D. "Childhood and adolescent characteristics of pedophiles and rapists." *International Journal of Law and Psychiatry* 9 (1986): 103–116.

Turner, N. "Animal abuse and the link to domestic violence." *The Police Chief* (June 2000): 28–30.

Urban, S. "Building alliances to safeguard animals and people." *New York State Office for the Prevention of Domestic Violence* (Fall 2002): 9–11.

USDA. "Humane treatment of dogs and cats: tethering and temperature requirements." *Federal Register* 61 no. 34386 (July 2 1996).

Veevers, J. "The social meanings of pets: Alternative roles for companion animals." *Marriage & Family Review* 8, no.34 (1985): 11–30.

Verlinden, S. "Risk factors in school shootings." Unpublished doctoral dissertation. Pacific University, Forest Grove, Ore., 2000.

Vermeulen, H. and J. Odendaal. "Proposed typology of companion animal abuse." *Anthrozoos* 6 (1993): 248–257.

Voith, V. "Attachment of people to companion animals." *Veterinary Clinics of North America* 15 (1985): 289–295.

Vollum, S., J. Buffington-Vollum, and D. Longmir. "Moral disengagement and attitudes about violence toward animals." *Society & Animals* 12, no.3 (2004): 209–235.

Walker, L. *The battered woman*. New York: Harper & Row, 1979.

——— *Terrifying love: Why battered women kill and how society responds*. New York: Harper & Row, 1989.

Wiehe, V. *Sibling abuse*. New York: Lexington Press, 1990. Worth, D., and A. Beck. "Multiple ownership of animals in New York City." *Transactions and Studies of the College of Physicians of Philadelphia* 3 (1981): 27–33.

Yllo, K. "Through a feminist lens: Gender, power and violence." Pp., 28–50 in *Feminist perspectives on wife abuse*, edited by R. Gelles and D. Loseke. Newbury Park, Ca.: Sage, 1993.

Zahn-Waxler, C., B. Hollenbeck, B., and M. Radke-Yarrow, M. "The origins of empathy and altruism." Pp. 21–39 in *Advances in Animal Welfare Science,* edited by M. Fox and L. Mickely. Washington, DC: The Humane Society of the United States, 1984.

Index

About the Authors

Trained as a social and behavioral scientist and researcher, **Dr. Pamela Carlisle-Frank** is the founder, primary researcher, and president of the Foundation for Interdisciplinary Research and Education Promoting Animal Welfare [FIREPAW, Inc.], a nonprofit research and education foundation committed to stop animal suffering. In addition to over two decades of experience as a researcher, educator and writer, Dr. Frank has extensive experience in the animal welfare and animal rights arenas. Dr. Frank's study of victims of violence began two decades ago. Her work in this area has included conducting empirical research studies, publishing professional articles, consulting and training domestic violence professionals, speaking at numerous conferences and seminars, and teaching university and college courses about human and non-human victims of violence. She has developed the Companion Animal Victims Educational Seminars [CAVES], offering profession-specific training about how to recognize and stop animal abuse. She can be reached at: FIREPAW, Inc., 228 Main Street, #436, Williamstown, MA 01267; Email: *DrPFrank@firepaw.org*; Web site: www.firepaw.org

Co-author **Tom Flanagan** is a retired Boston law enforcement officer as well as founder and coordinator of the Link-UP Program, a network linking law enforcement, animal control, social services and other municipal agencies to stop violence directed toward animals. Flanagan is frequently called upon to educate and train law enforcement and municipal agencies. A dynamic speaker and gifted storyteller, Officer Flanagan also conducts numerous public speaking engagements and training sessions on stopping animal abuse. In his role as vice president of Link-UP Education Network, Flanagan conducts professional conferences on how to recognize and stop animal abuse including the recent "Breaking the Links of Violence: Proactive Steps to Success" Conference held at Northeastern University in Boston, Massachusetts. Officer Flanagan currently works as a humane enforcement officer for the Animal Rescue League of Boston, Massachusetts. He can be reached at: ARL, P.O. Box 265, Boston, MA 02117, Email: tflanagan@arlboston.org.

Phil Arkow is an internationally acclaimed lecturer, author and humane educator. He chairs the Latham Foundation's Animal Abuse and Family Violence Prevention Project, under whose auspices he has written two manuals and a textbook to cross-train employees of animal shelters, veterinarians, child protection agencies, and domestic violence prevention programs to recognize and report each other's forms of family violence. He teaches three on-campus and distance-education courses on Animal-Assisted Therapy and Animal-Assisted Activities at Harcum College in Bryn Mawr, PA and Camden County College in Blackwood, NJ. He writes "Pet Pals," a biweekly newspaper column on pet care. Active in the animal care and control communities since 1973, he has served on national boards and advisory committees of the American Veterinary Medical Association, the Delta Society, the National Animal Control Association, and the American Humane Association. He can be reached at: 37 Hillside Road, Stratford NJ 08084 (856) 627-5118 arkowpets@snip.net; www.animaltherapy.net

James Knight, *DVM* was born and raised in Michigan where he became a dairy farmer, operating the family business from age 17 to 21. After training as a Special Forces Medic and serving in Viet Nam, he enrolled at Michigan State University in the Veterinary School, graduating in 1973. He first entered veterinary practice in Glendale, Arizona and, with a classmate, formed Academy West Animal Hospital. After 12 years in Arizona he sold his practice and moved to Massachusetts to accept a position with USDA-APHIS. Returning to private practice he worked in two low-cost spay/neuter practices and shelters and in 2002 accepted the position of Director of Animal Science Programs at Becker College in Leicester, Massachusetts. He also co-owns Canterbury Tails Veterinary Clinic with his wife, Anne Rylestone, DVM, Ph.D. Dr. Knight is President and Founder of Link-UP Education Network and a Founding Member and Member of the Board of Directors of Massachusetts Animal Coalition. He can be reached at 344 Old Greenwich Plains Road, Ware, MA 01082.